EMBROIDERY

EMBROIDERY

consultant editor Pauline Brown

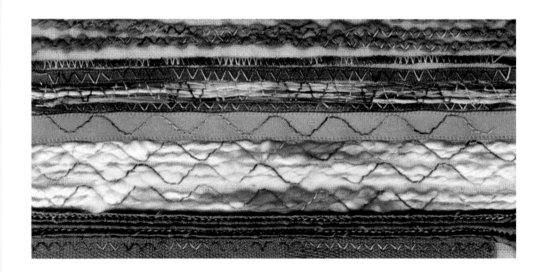

TIGER

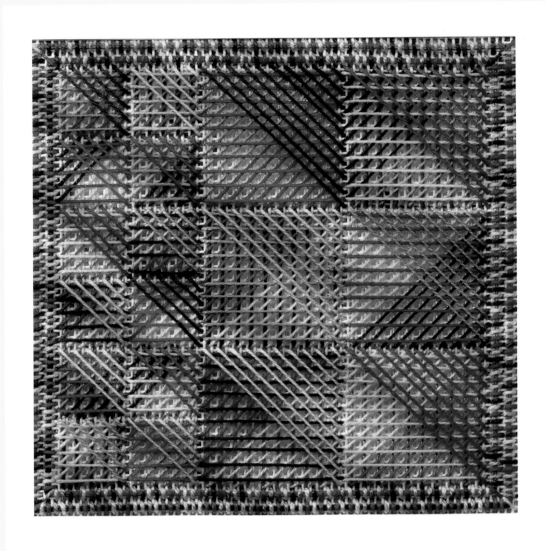

This edition published in 1990 by
Tiger Books International PLC, London
First published 1987 by

William Collins Sons & Co Ltd
London · Glasgow · Sydney · Auckland · Johannesburg

Conceived, edited and designed by
Marshall Editions Ltd,
170 Piccadilly, London W1V 9DD

Consultant editor/Author of
Design Your Own
Pauline Brown

Managing editor   **Ruth Binney**
Editor   **Carole McGlynn**
Sub editor   **Hazel Harrison**
Editorial assistants   **Vivienne Quay**
                         Pat Hunter

Art editor   **Daphne Mattingly**
Art assistant   **Richard McAndrew**

Picture coordinator   **Zilda Tandy**
Picture assistant   **Sarah Wergan**

Production   **Barry Baker**
Production assistant   **Rosanna Scott**
Production secretary   **Nikki Ingram**

ISBN 1-85501-156-9

Typeset by Filmtype Services Ltd, Scarborough, UK
Reproduced by Reprocolor Llovet S.A.,
Barcelona, Spain
Printed in Singapore

CONTENTS

EMBROIDERY is a unique book designed for anyone, irrespective of their experience, who wants to explore the craft of embroidery in an original, imaginative way. How you use the book will depend on your level of skill and on your goals as an embroiderer; but our hope is that through its use both your skill and your goals will develop enormously.

Three distinct, but interrelated parts make up the book; the Embroidery Design Collection of patterns, plus the two opening sections of this book, 'Design Your Own' and 'Embroidery Basics'. The 31 patterns each give complete instructions for making an embroidered piece of work, be it a garment, a household item, a picture, panel or a wall-hanging. The designs have been carefully selected to cover a wide range of techniques and to cater for different tastes as well as varying levels of embroidery proficiency.

A moderately experienced embroiderer can use many of the patterns without referring to the other pages of the book. For the beginner or the embroiderer whose experience does not extend to a particular technique, the book will provide invaluable guidance; cross-references are given where helpful.

Design Your Own is a comprehensive exploration of design as the 'heart' of embroidery. It begins with an introduction to the equipment required for embroidery—design tools and materials as well as the needles, the amazing diversity of threads and the wealth of different fabrics that come into play in modern embroidery. The principles of good design as found in any art form are explained, and then applied to embroidery techniques in particular. The various design sources and the media through which to interpret them are explored in detail—from using photographs and drawings to creating patterned designs with cut paper shapes, collage and geometric forms. This helps to establish as broad a base as possible from which to embark on your own original embroideries.

Readers are encouraged to be innovative with backgrounds too—an often neglected aspect of embroidery—by using fabric dyes or paints creatively.

The rest of this part of the book is concerned with free, experimental interpretation of the various embroidery techniques. It is intended to be used hand in hand with the Embroidery Basics section, and to take you a stage further. Once you know how to work any of the surface stitches in a conventional way, you will be receptive to ideas for trying them out using an unusual bouclé thread, for example, to produce a rough texture, or imaginatively varying the spacing for tonal effects.

All of the 'experimental' sections in Design Your Own cover an important element of embroidery design: colour, texture, lines and shapes, fabrics, threads and stitches. Each one relates to a range of embroidery techniques and should be treated as broadly as possible. Creative smocking, for example, is discussed in the section entitled 'Experiment with Fabrics', since it is a means of manipulating fabric, though it is also relevant to 'Texture', since it is a way of creating textural effects, and to 'Lines and Shapes' as it is also a basically linear exercise. The demarcations are not rigid—the intent is to extend the embroiderer's scope. Specially commissioned embroidered 'samples' illustrate this experimental approach. It is hoped that these will stimulate the embroiderer and give inspiration for including similar creative ideas in a finished piece of work.

Whether or not you feel inclined to use any of these examples in a practical way, simply reading and studying them will help you to understand the process of embroidery design. When you do begin to design your own pieces of work they will serve as inspiration and guides.

In Embroidery Basics (pp. 62–140) you will find detailed, illustrated instructions for all the essential embroidery techniques from surface stitchery and canvaswork to related crafts such as quilting and appliqué. This section of the book is especially valuable for its illustrated library of stitches (64 in Surface Stitchery and 50 in Canvaswork), many of which are used in other forms of embroidery too. Many of the canvaswork principles and stitches, for example, apply to other counted thread methods such as blackwork, drawn and pulled thread work, cross-stitch and Assisi work.

Any unfamiliar terms or techniques in a Design Collection pattern can be clarified by referring to this section of the book. For the complete beginner, Embroidery Basics will, of course, be the starting point.

THE EMBROIDERY DESIGN COLLECTION

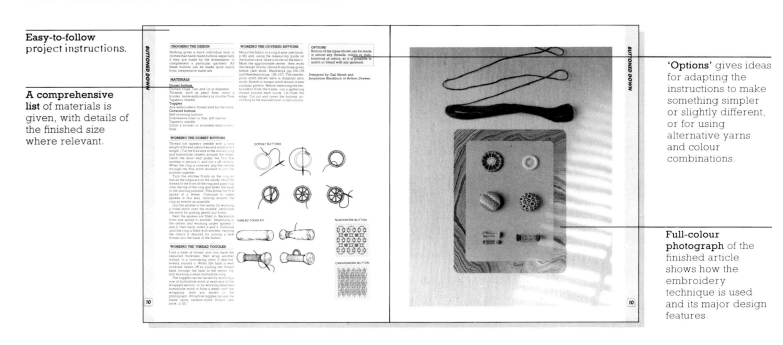

Easy-to-follow project instructions.

A comprehensive list of materials is given, with details of the finished size where relevant.

'Options' gives ideas for adapting the instructions to make something simpler or slightly different, or for using alternative yarns and colour combinations.

Full-colour photograph of the finished article shows how the embroidery technique is used and its major design features.

DESIGN YOUR OWN

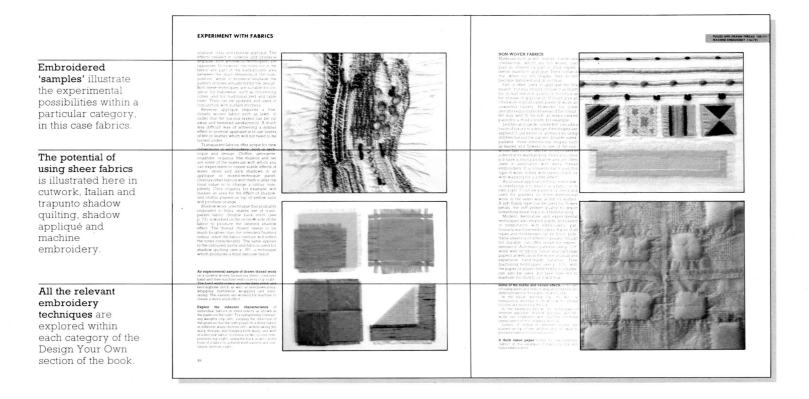

Embroidered **'samples'** illustrate the experimental possibilities within a particular category, in this case fabrics.

The potential of **using sheer fabrics** is illustrated here in cutwork, Italian and trapunto shadow quilting, shadow appliqué and machine embroidery.

All the relevant **embroidery techniques** are explored within each category of the Design Your Own section of the book.

EMBROIDERY BASICS

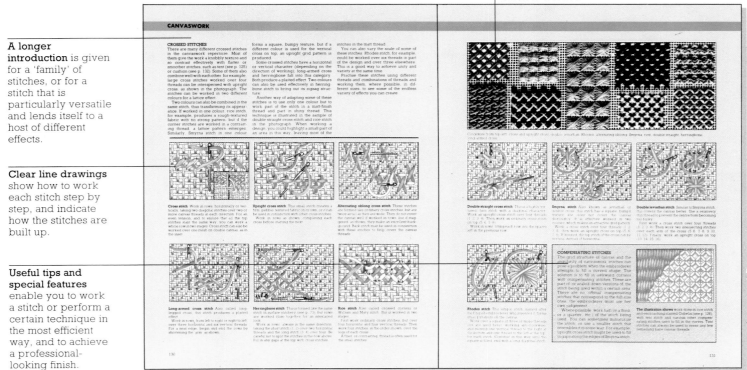

The photograph shows the stitches or technique explained on that page; each stitch is worked over a large enough area to show some of the textural and two-colour effects that can be achieved.

A longer **introduction** is given for a 'family' of stitches, or for a stitch that is particularly versatile and lends itself to a host of different effects.

Clear line drawings show how to work each stitch step by step, and indicate how the stitches are built up.

Useful tips and **special features** enable you to work a stitch or perform a certain technique in the most efficient way, and to achieve a professional-looking finish.

DESIGN YOUR OWN

All design begins with an idea, and the inspiration for an embroidery design can come from many sources. Ideas abound if you are sensitive enough to your surroundings to recognize the potential all around you. Being visually aware means seeing not only nature's most dramatic effects, such as a wonderful sunset or the spectacular colours of autumn, but looking closely at less obvious features, like the pattern of brickwork, the texture of lichen on a rock; the rusty colours in a heap of scrap metal; the shape and lines made by rooftops and chimneys – all of which could be translated into a design for embroidery.

Any research you can do will pay dividends in terms of widening the scope of your designs, so visit your local library and museum; go to exhibitions whenever you can, particularly of crafts, and try to analyze the designer's source of inspiration; also note the use of shape, pattern, texture and colour. Look at old embroideries in museums or ethnic or peasant work if you get the chance on holiday – ideas for techniques or subject matter may well evolve from these. Carry a notebook or sketchbook around with you and make notes and/or sketches to remind you of what you have seen.

There is no reason to feel daunted by the prospect of making your own designs. Even if you cannot draw well, there are many other ways to start off. You can design from photographs – your own or one in a magazine – with paper shapes, even by 'accident' using ink blots; or you can create more rigid geometric designs based on lines or shapes; all these subjects are covered in detail on pages 22–9.

The range of possible design sources for embroidery can be roughly categorized as follows. *Natural forms*, which include the elements – skies, water, landscapes – as well as all forms of plant life, and animals, insects, birds and fish. *Man-made forms*, which cover a wide range of possibilities such as your own home (from the whole exterior to a small corner of one room), or machinery of all kinds; a wheel, for example, could translate well into a design for a circular quilted cushion. *Geometric forms*, based on lines such as stripes or zigzags, or shapes such as squares, triangles or circles, any of which may be seen in a garden wall, a window frame or even a printed fabric. *Lettering*, which has traditionally played its part in embroidery design, particularly in the form of samplers. Letters and numbers can also be adapted to form a design in their own right, as in interlocking monograms.

There is no format to designing your own embroideries. You may hit upon an idea for a design – say, a bowl of fruit – before choosing the embroidery technique; you might then decide between

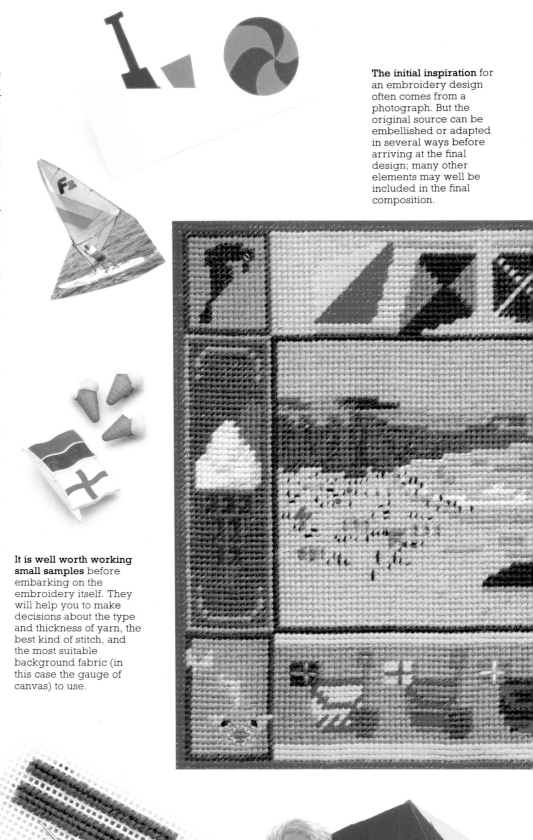

The initial inspiration for an embroidery design often comes from a photograph. But the original source can be embellished or adapted in several ways before arriving at the final design; many other elements may well be included in the final composition.

It is well worth working small samples before embarking on the embroidery itself. They will help you to make decisions about the type and thickness of yarn, the best kind of stitch, and the most suitable background fabric (in this case the gauge of canvas) to use.

surface stitchery, appliqué or even black-work, and adapt your design accordingly. Equally, you could be keen to do some quilting, for example, and then look around for a suitable design motif – it might be based on shells, or more abstract swirling forms. Whatever the starting point, you will then have to compose your design, arranging the elements into a coherent whole; considerations of line, space and form all play a part in a success-ful composition. At the same time you will have to make decisions about what colours, fabric, threads and stitches to use. Any one of the latter elements could even be your initial inspiration – an unusual textured fabric or some exciting knitting yarns might trigger off an idea for a wall-hanging worked freely in surface stitchery.

It is important to familiarize yourself with the range of categories within the craft of embroidery before you can fully realize the creative scope it offers. The narrow view of embroidery, as simply the appli-cation of decorative stitches to a back-ground fabric, is an outdated one. Contemporary embroidery is regarded as a textile art form that encompasses wide-ranging techniques, most of which can be done in either a traditional or a more experimental way.

Surface stitchery, with its multitude of stitches, is the most obvious category; its scope today is virtually infinite, with the range of different threads available and stitches that can be worked as freely as you like. Metal thread embroidery, a sur-face stitch method that in the past was used only for ecclesiastical and ceremonial work, is today adapted for evening bags, belts and embroidered jewellery. The recent advent of sophisticated domestic machines, incorporating numerous embroidery stitches, has created a technique in its own right. Free machining can produce with a needle an impression akin to drawing. Delicate lacy effects can also be achieved with one of the dissolvable agents such as vanishing muslin. Depending on your design, or how it is adapted, almost any of the embroidery methods can be employed in the creation of exciting pieces of work.

Designing your own embroideries not only allows you to produce original pieces – be they pictures, wallhangings, gar-ments, or accessories to complement your home; it also gives enormous scope as a means of self-expression. The processes involved in the refining of a design idea – from the original inspiration and planning the composition to the selection of colours, fabric and threads – all help you to build confidence and develop a range of skills that will allow creative freedom. Working to your own designs is what elevates em-broidery from the application of technique to a creative and expressive art form.

A border can finish off an embroidered picture perfectly. It may be continuous or made up of repeating motifs, as here. The chosen motifs might duplicate an element found in the main part of the design or can simply echo its subject or mood.

In a single stitch embroidery – like this canvaswork picture worked almost entirely in tent stitch – the choice of colours and threads is especially important. The strong, bright shades chosen here suggest the atmosphere of a hot summer's day.

It is not necessary to go to great expense when collecting equipment to help you design your own embroideries—some of the best ideas have started life sketched on the back of an old envelope. As you progress, you can gradually build up the design equipment you need, buying the best quality that you can afford. You will probably find that you are happier working with certain media than with others—some people enjoy the freedom of working with charcoal, for example, while others may find it messy. If you enjoy working in colour a box of watercolours or some tubes of gouache may be ideal for you, or you may prefer a collection of felt-tipped pens and coloured pencils.

The paper you choose for sketching or designing is also a matter of personal choice. If you find a large blank sheet of pristine white paper daunting, choose a sketchbook with smaller sheets, maybe of coloured or textured paper. Keep all your reference material—cuttings, snippets of fabric and threads, sketches, stitch experi-ments, written notes or ideas—together in a folder or scrapbook.

Most of the items listed on these pages are available from stationers and art shops, or from specialist needlecraft stores. Experimentation with different media will enable you to acquire a reper-toire of design methods which will, in turn, broaden the scope of your embroideries.

DRAWING EQUIPMENT

Pencils of graphite are made in grades of hardness (8H—8B) for different effects. Hard pencils (H) produce fine grey lines; soft (B) make thicker, blacker marks. Experiment to see which you prefer. A plastic or a putty rubber is the best type of eraser. Coloured pencils are available in a huge range of colours, as are felt-tipped pens, magic marker pens and coloured inks. A waterproof fabric marking pen is essential for marking the outlines of a design on to canvas and you will need either dressmaker's chalk (in block or a pencil form), or a water-erasable pen for transferring a design in surface embroidery.

If you use the pricking and pouncing method of transferring a design, you will need pounce powder. Pounce is a mixture of chalk and charcoal, both available in stick form from art shops. These need to be crushed to a powder. Depending on the colour of the intended background fabric, use more or less charcoal. Powdered dressmaker's chalk, which comes in several colours, is a useful alternative.

Wax crayons give a soft-edged, semi-opaque effect; they are also used for making rubbings. Charcoal, usually made from willow, is good for bold, free work. However, it smudges easily and should be used with a fixative. You could also try conté crayons and pastels.

The two types of paint most popular with embroidery designers are watercolour and gouache. Watercolours, available in blocks or tubes, give a light, transparent touch; gouache, sold in tubes, is opaque and gives a more solid, bolder effect. Both

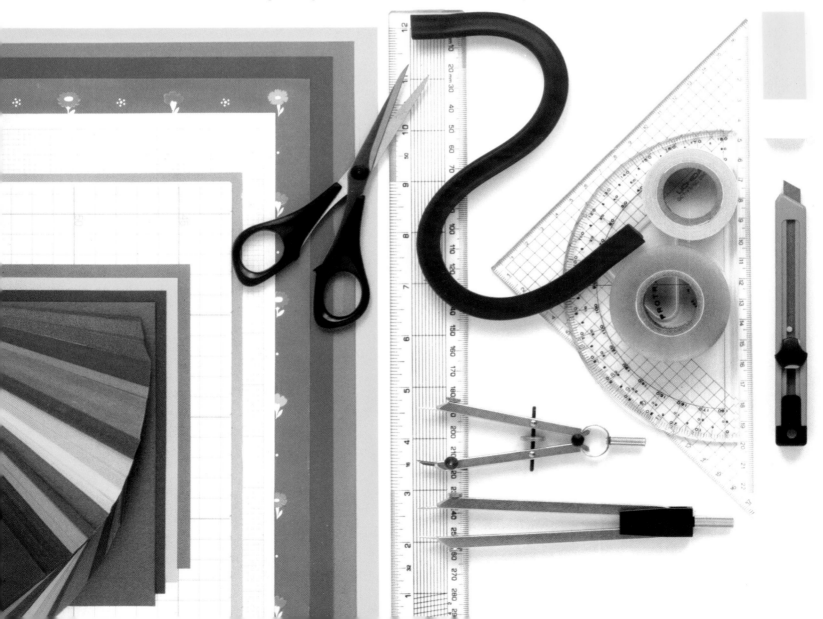

types of paint are water-based and come in a wide range of intermixable colours.

Brushes are available in sizes 000–12, the last being the largest. The best brushes have sable hairs and are consequently extremely expensive. Cheaper varieties are made in materials such as squirrel, or synthetic fibres. When you are beginning to design, three or four brushes in a range of different sizes should suffice.

TYPES OF PAPER

Sketchbooks and pads, usually containing cartridge paper, can be bought in a number of sizes from A2 to A6. Choose the size with which you feel happiest. Some people prefer working on a large scale, while others will make minute sketches. You can always alter the scale from the original drawing by enlarging or reducing it (see p. 21). A layout pad contains paper of a thinner quality, thin enough for tracings yet heavy enough to take crayons or paint.

Tracing paper is useful for copying, altering and adapting designs. It will assist you in making repeat, overlapping and mirrored images. Greaseproof paper is a cheaper alternative and is better than tracing paper for transferring designs by the tracing and tacking method, since it tears away easily. Tissue paper will be useful in preliminary experiments for embroidery on transparent fabric. It is available in a range of colours, which will blend if overlapped.

Graph paper, in pads or large size sheets, will be needed for working out charted designs, such as cross stitch, Assisi work, Florentine and some geometric canvaswork. Squared dressmaker's pattern paper is good for large-scale projects and garments, as the sheets are very big. Other papers, such as sugar, coloured sticky-backed, patterned craft, wrapping, corrugated, metallic finish etc. may be added to your collection for making collages, preparatory to appliqué designs. Those with interesting surfaces may help you make decisions about the use of texture in a design.

IMPLEMENTS AND ADHESIVES

Keep a special pair of scissors specifically for cutting paper as they will blunt rapidly. Alternatively, use a craft knife with replaceable blades. In conjunction with a metal rule or straight edge and a cutting board, a craft knife is essential for cutting mounts, stencils and geometric shapes.

Choose an all-purpose adhesive which will stick everything from paper to fabric; or miscellaneous objects such as buttons, beads and pieces of wood. Masking tape or transparent adhesive tape will be necessary for holding drawings or tracings in place while you work. Double-sided adhesive tape is useful for collage, mounting and for making bound mounts.

A ruler is invaluable, both for measuring and drawing straight lines. The following drawing aids can be bought as the need arises: a pair of dividers for plotting points; a pair of compasses for drawing circles and arcs; a flexible curve; a set square for geometric designs; a protractor for measuring and dividing angles.

Embroidery is created simply by the decorative relationship between fabric and thread. These materials *are* the embroidery, so their importance cannot be over emphasized. Your choice of fabric, thread and needle will depend to some extent on the embroidery technique you choose, as well as on the design and the planned subsequent use of the work.

Traditionally, certain fabrics were deemed to be suitable for a given method. While this still holds true, experimenting with fabric and thread will prove that almost anything is possible, provided you take into consideration any restrictions imposed by the inherent characteristics of the technique you propose to use.

NEEDLES

The needle is your most important embroidery tool, and it is essential to choose one that is suitable for the piece of work. The correct type and size of needle will be dictated by the technique being used, the background fabric and the yarn. Guidance is given under the individual techniques explained in the Embroidery Basics section of the book (pp. 62–141). Needle size is designated by number, the lowest number signifying the longest and thickest needle in each category.

As a general rule, if the needle is too small for the thread, it will make too small a hole, causing the thread to become frayed as it passes through the fabric. If you find it difficult to pull the thread through the fabric, change to a larger needle. Never use blunt, bent or rusty needles; they can damage the fibres of your fabric and thread.

Embroidery or crewel needles have long eyes to take one or more threads of stranded cotton or wool. (Sizes 1–10)
Betweens or quilting needles, traditionally used by tailors, are short with small round eyes. They are suitable for quick, even stitching, such as that used in hemming or quilting. (Sizes 1–10)
Darners and long darners are, as their name implies, longer than other needles and manufactured for darning.
Tapestry needles have large eyes and blunt points which slip easily between the weave of the fabric without damage. Apart from use in canvaswork they are essential for work on evenweave materials, i.e. pulled work, blackwork, drawn thread and needleweaving. (Sizes 13–24)
Chenille needles are similar in shape to tapestry needles but have sharp points. They are short with large eyes, and were originally used for chenille work, which uses a furry yarn. Today they are ideal for embroidering with thick knitting or weaving yarns, ribbon, raffia etc., particularly on closely woven fabrics. (Sizes 13–24)
Beading needles are for threading beads,

sequins and pearls as they are extremely long and fine with long eyes. They tend to bend in use and should be replaced as soon as they do. They are also used in metal thread embroidery for threading metal purls (small coils of gold wire). (Sizes 10–15)
Leather needles are a specialist item used by glovemakers and leatherworkers. Use them if you are working with leather, suede, plastic or vinyl for appliqué, since their triangular points will pierce the fabric without tearing. (Sizes 1–8)
Bodkins, with flat or round eyes, are for threading cords, tapes, ribbons and elastic.
Circular needles, used by upholsterers,

THE RIGHT NEEDLE FOR THE JOB

Technique	Needle
Appliqué (fabric)	Crewel
(leather/plastic)	Leather
three-dimensional	Circular
Beadwork	Beading or fine crewel
Broderie anglaise	Crewel
Canvaswork	Tapestry
Counted thread	Tapestry
Cutwork	Crewel
Free embroidery	
(fine)	Crewel
(heavy)	Chenille
Metal thread	Fine crewel, between or beading
Quilting	Between
Shadow work	Crewel
Smocking	Crewel

Crewel size 7

Crewel size 3

Quilting

Darner

Long darner

Tapestry size 24

Tapestry size 18

Chenille size 24

Chenille size 18

Beading

Leather

Large-eyed wool

Bodkin

Circular

are good for awkward jobs, particularly for three-dimensional embroidery.

If you have poor eyesight which makes needle-threading a problem, either use one of the large-eyed needles in the range or try the easy-threading needles which have a slot-eye into which the thread is pulled.

YARNS

Thread or yarn is an integral part of any embroidery, and virtually anything that can be threaded through the eye of a needle can be put to use. The variety of yarns available can be overwhelming—not only are there plenty of specialist embroidery threads in a full range of colours but, with the continuing popularity of knitting and crochet, each season produces a whole new selection of versatile textured yarns.

For experimental and non-traditional work the use of bouclé, chenille and other novelty wools and cottons can bring exciting possibilities to your designs. You can also experiment with other unconventional materials such as raffia, tape, ribbons and string—in fact anything with which you can sew. Fabric such as nylon, chiffon, jersey, suede and leather can be cut into strips. For a thread exactly matching the background fabric, it may even be possible to withdraw some of the weft (horizontal) threads and use these.

All the specialist embroidery threads, and some knitting and crochet yarns, are available from mail order suppliers, whose service is usually both quick and reliable. You can either purchase shade cards from these suppliers or they will send a returnable selection of these. (See list of suppliers on p. 144). Some carpet and woollen mills sell their 'thrums' (warp ends left over from weaving). These are usually sold by weight and can be incorporated in wallhangings and canvaswork.

Apart from the aesthetic qualities of colour and texture, you will need to choose your thread in relation to the weave of the ground fabric. Bear in mind too, any constraints imposed by your chosen technique.

SPECIALIST EMBROIDERY THREADS

Stranded cotton, available in a good choice of colours, both plain and shaded, is probably the most widely used embroidery thread. It has a pleasing lustre and is adaptable in that the six strands can be split to produce a number of thicknesses. It is useful for traditional surface stitches and can be incorporated in canvaswork. In blackwork you can use it to achieve a change of tone by varying the thickness used. One drawback of stranded cotton is that it can separate out when used in a long stitch. It is not a good idea to use it on smocking, for example.
Pearl cotton (perlé), a shiny, twisted 2-ply yarn, comes in both balls and hanks in three thicknesses, 3, 5 and 8, with 3 being

the coarsest. It is suitable for surface embroidery and canvaswork.

Coton à broder is a fine non-stranded thread with a slight sheen; it is good for counted thread embroidery and smocking, since there are no strands to separate.

Soft embroidery cotton is a tightly twisted, matt, 5-ply thread and is mostly used for couching or on coarsely woven fabrics.

Flower threads, 100 per cent cotton and dyed with natural and vegetable dyes, are chosen for their high degree of lustre.

Silk threads, available in twisted, twisted buttonhole and 6-stranded floss, can be used in most types of embroidery wherever a lustre is required. It is the thread usually chosen for shadow work. Waxed silk thread is often used in conjunction with gold or silver in metal thread embroidery.

Linen threads are less widely available than cotton, but specialist shops stock them. They have a dull finish and are used in smocking and counted thread work.

Embroidery wools are primarily manufactured for canvaswork but can be used on many other backgrounds, provided the weave allows. They include very fine 2-ply crewel wool, 3-stranded loosely twisted Persian wool, 4-ply tightly twisted tapestry wool and the thicker rug wool.

Machine threads, which can also be used for hand work, include ordinary sewing cotton and the thicker button twist. There is also a large range of cotton and rayon machine embroidery yarns in several thicknesses, and more recently available, some metallized and textured examples.

Metal threads come in gold, gold plate, silver, aluminium or copper. They are most easily purchased by mail order (see p. 144). Most metal threads are laid on the background surface and couched. They range in thickness from tambour (very fine) to heavy cords and braids.

Top right to bottom left: soft embroidery cotton, linen thread, coton à broder, stranded cotton (2 colours), sewing threads, pearl cotton (sizes 5 and 8), tapestry wool, crewel wool, Persian wool, bouclé wool, silk embroidery thread (2 colours), silver lurex thread (top); ribbon (2 widths) and beads.

The selection of metal threads includes: top —pearl purl in three thicknesses; centre— gold Russia braid, tambour, gold plate, imitation Jap gold cord; bottom—smooth purl in two thicknesses, gold check purl, white gold twist.

Purls consist of a length of wire coiled like a minute spring. Pieces can be cut off to the required length and then threaded and sewn down.

TRADITIONAL THREADS FOR EMBROIDERY

The techniques below were traditionally worked in these specific threads. However, experimentation with other yarns will provide exciting and unusual effects.

Technique	Thread
Appliqué	Cotton thread
Beadwork	Waxed cotton thread
Broderie anglaise	Coton à broder
Canvaswork	Tapestry and crewel wool
Counted thread	Linen and coton à broder
Cutwork	Stranded cotton and coton à broder
Free embroidery stitches	Stranded cotton
Metal thread	Gold, silver, with waxed silk thread
Quilting	Cotton thread
Shadow work	Fine cotton or silk thread
Smocking	Linen or coton à broder

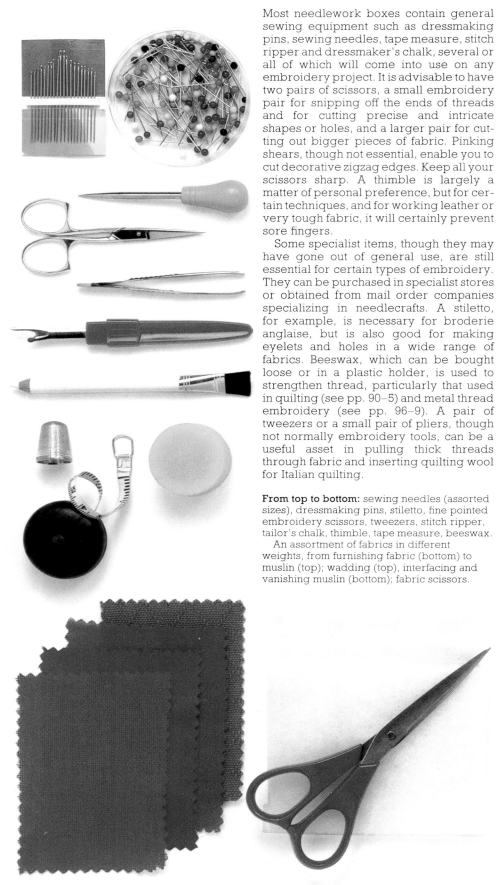

Most needlework boxes contain general sewing equipment such as dressmaking pins, sewing needles, tape measure, stitch ripper and dressmaker's chalk, several or all of which will come into use on any embroidery project. It is advisable to have two pairs of scissors, a small embroidery pair for snipping off the ends of threads and for cutting precise and intricate shapes or holes, and a larger pair for cutting out bigger pieces of fabric. Pinking shears, though not essential, enable you to cut decorative zigzag edges. Keep all your scissors sharp. A thimble is largely a matter of personal preference, but for certain techniques, and for working leather or very tough fabric, it will certainly prevent sore fingers.

Some specialist items, though they may have gone out of general use, are still essential for certain types of embroidery. They can be purchased in specialist stores or obtained from mail order companies specializing in needlecrafts. A stiletto, for example, is necessary for broderie anglaise, but is also good for making eyelets and holes in a wide range of fabrics. Beeswax, which can be bought loose or in a plastic holder, is used to strengthen thread, particularly that used in quilting (see pp. 90–5) and metal thread embroidery (see pp. 96–9). A pair of tweezers or a small pair of pliers, though not normally embroidery tools, can be a useful asset in pulling thick threads through fabric and inserting quilting wool for Italian quilting.

From top to bottom: sewing needles (assorted sizes), dressmaking pins, stiletto, fine pointed embroidery scissors, tweezers, stitch ripper, tailor's chalk, thimble, tape measure, beeswax.
An assortment of fabrics in different weights, from furnishing fabric (bottom) to muslin (top); wadding (top), interfacing and vanishing muslin (bottom); fabric scissors.

FABRIC
Whether the fabric is principally the background to the embroidery or part of the applied decorative effect, choosing the right material is crucial. Each type of fabric has its own particular characteristics and you need to consider the design, the technique used and the practical use, if any, of the proposed work, when selecting a fabric. Firstly it is essential to know the properties of the whole range of fabrics.

Fabric can be categorized in different ways. Look first at its structure: is it woven, knitted, or non-woven? Woven fabrics made on a loom are structured, with warp threads running the length of the fabric and weft threads interweaving them at right angles. The weave can be plain or patterned and in any fibre. Evenweave fabrics, used for the counted thread methods of embroidery, have distinct, well-spaced warp and weft threads. To check whether a fabric you may have is evenweave or not, count the warp and weft threads over 5 cm—there should be an equal number.

Knitted fabrics, such as jersey, are constructed with a continuous yarn which gives elasticity. They are malleable and drape well but they tend to be difficult to use as a background fabric for embroidery unless mounted on a firm backing. If you are embroidering on to a garment made of knitted fabric you should back the area to be embroidered with a woven fabric first.

Non-woven fabrics include felt, leather, suede, kid, plastic and bonded interfacings. Their main advantage is that they do not fray and are firm to handle. This makes them particularly suitable for appliqué. The bulk of felt also makes it an appropriate fabric to pad out motifs or shapes in appliqué and shadow quilting.

Having ascertained the structure of your fabric, now look at the fibres. Are they natural or synthetic? It is sometimes difficult to tell without reading the fabric content tag, since a vast range of man-made and synthetic fabrics are now produced to simulate, or made into fabrics mixed with, natural fibres.

The natural fibres include cotton and linen, both of which come from plants, and silk and wool, derived from animal sources. Materials made from these usually wash and iron well, are pleasant to handle and can be manipulated satisfactorily. They are also suitable for dyeing in either hot- or cold-water dyes and will readily accept fabric paints. Cotton dress fabrics, including lawn, poplin, calico, towelling, voile, brushed cotton, velvet and corduroy can all be used as backgrounds for embroidery, or for hardwearing, washable clothes on which embroidery is worked. Household items such as table mats, cushions and quilts also make up well in cotton.

Linen can be fine or heavy and either evenly woven or with a slub effect. Traditionally used for table and bed linen because of its fine washing and wearing qualities, it is also suitable for clothes and, depending on its structure, may be appropriate as a basis for counted thread decoration. Natural hessian and jute make good background fabrics (though the dyed varieties tend not to be colourfast).

Silk is available in various types and weights from fine Honan silk through to silk tweed, as well as the transparent organzas, chiffons and georgettes. Although expensive, it has a unique lustre, will press into pleats and tucks yet also has good draping qualities. It is suitable for surface stitchery on fine garments and evening bags, for embroidered wall panels and for appliqué and smocking.

Wool, though traditionally rarely used as a background for embroidery, can be made up into warm garments such as stoles and scarves, then decorated with surface stitches. Its soft texture can enhance a piece of appliqué, and fine woollens such as crêpe and challis can successfully be smocked.

Synthetic fibres are produced either chemically or from sources such as coal, wood and petroleum. Many need little or no ironing, which makes them suitable for easily laundered clothes and household items. Their visual resemblance to natural fibres means that they can generally be used in the same way as these, though some have a resilience which makes them more difficult to pleat or tuck crisply. They vary in their acceptance of hot- and cold-water dyes, depending on their content, but they can all take fabric paint.

Wadding is a useful material made of synthetic fibres, usually terylene or Courtelle. It is sold by the metre in three weights and several widths and is both washable and dry cleanable. Its main use is in quilting or for padding and stuffing three-dimensional embroideries.

Interfacings are non-fray, bonded materials, produced to stiffen or give added support to fabrics. They are useful for appliqué and for backing finished embroideries. They can either be ironed or sewn on; the latter type can be painted and dyed.

Furnishing fabrics have either a natural or synthetic fibre content or a mixture of both. They are particularly good for wall-hangings and embroidered panels since they are wider than dress fabrics and heavier in weight, which gives the greater substance needed for large-scale embroideries. Furnishing sheers and loosely woven acrylics and linens are suitable for pulled and drawn thread work; furnishing nets can be pattern-darned or used for transparent effects.

Specialist embroidery fabrics, normally

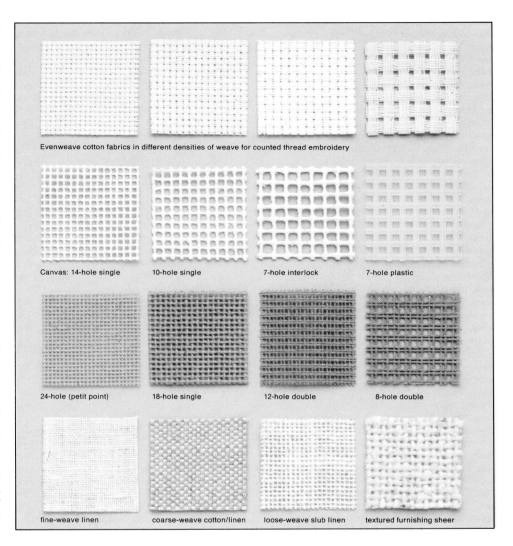

Evenweave cotton fabrics in different densities of weave for counted thread embroidery

Canvas: 14-hole single   10-hole single   7-hole interlock   7-hole plastic

24-hole (petit point)   18-hole single   12-hole double   8-hole double

fine-weave linen   coarse-weave cotton/linen   loose-weave slub linen   textured furnishing sheer

in cotton or linen, are available in a selection of different widths from 56cm to 160cm. Some are specially woven to lend themselves to a particular embroidery method. Evenweave cottons and linens are all intended for counted thread designs such as cross stitch, pulled and drawn thread work and blackwork. They come in varying densities of weave, from fine to coarse, and your choice of fabric for these techniques will depend on the size and scale of the design. Those plain weave fabrics produced with surface embroidery in mind, like fine linen, are most appropriate for traditional designs on such items as table linen.

Vanishing muslin and water-dissolvable fabrics are two materials used for making lacy effects in machine embroidery—the first disappears in contact with a hot iron, the second with boiling water (see p. 121).

Canvas is a specially woven material in either cotton or linen for the technique of canvaswork (needlepoint). Your choice of canvas will depend on the size and intricacy of the design (see pp. 122–3).

There are two types of woven canvas, single and double, each available in several widths from 60–100cm and with a wide range of mesh gauges. Canvas gauge has not yet been metricated and is given as the number of threads (or, in the case of double canvas, holes) per inch. They range from fine petit point canvas with 24 threads per inch (2.5cm) to coarse rug canvas with 4 threads per inch (2.5cm). Single canvas is more useful than double since it is difficult to adapt the double variety for the large number of textured stitches used in canvaswork.

A recent innovation is a rigid canvas made of plastic with six holes to the inch. This can be used for such items as boxes, pencil cases, coasters etc.

In addition to the use of dress, furnishing and specialist embroidery fabrics, certain embroideries demand a more unusual approach. Wallhangings and pictures can include any type of textile. Some progressive embroiderers are even incorporating paper and plastic in their designs for decorative panels.

Design incorporates the selection and arrangement of different elements to form a satisfactory composition, whatever the nature of the piece of work. In the case of embroidery, these elements include shapes and spaces, line, colour, texture and pattern—all of which must be brought together with regard for any limitations imposed by the technique, as well as such practical considerations as time and cost involved or whether the item is washable. A successful composition will command notice unselfconsciously, and will avoid being a confused jumble of shapes or colours assembled in haphazard fashion. A pleasing design will be well-proportioned; it will have balance and a focal point or areas of interest, as well as lines of sight to draw your attention.

You may already have a natural talent for design—a sense of colour, proportion and balance—and be able to draw and sketch well; or you may feel that you are lacking in these qualities and that you need some help in this direction. (Don't worry about your drawing skills for a start; there are other ways to put together a working plan.) Remember that you are constantly applying design principles in your daily life; you choose and coordinate your clothes, use cosmetics, decorate your home, hang pictures, arrange indoor flowers or plan out a garden—all of which require you to make decisions as to the final look of the job in hand. In the same way, when planning a design for embroidery you will arrange the elements in a way which pleases the eye, and as your design experience increases you will soon recognize if something is unsuitable.

When making a composition you should be aware of certain traditional design concepts which can serve as guidelines and may prevent errors creeping in which cannot later be rectified. You need not follow the time-honoured laws of composition slavishly, but like any artist you will be better off if you understand them before going your own way. They distill what the human eye has found pleasing over the course of centuries. Just as needlework itself possesses a venerable history, so do the basic principles of design.

PROPORTION AND SCALE

Proportion in a design refers to the relationship between the size of one element and another. It is important to get the proportions right at the beginning as it is difficult to make alterations to them at a later stage. You need the correct organization of amounts and areas to give your basic plan a satisfactory balance. Embroidery projects call for particular choices to be made in the matter of scale. The scale of a practical article is frequently dictated by its use or surroundings—a chair seat must fit the chair or a garment the wearer; a wallhanging or picture should relate suitably in size to the space in which it is displayed. As far as the design itself is concerned, bear in mind that the scale of the embroidered area must relate in size to the overall shape, and that the undecorated background space should work effectively as part of the design.

BALANCE: SYMMETRY AND ASYMMETRY

The most well-balanced design (although not necessarily the most interesting) is one based on symmetry. A symmetrical design is one which, when cut through the centre either horizontally or vertically, results in two mirrored halves. This makes for a rigidity and formality which might well have a place in border designs or samplers, or on household items such as table linen with strong regular patterns. In terms of clothing, a symmetrical embroidery design would suit, for example, the fronts of a waistcoat or jacket. Its effect is generally less satisfactory for embroidered panels and wallhangings.

If it is overused, this type of balance can be limiting and monotonous. However, symmetry can be relieved in a number of ways—for one, by retaining the outline exactly, but changing the details within (colours, stitches, fabrics, textures). This would be the more creative approach. Another way of altering symmetry is to work a counter-change design. An example of this would be where the motif in one half was black on a white background, and the reverse colours in the other half. A counter-change design has great strength and in repeat patterns can make for added interest. Although normally effected by the reversal of colours, counter-change can also be achieved by reversing stitches or qualities of texture.

Asymmetry (without symmetry) characterizes a design of unequal balance and tends to create a more interesting and lively impression than does strict symmetry. Although the halves of the design are not identical, they still need to be balanced. In an asymmetrical composition, you need, for instance, to offset dominant elements on one side with smaller components of a similar weight on the other to prevent the design looking lopsided. The same applies to the tonal and textural qualities of the composition. For example, a heavily padded or brightly coloured focal point placed on the right would need to be complemented with smaller areas similarly worked on the left so that it would not become isolated in space.

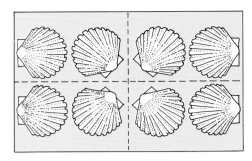

A symmetrical design: cut in half either horizontally or vertically one half is a mirror image of the other. The result is somewhat formal and regular.

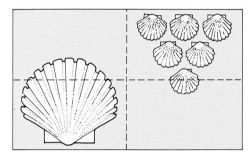

An asymmetrical design: the large motif in one corner is balanced by the arrangement of small units in the opposite corner. Such a design has an interesting and lively quality.

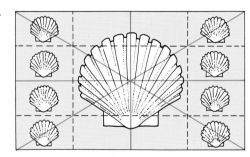

The large shell is undoubtedly the focal point, but it is balanced by other areas of interest in the design. Grid lines dividing the space into thirds and quarters help to plan out harmonious proportions.

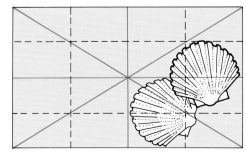

Do not be afraid of empty space – it can be an important part of the design if planned carefully. Taking a motif off-centre prevents it 'floating' in space. The proportion of the total area filled works satisfactorily.

FOCAL POINTS/AREAS OF INTEREST

If a design has a focal point, it will form the heart of the composition—the most important, most colourful or largest textured area. In a symmetrical design, the focal point is most likely to be placed centrally with other less important elements surrounding it. In an asymmetrical design, if the focal point is moved slightly away from the centre, a more interesting composition is possible.

The other areas of interest in a design, although secondary to the focal point, should relate to it in some way—by shape, colour, texture or connecting lines. Sometimes a good design may consist only of isolated and unrelated shapes, but a more harmonious effect is likely to be produced if the elements are overlapped or connected in some way.

HARMONY AND CONTRAST

Harmony in a design can be achieved by using similar shapes and sizes, textures, lines and colours. A harmonious work is easy to understand and does not offend the eye. However, perfect harmony can produce rather uninspired designs: a small amount of contrast may be needed to provide a spark, enlivening the overall quality of the piece. The means for introducing contrast to an embroidery design include texture (such as beads or knotted stitches on an otherwise flat design); colour (by using complementaries—see p. 40) or by using elements of shapes and sizes different from those in the main part of the design.

PRINCIPLES OF PATTERN

The arrangement and repetition of single motifs or units to form a pattern is an essential ingredient of embroidery design. The pattern's complexity or simplicity is determined by the designer, taking into account the proposed technique and the intended use of the finished article. Some techniques, such as canvaswork, lend themselves well to intricate patterns; others, such as quilting and appliqué, rely on different effects which are best kept uncomplicated. The elements of an all-over pattern can be arranged in a variety of ways—straight, brick, half-drop or random. Patterned borders are often made up of evenly distributed repeat or mirrored images (see pp. 58–9).

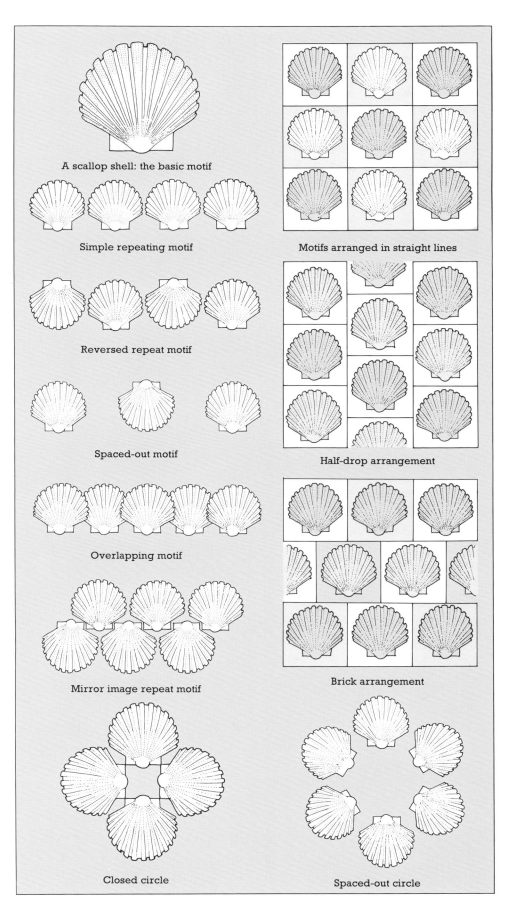

A scallop shell: the basic motif

Simple repeating motif

Reversed repeat motif

Spaced-out motif

Overlapping motif

Mirror image repeat motif

Closed circle

Motifs arranged in straight lines

Half-drop arrangement

Brick arrangement

Spaced-out circle

TYPES OF DESIGN

The type of design you settle on will depend on both your style preference and on the technique you intend to use; some methods lend themselves to realism, others to stylization or abstraction.

Realistic or naturalistic designs A realistic design is one which imitates as nearly as possible the form, colour and texture of the subject. Naturalism is perennially popular because people enjoy producing instantly recognizable images—easy to relate to, but challenging in their fine details. There are several approaches to a realistic design. If you are skilled at drawing or painting, you can work from an existing sketch you like, or produce one with a specific embroidery technique in mind. As an alternative to drawing, borrow your idea from a photograph or painting (see pp. 22–3). Do avoid copying other people's embroidery; there is never a shortage of original references from which to work. A landscape can be duplicated in surface stitchery with colours and textures faithfully reproduced; a picture can be recreated in appliqué with areas in high or low relief, padded to resemble the actual forms of the subject.

Stylized or decorative designs Stylization is a deliberately altered view of reality in which the artist freely emphasizes those aspects of the subject she feels are most characteristic, while playing down the less important details. Lines may be straightened or exaggerated, plain flat areas given pattern and surface texture; elements may be eliminated to suit the technique or the materials used—but the subject never loses its basic identity. One method of stylizing a design is to trace from your original reference using a pencil and ruler, thus eliminating all the curves. The rather formal, rigid outline this gives you can be used for simple appliqué shapes or for counted thread methods. A bird, for example, would assume a geometric outline; areas of head, breast and wings could then be divided and worked in whatever stitches you prefer, without the need to reproduce the exact look of the feathers.

A more ornamental method of stylization is to retain the original outlines of the subject, but add decorative features. How this will be done depends on the proposed technique. A butterfly motif could be completely covered in beads; a street scene stitched in blackwork patterns. Colours can be altered from nature—a seascape in black and white; a rose in gold or silver thread; a penguin quilted in colour or a parrot in monochrome. Textures, too, can reverse reality—ballet slippers in chunky wools or sheep quilted in satin.

Symbolic designs A symbolic design carries stylization a stage further, eliminating all superfluous decoration and detail so that the image is reduced to a minimum —purely an emblem of the original subject. A tree reduced to symbolic form, for instance, would be suitable for a cross stitch or Assisi work design.

Abstract designs The term abstract applies to a number of concepts. You can have abstractions of natural subjects, such as flowers, but these will be so far reduced in form as to be scarcely recognizable. The original flower is merely the inspiration for the abstracted shape. Abstract designs can also be based on geometric forms, lines or random shapes; on cut paper (see p. 24); on found objects and assorted accidental means (see p. 26). Abstract designs can also give expression to abstract thoughts or feelings—happiness, anger, warmth, loneliness, passion. There is scope for virtually every embroidery technique; the interpretation is in the hands of the designer.

DESIGNS FOR SPECIFIC TECHNIQUES

Whatever type of design you are embarking on, it is nearly always worthwhile to make a working drawing. This helps both to clarify your ideas and to eliminate any errors in the proportions of the design which might be difficult to alter at a later stage. You need draw no more than the design's essential elements; details can be added later. In any case, a totally worked out plan leaves no room for any adjustments or embellishments. A design which is allowed to develop spontaneously as work progresses has more vitality and should give a more satisfying and original result. In any creative field from fiction to film-making the finished piece is more likely than not at variance with the initial working plan. Give your embroidery the same flexibility. The working drawing will need to be made with the embroidery technique in mind; some adjustments or simplifications may well have been incorporated already.

Surface stitchery Surface stitchery is probably the most versatile embroidery medium. The wide variety of stitches combined with the profusion of threads available in all colours, thicknesses and textures make it suitable for any type of design—realistic, stylized, abstract or symbolic. The success of the design hangs on the ideal selection of stitches and threads. When working a naturalistic design, try to make the direction of the stitch compatible with the subject—matching the upward thrust of growing ferns or the lateral motion of water, for instance. The stitch chosen will also need to interpret the texture of the original—such as satin stitch in silk for a smooth area, French knots in thick wool clustered together for a chunky effect.

Appliqué Appliqué generally calls for bold designs which take into account the cutting out of the applied shapes. If you do choose to work with delicate and fairly intricate pieces, a double-sided bonding

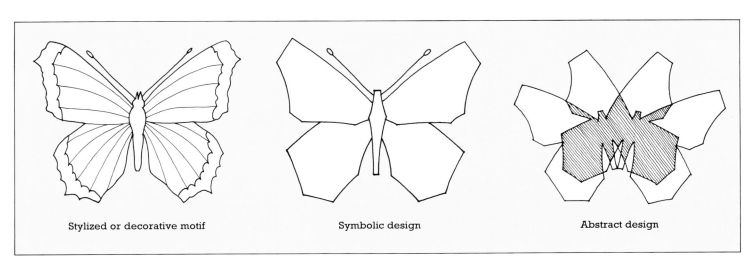

Stylized or decorative motif   Symbolic design   Abstract design

Broderie anglaise

Appliqué

Reverse appliqué

Wadded quilting

Italian quilting

The original design source — a realistic painting of a butterfly

Surface stitchery, incorporating herringbone, fern stitch, long and short stitch on the wings; padded satin stitch for the body; stem stitch and French knots for the antennae

Goldwork, including gold plate, couched gold thread, padded kid, bugle beads and sequins secured by a bead on the wings; padded couching for the body; gold cord antennae

Counted thread techniques: canvaswork, cross stitch and Assisi

19

material helps; but care must be taken to prevent fraying or loss of definition of the outline. You will need to simplify your design slightly for most types of appliqué, paying particular attention to narrow shapes and points which are difficult to use satisfactorily. Cut paper designs make a good basis for appliqué methods as they rely on shape rather than line for their immediate impact.

Reverse appliqué requires special treatment. You separate the design into individual elements, rather like a stencil, working from the top down. These elements are then divided by a series of parallel lines to correspond with the several layers of fabric this technique uses, similar to contours, which will take the form of layers of fabric.

Quilting Designs which have been considerably simplified or reduced to outline work best with wadded and stuffed quilting methods. Quilting relies for its effect on the shadows cast by the uneven surface, therefore it is essential that a large proportion of the surface is left unworked: the more quilting there is, the flatter the work becomes and . the effect is diminished.

Designs which contain parallel lines are suited to Italian quilting. This method permits easy interpretation of, for instance, the trailing, sinuous curves of Art Nouveau or the interlaced patterns of Celtic art. Other subject matter would need to be adapted by breaking it down into a series of parallel lines which is the chief characteristic of this technique.

Metal thread Metal thread is a highly decorative technique, particularly suitable for stylized designs. Areas can be filled with textured purls or couching; the latter form lends itself to linear patterns in which the metal threads can be laid in long lengths.

Cutwork Cutwork relies on the correct distribution of the design's main elements; they must overlap or connect in some way, as the background area will ultimately be removed. This in turn creates a pattern of spaces which needs your careful consideration as it forms an important part of the overall design. Shade the spaces in on your working drawing to judge the effect.

Broderie anglaise The special characteristic of the broderie anglaise technique is that the design consists of the overcast holes. The holes must be sufficiently close together to form a coherent pattern. To help plan your design, you can use small objects such as buttons, moving them about until you come up with a satisfactory arrangement.

Cross stitch and Assisi work Cross stitch and Assisi work operate on a grid principle and therefore the most suitable designs are simplified silhouettes or symbols which are easy to adapt in this way.

In both types of embroidery each stitch covers two intersections of the evenweave fabric. Cross stitch is used to create the motifs themselves; in Assisi work the stitches cover the background instead. For instructions on how to transfer your design to graph paper, see page 102.

Blackwork Blackwork relies for its success on the correct interpretation of the tonal values of the design. The most suitable designs are those based on spaces rather than lines, although line stitches can be added to the surface to delineate and emphasize the forms. The subject matter may be realistic or stylized. You can work from a collage made either of black and white photos or of cut or torn newspaper shapes carefully chosen for their tones.

Drawn thread designs The nature of the drawn thread technique limits designs to those based on vertical or horizontal bands, with or without adjoining squares or rectangles. When planning the work you may find it helpful to use strips of cut paper which you can arrange to form your design.

Pulled work Pulled work, like blackwork, is best executed using a simplified or stylized design. The pattern derives its impact from shapes, although outlines can be added at a later stage if essential.

Smocking Embroidered smocking designs are a decorative addition to smocked or gathered fabric. Traditional designs are based on a series of straight and zigzag stitches, such as honeycomb and chevron. You can experiment by working lines unevenly or by creating textured areas to contrast with unworked portions of your pattern.

Machine embroidery You can incorporate the automatic patterns for embroidery available on many sewing machines into your design. They provide useful decorative effects, particularly with stylized work. Alternatively, free machining, which emulates drawing, is an excellent medium for realistic effects.

Canvaswork Canvaswork lends itself readily to geometric designs, based on the grid of the canvas. You can either work freely or plan your design first by making a line chart (see p. 29). Pictorial canvaswork does not require a detailed graph of the design. It is better to make a simplified plan of proposed stitch patterns; transfer only the outlines to the canvas and fill in the spaces accordingly, using compensating stitches (see p. 127) to cover any gaps. This will result in a stylized and decorative appearance.

For a more realistic effect, the entire design could be carried out in tent stitch, with precise use of colour so as to depict the subject most naturally. For this, your original design should be either painted in oils (see p. 123) or worked out using a box chart (see p. 29). In the latter case, each

box would signify one stitch worked over one intersection of canvas. You do risk losing spontaneity with this type of design; if you prefer, you can disregard the grid of the canvas to some extent and rely on surface stitches added later to heighten realism. The intricacy of the design will determine the choice of canvas. A finely detailed piece will require a small mesh; a less intricate one, a larger mesh.

Design is choice: ask yourself the following questions to help you with your initial plan.
What shall I make?
Where will it go?
What will the size and shape be?
Which technique or combination of techniques shall I use?
What is my design source?
Which type of design—realistic, stylized, abstract, symbolic?
Which colours, textures, patterns, shapes, lines?
Which fabrics and threads?

ENLARGING AND REDUCING

Often the scale of your preparatory sketch or source material will need to be altered—enlarged or reduced—to make it practicable for your proposed design. You can do this in several ways: first, you could redraw it to the required size; or you could take it up or down using a photocopier. A third alternative, however complicated it might sound, gives you the option of incorporating a distortion or elongation that would improve the piece.

Using a large piece of paper, make a tracing of your original drawing and enclose it within a rectangle.

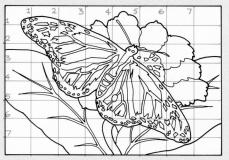

Make a grid of the rectangle by halving and quartering it, adding further equal divisions as necessary. The more complex the design, the more grid lines you will need. Number the squares vertically and horizontally.

To make your enlargement, draw a diagonal line from the bottom left to the top right corner, extending it well beyond the rectangle. Decide on either the height or width of your proposed enlargement and extend the right-hand side line or the top line accordingly. Draw a line at right angles to this to meet the diagonal. Then join up the remaining sides to form the enlarged rectangle. Divide the large rectangle into a grid containing the same number of squares as the original tracing. On both grids, assign matching numbers or letters to the vertical and horizontal lines. Copy the design section by section on to the larger rectangle, making sure that each part corresponds correctly to the original drawing.

To make a reduction, simply reverse the enlarging process by drawing a smaller rectangle. Again, divide it into the same number of squares as the original and make your copy.

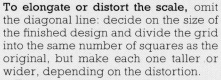

To elongate or distort the scale, omit the diagonal line: decide on the size of the finished design and divide the grid into the same number of squares as the original, but make each one taller or wider, depending on the distortion.

To alter the perspective, you can change the grid in a variety of ways. Here the squares remain the same width but have been made less deep, so that the butterfly is foreshortened but appears wider.

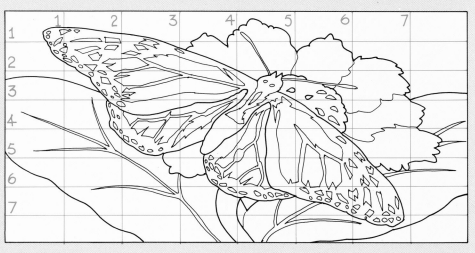

DESIGNING FROM DRAWINGS AND PHOTOGRAPHS

The source material for embroidery designs can take many forms. But designs produced from your own sketches and drawings are likely to produce the most original embroideries. In drawing a subject you get to know it intimately—it will lead you to an intuitive feel for the essence of the piece, for which shapes, lines or forms you wish to play up or to eliminate.

If you are already a competent artist, this is of course a great asset. However, with some practice, most people can draw up a satisfactory working scheme for an embroidery design. In this instance you are not trying to paint a portrait, landscape or still life as a work of art in its own right, but to produce an adequate plan or pattern from which you can achieve a pleasing piece of work. Remember that it is the final embroidery that is all-important.

If you like the idea of sketching, carry a small sketchbook with you whenever you can; it will enable you to make thumbnail sketches as well as a few notes whenever appropriate. It is a good idea to include, in words, your impressions of mood, colour and texture, since these will help formulate the prospective design as well as your choice of fabric, thread and technique.

The materials you use for drawing are largely a matter of personal choice and you should try out different media; coloured pencils, paints, wax crayons and charcoal all have different qualities, some of which may suit your way of working better than others.

In addition to a sketch pad of your own drawings or paintings, it is a good idea to make a scrapbook of items which intrinsically appeal to you. Pictures invariably spark off ideas for embroidery designs. Postcards from well-loved holiday places or visits to museums and art galleries all provide tangible reference as well as abstract images. Some birthday and greetings cards provide interesting sources of reference for decorative embroidery.

Books are a rich source of inspiration, too. If you enjoy outdoor pursuits such as gardening, birdwatching or walking, you will probably have books relating to your hobby which will be full of nature reference. It is well worth looking in children's books, since they often contain detailed or decorative illustrations suitable for interpretation in stitchery, or bold oulines which could be adapted directly for appliqué. Your local library will of course provide much more material. Whatever your idea or inspiration it can be interpreted realistically, or adapted to stylization or abstraction.

Magazines and colour supplements are another good source of ideas. Look at advertisements that use interesting photographic images—distortions, reflections, shadows—whose unusual effects could well be exploited in embroidery. Medical journals, as well as books on biology and botany, often include photographs of highly magnified subjects, which make exciting foundations for abstract ideas. At the other extreme, aerial photographs eliminate all detail, but reveal distinctive pattern and shape.

In some ways it is better to use your own camera, if you have one, to gather original source material, since you can select the exact subject for a specific design idea. If you do own a camera, always take it with you on excursions; do not limit its use to special occasions and your annual holiday. Treat it as a useful tool to help you record impressions, without worrying too much about the artistic merits of the photograph.

Photographs are the most authentic reference for portraits, which can successfully be carried out in several embroidery techniques, especially surface stitchery and canvaswork. A close-up lens will help you to record detail—the centre of a flower-head, the ridges and indentations on tree bark, the pattern and colour of lichen on a rock, the texture of moss between paving stones.

Very often a part of a photograph or drawing can be taken out of context and successfully used. To do this, cut L-shaped pieces of paper as shown opposite and use them to form rectangles or squares of varying sizes, selecting and isolating different areas of interest. Look carefully at the composition before arriving at a final decision: consider the possible focal points and the distribution of pattern and texture and evaluate these in the context of the technique used. Unnecessary background spaces can always be left out so that the focus is directed to more interesting parts of the design.

If you make a tracing of your source material you can interpret it freely: some unexpected areas can be shaded in and accentuated, or background shapes and spaces can be made more important than foreground elements; certain parts of the design can be eliminated, others emphasized. The removal of detail, leaving only the main lines, will reduce the subject to a symbol (see p. 18) and this is a sound basis for simple appliqué, Assisi work or cross stitch. Repeat patterns and overlapping images can all be made from your original source, using tracing paper as an aid.

Remember that your source material, whether magazine cuttings, drawings, photographs or slides, should be used as a starting point only. Do not try to reproduce it exactly in embroidery. It is better to consider it as an initial source of inspiration, which can then be adapted to your needs and to that of the embroidery technique.

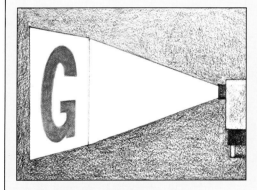

Slides, though not generally as useful as colour or black and white prints, have an advantage for designing large-scale embroideries such as wallhangings and large panels. The advantage of a transparency is that it can be projected on to a sheet of paper (as long as it is vertical) enlarged to any size, and the design drawn in. It is essential that the projector is placed correctly to ensure that no distortion occurs.

Slides, if projected on to objects such as boxes, bags or garments, can give unexpected and unusual effects which could develop into highly original work. Projecting a letter on to a box produces an interesting three-dimensional distortion which can be exploited in an exciting embroidery design.

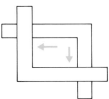

Cut L-shapes out of paper or card and move them around to 'frame' different areas of a photograph.

Your choice of embroidery technique will influence which portion of the photograph you isolate as the basis for a design. This area might lend itself to appliqué or shadow appliqué, whereas a detail from the foreground might be more suitable for surface stitchery.

Taking a drawing from a photograph, or from part of it, blurs the edges and makes it more abstract. Though the photograph may be your initial inspiration, the drawing might translate more readily into a working design for embroidery.

Abstract effects can be made by cutting photographs or drawings into strips and moving them up and down to create a sense of movement. The strips can also be rearranged in a different order, or reversed, for a more complex design. Though these strips are interspersed with blank strips of paper, they still form a coherent whole.

DESIGNING WITH PAPER

Apart from the obvious use of paper as a background for drawing or painting (see p. 23) different qualities of cut or torn paper can be a valuable aid to embroidery designs, particularly for those who are nervous or inexperienced at drawing. Every needleworker is adept with a pair of scissors, and paper is cheap, expendable and easy to use.

There are many types of paper available, from art supply shops or more general stores, ranging from those manufactured for specific design purposes, such as graph and tracing paper, to the decorative variety sold for collage, wrapping or display.

Tracing paper is one of the most versatile design materials, and has many uses apart from transferring designs to the fabric. It can be used for adapting and altering designs, repeating and overlapping motifs, producing mirror images of drawings and sketches, or as a design element cut from paper.

Paper designs have the advantage of immediacy; they are quickly executed, can be altered or adjusted without endless rubbing out and give bold, strong designs —a great advantage for the timid designer. They are particularly suited to those types of design in which shapes need to be filled in, rather than those which rely on lines for their effect; included in this category would be blackwork, canvaswork, pulled work, appliqué, wadded and trapunto quilting.

COLLAGE
For a first experiment, cut out a few random shapes of different sizes from paper and move them around on a contrasting background. They can be pushed close together in a group, with some overlapping, or gradually scattered over the surface. They can also be arranged to fill a specific shape relating to that of the finished project—a rectangle or circle for a cushion, an oval for a table centre, or a square for an embroidered pocket.

Paper that has been torn gives a softer-edged effect. This can translate well into designs based on natural forms—landscapes, hills, bushes. A collage of tree forms made up from pieces of torn paper in different tones could easily become a design for surface stitchery. Use striped wrapping paper to represent lines of band stitches or canvaswork or see how metallic papers can lend themselves directly to designs for metal thread embroidery. Brightly-coloured torn tissue paper can interpret skies or water; newsprint could be used for the same features on a darker or stormy day.

When areas of coloured tissue paper are overlapped an additional colour is produced, and a third shape also. In arranging the pieces, look carefully to make sure you have a well-balanced composition. In addition to a delicate appliqué panel, this material could lead to a design using shadow work or shadow quilting.

A collage made with carefully selected cut-out shapes from a newspaper can provide inspiration in a technique such as blackwork, which relies for its effectiveness on the tonal values of the design. Black and white photographs and newspaper cuttings can also be enlarged and used as a basis for blackwork designs.

FOLDED AND CUT PAPER
Cut paper designs of the sort children create for friezes can be a good source of ideas for borders, worked in different techniques ranging from cross stitch and Assisi work to appliqué.

A variation on this theme is to fold a square or circle of paper into eight and cut out a shape against the central folded edge, which will produce the type of design known as Hawaiian appliqué. It is suitable for a cushion or for a repeated block to be made up into a quilt. If your cut-out design contains a number of large holes rather than a single shape, it could adapt well to a cutwork design for a camisole top, for example.

REPEAT MOTIFS
The effect of repeat motifs can be clearly seen if you cut out several identical paper shapes. These can then be arranged to form a great variety of patterns: straight, brick or half-drop arrangements (see p. 17); they can be reversed, placed at an angle in rows or in circles; they may be scattered or overlapped to suit your purpose. They will lend themselves to numerous interpretations in embroidery, and are particularly suitable for border designs (see pp. 58–9).

EXPLODED DESIGNS
The principle of exploded designs is that, since all the elements have been cut or torn from a single piece of paper, they will be harmonious shapes that will relate well to one another. Place the cut shapes together on a contrasting background like a jigsaw puzzle. Now gradually draw the pieces apart, without altering the direction in which they lie, until you have a pleasing arrangement. Look carefully at the spaces left between the cut shapes, bearing in mind that the background area is part of the design.

For designs to fit specific areas, for example the flap of a handbag, cut out two pieces of paper—one for the background the exact size and shape of the finished work, and a contrasting piece in the same shape but considerably smaller. The smaller shape can be cut and exploded, and the pieces juxtaposed to form a well-balanced design. Exploded designs translate well into many embroidery techniques, including quilting, appliqué, stitchery and canvaswork. In canvaswork you would also need to fill the background areas with contrasting stitches.

STENCILS
All types of stencils lend themselves readily to use in repeat designs, since only a single motif needs to be cut and the stencil can be repositioned for subsequent use. Such designs can be quilted, embroidered with surface stitchery, or painted with fabric paint, using a stencil brush or spray-gun (see p. 33).

The use of a stencil in paper or, preferably, in card can be directly applied to the method of reverse appliqué, since its fragmented elements reflect the type of design necessary for this technique.

To adapt a design for a stencil, it is necessary to simplify the original motif and to separate each element of the design from its neighbour.

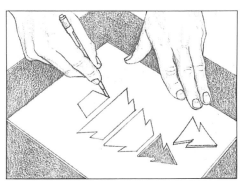

Draw the design on to thick paper or card, then carefully cut out each shape with a craft knife, using a cutting board.

One advantage of tissue paper is that when two colours are overlapped a third is produced. In embroidery terms, this can be exploited through an appliqué design using transparent fabrics such as net, organza or chiffon.

Hawaiian appliqué motifs are made by folding a square of paper into quarters and again diagonally from the centre into eight, and cutting a shape against the folded edge. Use the resultant paper pattern to cut out a motif in fine cotton.

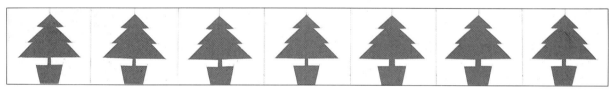

If you fold a strip of paper concertina fashion and cut holes or shapes in it, it can result in an interesting repeat motif, suitable for a border.

For an exploded paper design, select a shape such as a circle and cut it into pieces; the cuts can be straight or curved. Replace the cut circle on a contrasting paper in different ways. Whatever the arrangement, it will have an inherent unity.

For a newspaper collage for a blackwork design, choose newsprint in as wide a range of sizes and densities as possible, and arrange the shapes to coincide with those of your original sketch or inspiration.

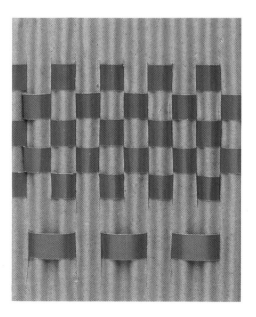

Strips of paper can be woven together, perhaps with strips of a contrasting paper, to form an abstract design. The textural qualities of these papers could be interpreted in corduroy and heavy satin, or in surface stitchery using, for example, lines of couching with long and short stitch or split stitch.

ABSTRACT DESIGNS

Abstract designs can evolve from almost any source; even a realistic image can be adapted, or reduced to its bare outline, so that it becomes pure pattern or design, barely distinguishable from its original form. Abstract patterns can also be based on geometric forms, lines or random shapes. However, one of the most direct routes to an abstract design is simply to play around with a pen, pencil or with found objects such as buttons or shells, until you create, almost by 'accident', a pleasing pattern.

If you are visually receptive, there is potential for abstract design all around you. A heightened visual awareness will help you to register unexpectedly interesting effects as you look around. Notice, for example, the rainbow colours and fluid patterns of oil spilled on the road, of cream poured on stewed raspberries, or of raindrops trickling down a window pane. Such ideas can all be adapted for embroidery design, so make sketches and notes or take photographs whenever possible. Save up ideas so that when you are looking for inspiration for a specific project, you can turn to your reference material and adapt it accordingly.

Studies of shadows and reflections can result in interesting embroidery designs; the shadow cast on a wall behind an object could be developed into a design using repeat images or overlapping shapes in transparent fabrics. Reflected images can also be worked as a counterchange design in different colours, or one technique could be juxtaposed with another to represent the reflection. For example, an embroidered picture depicting a lakeside scene could have the top half done in canvaswork, and the bottom half in cross stitch or Assisi work on linen. Alternatively, the top could be carried out in appliqué with the lower half in shadow quilting.

DESIGN BY ACCIDENT
A simple way to make a mirror, or reflected, image is through an ink or paint blot. Make a large blob of ink on a piece of paper, fold the paper in half and press the liquid away from the fold. Weird insect and butterfly shapes will emerge, which can be adapted for the technique you have chosen to embroider. If you try this with tissue paper, the design produced will have indistinct feathery edges suitable for a delicate treatment.

You can make a transfer printed blot in the same way. Iron off the print on to a piece of fabric made of synthetic fibres, such as polyester, and embellish the design with stitches, quilting or beads. Paint or ink can be splashed, dripped or blown with a straw across the surface of paper; try out different types of liquid and paper but remember to protect the surrounding surfaces.

Doodles sometimes produce sketches that can be adapted for use in embroidery. Doodles depend on your mood and personality; some are flowing and rhythmic, others more rigid and geometric. Flowing lines could well be interpreted successfully as a design for stitchery or Italian quilting. A geometric pattern may well be adapted to one of the counted thread methods such as pulled or drawn thread work, blackwork or canvaswork.

Accidental methods will, by their very nature, tend to produce random, free designs, lacking in control. The asymmetric, uncontrolled quality may be part of the appeal, but, in most cases, the blot, splash or doodle will need some form of adjustment before serving as your embroidery design. This is best done before committing the design to fabric, though it may sometimes be possible to make alterations at a later stage as long as you are aware that this needs to be done.

Once you have chosen the embroidery technique to use, the blot or doodle can be altered accordingly to accommodate any restrictions or characteristics imposed by that technique. In any case it will be neccessary to take a tracing of your accidental source material, simplifying and eliminating any areas or elements that you think need improvement. Decide on a focal point or areas of special interest and colour or shade these in; thicken some lines to add emphasis.

Most accidental designs can also be made into repeat motifs, borders or mirror images; they may be charted for counted thread techniques, padded for quilting or cut away in cutwork or broderie anglaise.

PATTERN MAKING FROM FOUND OBJECTS
Many inexperienced designers find it difficult to draw a design on paper. One way round this problem is to arrange 'found objects' into patterns. Make a collection of small, everyday items such as buttons, beads, nuts and bolts, pegs, paper clips, matches, seeds, pasta of different shapes. Choose a background paper or fabric, and make a window mount to coincide with the size and shape of the finished design. This could be a rectangle, square or circle for a cushion or an abstract panel, or could take the specific shape of the article you are designing—handbag flap, spectacle case or garment, for instance.

Select three or four different types of object from your collection and begin arranging them in a design. This may take the form of a repeating all-over pattern, a border, a circular, swirling design or a symmetrical or asymmetric scheme. Decide on points of interest and, as you move the pieces around, take into account the spaces between them. Look at the overall shape and make sure that the arrangement of the objects relates to the entire area. Once you feel satisfied with the plan, the items can be glued down to paper and then traced or photocopied.

Certain objects, such as small beads, would make a good basis for a broderie anglaise design, the beads representing the characteristic holes. Curtain rings or coins of different sizes could be the inspiration for a surface stitchery design using buttonhole or woven wheels, spiders' webs or circular couching; alternatively, the design could be interpreted in circles of appliqué.

Making a seed collage—with beans, peas and lentils as well as fruit and flower seeds—is fun, and the collage can be the starting point for flowing designs based on natural forms, both realistic and abstract. Seeds can also be showered to form exploding designs or random patterns. These lend themselves to interpretation into embroidery using a mass of French knots or beads. The effects made by an arrangement of pasta shapes could be exploited in quilting or even metal thread embroidery.

String, if cut into various lengths, arranged into patterns and stuck down, can also be manipulated to suit your purpose. Alternatively it can be left in a length, and dropped at random on to a background for a flowing, linear design. This also works well with strings of beads, and could be developed into an Italian quilted design or a line stitch sample.

An ink or paint blot is one of the simplest ways of achieving a symmetrical design for embroidery. The shape could be filled in with surface stitchery or blackwork patterns, or its outline simplified in a tracing in order to use it for appliqué.

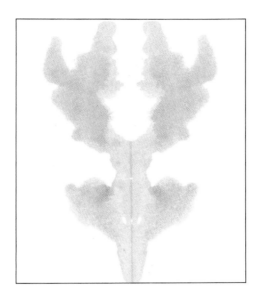

Blowing paint through a straw across a paper surface will produce an abstract, fluid shape which could be transferred to the fabric using transfer paints. This type of design is appropriate for a technique such as quilting.

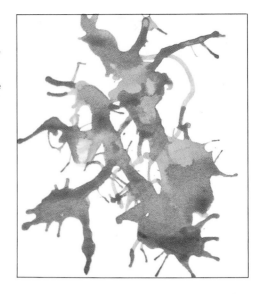

Buttons of different sizes can be arranged alongside each other to work out a scalloped edge, for example. Depending on their shape, they might equally represent the circular or teardrop-shaped holes of broderie anglaise.

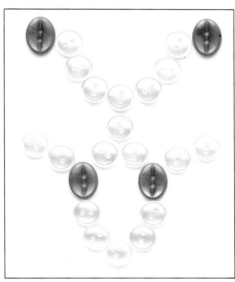

A pleasing arrangement of seeds, peas and beans could create a design suitable for beadwork or for surface stitchery, combining massed French knots and a variety of band and filling stitches.

A pasta collage might suggest an interesting basis for metal thread work, using a combination of purls and braid.

String stuck down in well-ordered lines could inspire a design for Italian corded quilting or surface stitchery, using mainly line stitches. A more representational shape, as here, could be interpreted in goldwork, with the metal threads couched down.

GEOMETRIC DESIGNS

Pattern-making—or the planning of abstract designs from geometric shapes—is a simple method that can be applied to many embroidery techniques from surface stitchery and appliqué to canvaswork and drawn thread. Inspiration can be taken from natural objects as well as pure geometric forms and adapted for a variety of embroidery methods. Some natural phenomena, though not obviously geometric in form, may contain circular or spiralling shapes—as seen in shells or pine cones; concentric circles can be seen in cross-sections of logs or onions, as well as appearing when a stone is dropped in water. Snowflakes are hexagonal. Many manufactured items, such as cogs, wheels and plates are circular, whilst straight-sided rectangular shapes occur in a diversity of man-made forms such as furniture and buildings.

Almost any design source, broken down to basic form or outline, will result in the evolution of a geometric shape capable of being modified for embroidery design. One of the simplest geometric arrangements is the stripe, which often appears in printed and woven fabrics. Stripes could be translated into bands of surface stitchery, drawn thread or canvaswork rows.

Rectangular shapes are suitable for bold pieces of appliqué, while circles could be treated similarly, or, on a different scale, could be developed into a design using stitches which naturally form circular shapes—buttonhole and woven wheels, spiders' webs and circular needleweaving. Straight-sided geometric shapes (squares, rectangles, triangles, diamonds and so on) will integrate well together in one project as will circles and ovals in another. It is, of course, possible to combine curved and angular elements in a single work, but more care will be needed in their placement if a well-balanced result is to be achieved.

Use a ruler and set square to draw squares and rectangles and a protractor for triangles, diamonds and parallelograms of specific angles. All these shapes will introduce a quality of strength and regularity to a design. They can be drawn precisely and arranged to form a pattern or a border; they can overlap or repeat. For a symmetrical design you will generally need an even number of shapes of each size; for a more interesting asymmetric design choose an uneven number.

Circles are intrinsically harmonious and restful shapes; a circle draws the eye to the area it encloses. Circles have a gentle movement and rhythm, in contrast to the strength and angularity of the straight-sided forms. There are many ways to draw circles, the simplest being to draw around circular objects such as saucers, lids, buttons or coins. (You can also use a selection of these items for pattern-

making, as shown on pages 26–7, for direct interpretation in embroidery.)

Another method for working out ideas is to use a pair of compasses, setting the distance between the point of the compasses and the end of the pencil to the radius of the intended circle. To divide the circle into petal shapes, place the point on the circumference and draw arcs. Concentric circles can be drawn by steadily decreasing the radius to make a series of different sized circles inside each other. These two ideas can be combined or adapted with limitless possibilities. Radiating lines, like the spokes of a wheel, can also be introduced. To divide the circle into uniform-sized segments, use a protractor and measure off the divisions, keeping the number of degrees at the centre constant.

Circles make good designs if several different sizes are used together; cut out a selection of paper circles and move them about, overlapping some, until you have a pleasing arrangement. Arcs can also be incorporated to 'reflect' the images.

COUNTED THREAD AND CANVASWORK

The counted thread embroidery techniques of cross stitch and Assisi work are done on evenweave fabric and their designs need to be drawn on graph paper in the form of a box chart. The standard cross stitch covers two intersections of the evenweave fabric, and each square on the graph paper represents one stitch. Canvaswork designs worked only in tent stitch are also charted in this way.

To transfer your design, either use squared tracing paper or trace the design directly to the graph paper by taping it to a window. Then redraw the design outline in steps, following the lines of the grid. Some curves may need accentuating otherwise they will flatten out when the embroidery is worked. Fill in the squares with appropriate colours or, in the case of Assisi work, fill in the squares of the background area with one colour and outline the motifs (which are left blank) in a contrasting tone.

The scale may need to be adapted to suit the finished design by enlarging or reducing (see p. 21).

Canvaswork lends itself readily to geometric designs, based on the grid of the canvas. If you wish to plan a design completely and not work freely, you will need to make a line chart. This differs from the box chart in that the lines on the graph paper signify the threads of the canvas, as opposed to the stitches to be worked. The actual stitches are drawn by lines, between the grid of the graph paper.

The form and structure of each stitch must be carefully shown; make sure the lines cross the graph paper as they would the canvas threads. If you are using a selection of stitches, each requiring a

different thread count, use a versatile module of 12 threads. Each module can incorporate stitches which cover multiples of two, three, four or six.

For pictorial canvaswork designs it is not necessary to plan a detailed chart; a freer way of working is explained on page 18. A design to be worked entirely in tent stitch, using different colours, is best represented by a box chart.

Florentine embroidery, with its characteristic zigzag patterns, is based upon a repeating stitch unit and is one of the simplest forms of embroidery to design yourself. The pattern of Florentine embroidery is established by means of Gobelin stitches, usually over an even number of threads, placed in step formation. To form a curve or a less sharp zigzag, blocks of two or more stitches are stepped instead of single stitches.

Once you have worked out your unit of design, this can be repeated horizontally along the row and subsequent lines in different colours worked in exact repeat formation. Alternatives such as motifs or four-way Florentine designs can also be tried, with the help of mirrors.

For this type of canvaswork, you need to draw up your design as a line chart, with the actual stitches drawn between the grid of the graph paper. If the design does not specify an exact width, start in the centre of the row and work horizontally toward one edge, repeating the pattern unit as many times as you wish. Then return to the centre and exactly mirror the row already worked, on the other side. If a precise width and number of units is stipulated the threads of the canvas used for the entire design should be counted and the pattern unit calculated to fit exactly. For example, a width of 48 threads could be divided into four patterns, each based on 12 threads.

An attractive variation on the row design is one containing motifs. The effect of this can be seen if an upright mirror is placed along the original horizontal pattern, thus producing a reflected image of medallions, lozenge shapes or diamonds. The resultant central spaces between the rows can be filled with Florentine or other straight stitches.

A further elaboration of this type of design is four-way Florentine, which consists of four identical triangular quarters, placed at right angles to each other along diagonal lines. You will need mirrors to help you formulate this type of design.

To chart the four-way design, draw horizontal and vertical lines on the graph paper to establish the centre. Then draw diagonal lines at 45°, intersecting the centre. Only a quarter of the design need be copied on to the chart, since this is repeated in the three remaining areas. Compensating stitches (see p. 131) will be needed to complete the diagonal edges.

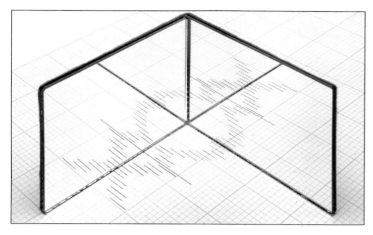

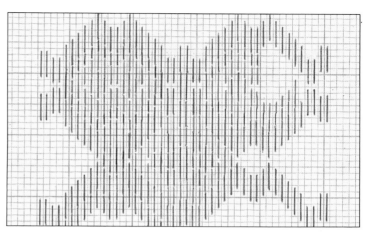

To establish a Florentine motif design, slide two mirrors along a row of charted Florentine stitches, placed at right angles to each other and to the stitches. When you find a part that mirrors well to form a suitable motif, draw in the perpendicular centre lines on which the mirrors lie, and mark the end of the pattern also.

On a piece of graph paper, chart the stitches between the marked lines, then repeat them as a mirror image on the other side of the vertical centre line. Chart the lower row to mirror the top row. Draw another motif next to the first and part of a second row underneath. The open areas between motifs may form secondary motifs.

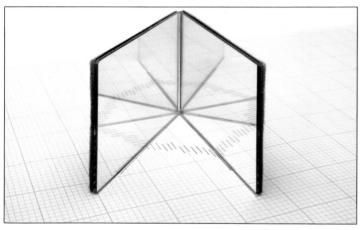

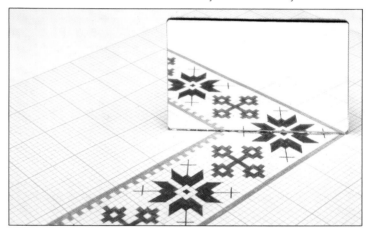

For a four-way Florentine design, place two mirrors on the row of charted stitches, one parallel to the stitches and the other at a 45° angle to the first; move them along the row to select the most appropriate part of the design.

The design for the corners of a continuous border can be worked out by placing a mirror at 45° diagonally across the proposed pattern. This will show a reflection at right angles. Move the mirror along the border design to select the most pleasing part for a corner.

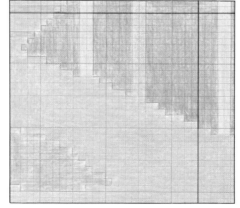

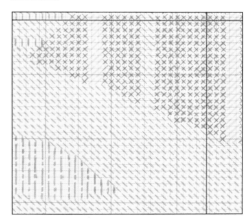

To chart a design for canvaswork, place the canvas over the drawing and count out the number of threads it covers in each direction. Measure these out on graph paper (any gauge); mark the centre lines. Transfer your design to the graph paper, square for square.

In a box chart, each square on the graph paper represents a stitch; the squares are filled in with the intended colours in different areas. Box charts are suitable for canvaswork designs worked in tent stitch only, as well as for cross stitch and Assisi work designs.

In a line chart, the chart is an exact duplication of how the different stitches will be laid over the canvas threads; draw the lines in the colours to be used. Use a line chart for Florentine patterns and for canvaswork designs worked in a variety of stitches.

CREATE YOUR OWN BACKGROUNDS

Once you advance beyond the simple application of decorative stitching to a plain fabric, your embroidery can become truly inventive. To achieve an original look, you should take advantage of the enormous design potential of backgrounds. As a visual dimension, the background is far too important to be left to chance; it can make or break a design even when playing a supporting role, and is so versatile it can assume an equal or even dominant character in relation to the other elements in your composition.

There are various subtle liaison techniques you can employ to pull your scheme together. Effective links between background and foreground can be made with pattern, colour or texture. The medium for a link might be a form of stitching—machine embroidery, pulled work or the application of a transparent fabric in harmonious colours, for example; alternatively, it might be a combination of fabric paints and/or dyes planned to team with the embroidery. Modifying the background as you like allows for totally original results.

Paint can be incorporated at any stage of the project—at the start, before embroidery begins; to highlight areas as the work progresses; or as a finishing touch. Paint can also be used to decorate the unworked areas of a canvaswork panel. In combining painting or dyeing with embroidery, always bear in mind the following points. The colour you apply should contribute something to the design which could not be achieved by embroidery alone, and the two methods should be carefully balanced in order to harmonize agreeably together.

FABRIC PAINTS
You should find fabric paints quite simple to use. There are three categories: all-purpose fabric paints, silk paints and transfer paints. Colours within the range for each category may be mixed, making possible infinite tonal variations. The paints are water-based and are generally made fast to washing and light by pressing with a hot iron. They can be applied either direct by brush or sponge; spattered, using a toothbrush; or sprayed on with a mouth spray diffuser or spray-gun.

All-purpose fabric paints All-purpose fabric paints are suitable for every type of fabric. First wash and iron the fabric, then mount it in a ring or stretcher frame, or fix it with masking tape to your work surface. Protect the work surface by putting paper beneath the fabric, and if working on a two-layered item such as a T-shirt or pillowcase insert either card or heavy cartridge paper in between the layers.

For small-scale and detailed designs use a fine brush and as little water as possible so as to avoid seepage along the grain of the fabric. For large areas of background, paints should be applied with a sponge; either the paint must be considerably watered down or the fabric must have been dampened first.

Silk paints Silk paints are specially manufactured for fine fabrics such as silk, thin cottons and synthetics. Choose the type made fast by ironing, rather than the more complicated steaming process. As silk paints are far more watery than the all-purpose fabric paints, they will spread by capillary action along the fibres of the fabric, giving a transparent water-colour effect. Beautiful backgrounds, such as sunsets, can be created by allowing different colours to blend together.

Transfer paints Only materials containing synthetic fibres can accept transfer paints. These paints are applied first to paper, allowed to dry and then ironed off on to the fabric. Be sure designs such as lettering and asymmetric motifs are painted in reverse, mirror-style, so that they appear correctly when transferred. Transfer crayons have similar properties.

SPATTERING AND SPRAYING
You can use any of the different fabric paints to create a spattered or sprayed effect for a background; however, silk paints tend to spread as their consistency is more watery. Those areas you do not intend to spray should be masked or shielded with card or paper; secure it to the fabric with masking or double-sided tape. Self-adhesive film, of the type sold for covering books, makes a good alternative to paper masks as it adheres to the fabric.

Spattering can be done with a toothbrush or mouth spray diffuser (see below). Guns for spraying are available in a wide range of models and can be used with either an aerosol can of airbrush propellant or with a more expensive compressor. Assemble and fill the gun according to the manufacturer's instructions, watering down your paint carefully to a milky consistency; make sure there are no paint lumps to block the nozzle. Holding the spray-gun about 20cm away from the surface, apply the paint with constant even pressure on the button, moving the gun back and forth at a steady rate. Most spraying is easily done with the work in a horizontal position (except when using a mouth spray diffuser).

Spraying or stippling with a stencil brush through a variety of different meshes will provide an interesting negative image. You can try rug canvas for a chequered pattern representing buildings or brick walls; or wire mesh of varying sizes for a texture and pattern unobtainable by ordinary painting methods.

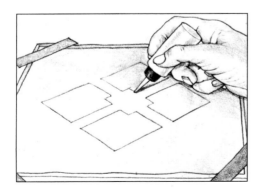

Gutta resist helps to control watery silk paints for more detailed or clear-edged designs. First iron the fabric, then tape it to a work surface covered with polythene. Apply the gutta resist to the fabric before painting to prevent seepage from one part to another; use the special applicator to ensure that the fabric is penetrated completely.

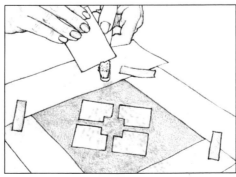

Use a toothbrush to get a spattered effect. Dip the brush into diluted or undiluted paint and, holding the head away from you, draw a piece of stiff card toward you over the bristles, at the same time directing the paint toward the fabric. The work can be in either a vertical or horizontal position. Practice to get correct coverage. Mask with paper or self-adhesive film the areas not to be spattered.

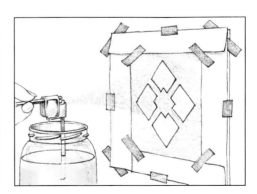

The mouth spray diffuser can be used with a stencil. Keep the work vertical. Put one end of the diffuser in paint watered to a milky consistency and put the mouthpiece in your mouth. Keeping the nozzle about 20cm from the work, take a deep breath and blow steadily and hard. Practice first. Mask the area beyond the stencil with paper or card stuck down with double-sided tape or self-adhesive film.

Blending occurs readily with brush- or sponge-applied silk paints. Their watery tints spread by capillary action through fine fabrics.

Sponging can produce a mottled effect like this when the paint has been dabbed on with a piece of plastic foam.

Gutta resist, a rubber-based solution, penetrates fine fabrics to prevent paint seepage, allowing for clear-edged designs.

Transfer paints, which bond with synthetic fibres only, are applied to paper first, then reversed on to the fabric and fixed by ironing.

Some fabric crayons can be applied direct and fixed with an iron. Masking tape gives the clean edges which contrast with the grainy colour.

Two-tone toothbrush spattering combined with the same mask used in two consecutive positions creates this special star-centre effect.

Use a mouth spray diffuser if you prefer a coarser, grainier spattered effect than is normally obtained by the toothbrush method.

Working with a stencil brush, use your chosen fabric paint sparingly and at full strength, applying it with a stabbing motion.

The rectangular motif of the stencilled and spatter-painted background is echoed by the outline-stitch quilting applied afterwards.

Dyeing colours fabric in a manner that is fundamentally different from painting, and home-dyed materials generally display tonal qualities of softness and luminosity quite distinct from the commercially dyed hues of shop-bought fabrics. If you are working with a natural fibre cloth, ordinary cold-water dyes are suitable for home use. You can mix them in order to produce original shades; just follow the manufacturer's instructions.

In addition to dyeing in solid colours, you can create unique background patterns by employing one of the resist methods. A resist method of dyeing is one that treats a portion of the fabric in such a way as to resist the penetration of the dye. Batik does this with wax; gutta resist uses a rubber solution; and tie-dyeing simply exploits the tight folds in the material which block the even spread of colour to create a variety of pleasing random-effect patterns.

The usual procedure for tie-dyeing is to tie the fabric with string, which prevents the dye from penetrating those areas most tightly bound. As well as different types of yarn, you can use rubber bands, paper clips, bulldog clips and clothes pegs to hold the fabric firmly and to produce characteristically different patterns. In tie-dyeing, chance always influences the final result. Exact repetition is impossible to achieve, but similar effects can be reproduced by repeating a prescribed technique.

If you are aiming for a specific tie-dyed effect, do allow time for experimentation. Keep comprehensive notes on the methods of folding and tying and on the length of dyeing time for future reference.

BASIC DYEING METHOD
To dye small quantities of fabric with the minimum of trouble, use cold-water dyes. A good range of colours is widely available and you can always mix your own new ones from these. Cold-water dyes are the rule for both natural fibres and viscose rayon; most synthetic fibres require hot-water dyes. Always follow the printed instructions faithfully, taking note of the amount of dye and water—particularly if you intend to repeat the colour in future. Dissolve every particle of powder completely, stirring the solution at each stage, and use the dyebath immediately as it will remain stable for only two to three hours after the salt and soda have been added.

Tie the fabric in the desired way, leaving a length of string with which to lower the bundle into the dyebath; this can be looped over the edge or tied to the handle, if you are using a bucket. First wet the bundle with plain water, then immerse it in the solution; stir continuously for a few minutes to ensure even distribution of the dye. Check for depth of colour frequently,

bearing in mind that it will be considerably paler when rinsed and dried. When you are satisfied with the shade, remove the sample from the dyebath, rinse thoroughly, untie, rinse again, dry and iron. If you like, the sample can then be retied and redyed in another colour to produce a greatly enhanced, multicoloured effect.

FOLDING AND TYING
The method used to fold the fabric will determine the nature of the pattern you get. There are numerous folding techniques. The simplest is to fold the cloth in half and bind it, which will result in a mirror image when dyed. Fabric can be folded in quarters, diagonally or in concertina fashion. Remember that the fabric on the inside of the sample will be the least likely to accept the dye, so ascertain which areas of the piece you would prefer darkest in colour and arrange these on the outside of the folded sample.

One of the easiest and most useful techniques is **marbling.** The random patterns produced are suitable for a selection of embroidery backgrounds. Voile and muslin can be marbled to evoke skies, vegetation or watery scenes; the effect can also be used simply to add interest to otherwise bland fabrics of different types.

To get a marbled effect simply crumple the fabric in your hand and tie it securely by binding it with string, raffia or strong cotton, criss-crossing the entire surface. Fasten with a knot.

You can use the folds and tying to control the pattern shape. For example, a **chevron** design can be made by folding a square of fabric in half lengthways, concertina pleating diagonally and binding straight across. Bulldog clips produce **rectangular** areas of resist which form interesting and regular geometric patterns on squares of fabric folded in different ways.

Circular motifs in a variety of shapes and sizes can be produced with the aid of such objects as buttons, pebbles and cotton reels. Just wrap the fabric around them and either bind with yarn or secure with rubber bands. The results are often flower-like dots, suitable for a garden scene, or for cutting out and embroidering individually on an appliqué panel. If you intend to make a regular pattern, plan the positioning of the objects and mark the fabric with a pencil before beginning. It will then be possible to see where each one should be placed even when the fabric has become distorted in the course of the binding.

A **sunburst** design can be produced by wrapping up an object such as a large button in the centre of a piece of fabric. The remaining bundle can then be bound at intervals with string to give concentric circles. If the sample is dyed a second

time, bind the string in the areas between the original bindings to produce a richer image. Experiment with fabrics of different textures, such as satin or transparent chiffon, and enhance the design with surface stitchery by hand or machine.

Individual, **stemmed flowers** can be created by proceeding as for the circular or sunburst motifs, using a small button for the centre of each flower. To make the stems, fold the fabric vertically just beneath the centre of each flower head and clamp a lath of wood with a bulldog clip along the edge of the fold.

Tritik is an interesting variation on the tie-dye theme. The resist is achieved by means of needle and strong cotton, rather than clamping or binding. It suits a fine fabric such as cotton lawn or muslin, which you stitch in your own choice of gathers, tucks, pleats or oversewing; finish by pulling the thread very tight before dyeing and unpick it afterwards. Tiny dots can be made by binding with thread, and outlines for designs can be made with a double row of tiny running stitches, or by oversewing along the line. Alternatively, you can machine the outline in a zigzag stitch through two or more layers of fabric if you would like to create a repeat motif.

Discharge dyeing, or tie-bleaching, will produce any of the patterns described above in reverse, leaving you with a positive image on a bleached background. Simply use non-colourfast dyed fabric with any of the proprietary brands of colour and stain remover, or experiment with a weak solution of household bleach and water using a 1:6 ratio.

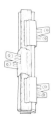

Rectangular patterns like this with the look of Indian Madras cotton are produced using bulldog clips on concertina folds. Cling film was also bound around the middle to prevent too much black dye penetrating.

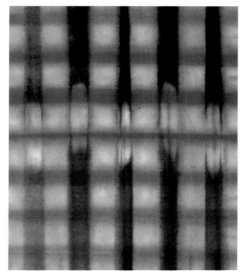

Marbling is one of the simplest effects to achieve. Simply crumple the fabric in your hand and bind it with string, criss-crossing the surface.

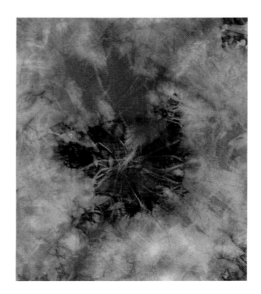

Chevron designs result when fabric squares are folded lengthways and concertina pleated diagonally, then bound straight across.

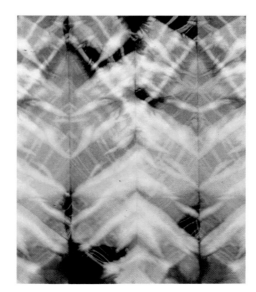

For sunburst patterns wrap an object such as a large button in the centre of the cloth and bind the remainder at intervals to form concentric circles.

The tritik method is similar to tie-dye, but uses pulled thread instead of binding to achieve the resist. Fabric is gathered, tucked, pleated or oversewn before dyeing.

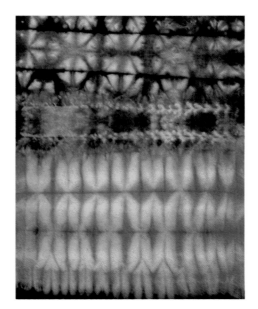

Circular motifs that sometimes look like the heads of flowers are made by securing pebbles or buttons in the fabric with string or rubber bands.

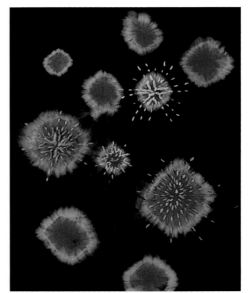

EXPERIMENT WITH LINES AND SHAPES

The basis of almost any embroidery design, when reduced to its essentials, is the use of line and shape: whether the design is pictorial, stylized or abstract it will depend for its success on the proportions of shapes and spaces, together with the direction and use of line.

USING LINES

Lines in all their forms constitute potent elements of embroidery, from the jagged zigzag lines of Florentine work to the gently curved contour lines used in quilting.

Lines are ever-present in natural forms. They can exist as pure pattern—think of the stripes on tigers and zebras, as well as on shells, pebbles and leaves—or in delineating shape, as in the linear elements of a landscape: imagine rolling hills with lines of ploughed fields converging toward the skyline, the lines of streaky cloud formations or of flowing water. Manmade forms also produce strong linear effects—for example, the curving structure of a flyover contrasted with the parallel lines of the motorway.

Lines appear in many forms—straight, curved, wavy, broken, zigzag, parallel. Horizontal lines in a design give a sense of calm and tranquillity, whilst vertical lines, by contrast, are stronger and more aggressive. Flowing curves usually depict gentle rhythms, whereas the angularity of zigzags suggests vigorous movement of a very different nature.

Subjects that are made up of related lines, rather like contours—woodgrain, rock strata, an avenue of trees, corn blowing in the wind, the folds on a garment or a draped fabric—can all be translated into harmonious embroidery designs. Such a subject could also be taken out of context, by isolating part of it in a window mount (see p. 23), to make an abstract project.

Several embroidery techniques rely particularly on linear forms. Many surface stitches naturally create lines (see pp. 69–75). Those such as back stitch or stem stitch produce thin lines; some, like Pekinese, are fairly narrow but decorative; others, such as buttonhole and loop stitch, make wide borders and bands. Their effects can, of course, be varied considerably, depending on the sort of yarn used as well as the way in which the stitch is worked (see pp. 50–57).

Running stitches, which make broken lines, have a much more tentative or subtle effect than broad chain stitch, which produces strong, solid lines. A dotted line can be achieved with coral stitch or couching, whereas bullion or French knots would make dotted lines with spaces between the dots. Lines that expand or diminish in width are easily made by using chain stitch combined with open chain.

Band stitches, when worked conventionally, form broader lines than line stitches. Wide, openwork stitchery can be achieved with up-and-down buttonhole or feather stitch, and very decorative effects can be made by juxtaposing several rows of complementary band stitches, such as double herringbone, chevron and open Cretan. Textural borders can be created using raised chain band or rosette chain.

Many quilting designs are based on intersecting lines or, like Hawaiian quilting, on concentric contour lines. Italian (corded) quilting, being made up of narrow padded parallel lines, lends itself to continuous curving lines. Stems and stalks can be depicted effectively in this type of quilting; interlaced patterns will make interesting border designs.

Many metal thread designs depend on the use of line, since the method of couching gold cord or threads plays a large part in the technique (see pp. 96–9).

Drawn thread work is composed of vertical or horizontal bands of threads withdrawn from the ground fabric. In its traditional form, this technique can be used either for borders or to execute formal, grid-based openwork designs. You can experiment with drawn thread work by varying the width of line; or by using the openwork areas as part of a stylized pictorial design: for example, as upright tree trunks with the foliage carried out in surface stitchery or pulled work.

Smocking designs are usually composed of a series of parallel lines worked in stem, cable and double cable stitch to form rows of different widths. Experimental effects could be tried by using lines which separate and then converge, or which are wavy rather than straight.

Machine embroidery, by its very nature, consists of rows of stitching, used to create thin linear effects. The width of line can be altered by adjusting the stitch-width control, and thicker, more textured lines can be produced by couching wool, braid or handmade textured yarns. Some automatic patterns will make decorative lines, particularly suitable for dress embroidery or for table and bed linen.

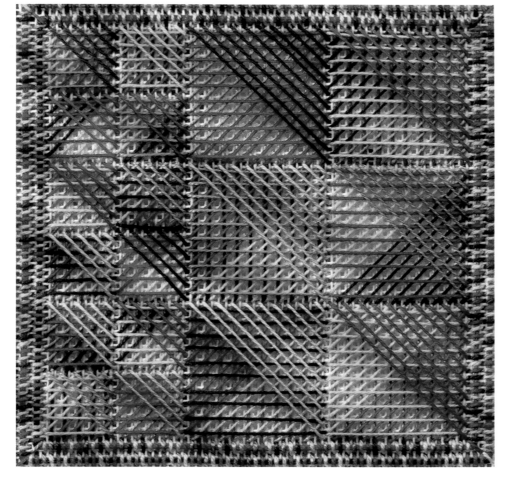

Lines can be used to build up shapes. In this experimental form of canvaswork, in which the canvas is allowed to show through the stitches, long lines of thread are worked in different directions to form a multi-layer grid-based design. The juxtaposition of primary colours adds a further dimension to this geometric embroidery.

The type of canvaswork known as Florentine embroidery relies on the structure of the related lines of stitches to form the wavy or zigzag patterns characteristic of this technique. The blocks of stitches stepped to establish curves can be combined with zigzags of single-stepped stitches for an infinite number of different patterns. Try experimenting with one basic unit in as many ways as possible (see pp. 128–9). Make a mirror image to create a medallion shape (see p. 29); alter the placing of the colours to give unusual effects; work the unit as a four-way sample.

USING SHAPES

When adapting a three-dimensional subject to a flat embroidery design it will be necessary to reduce the object to basics, so that you are left with an outline which encloses a shape. It may help to classify a shape—is it geometric or free-form, simple or involved? Can it be broken up further into smaller areas?

Make a selection of items that attract you purely for their shape—it might include a hand-crafted pot, a piece of sculpture, or a handful of smooth pebbles—and try to analyze the reasons for your choice. It may be the perfectly regular form of the pottery, the asymmetric curves of the sculpture, or the related shapes in the pebble collection. A design that uses related shapes is easier on the eye than one containing a number of unrelated elements. For example, a geometric design made up of squares and triangles, or one developed from an exploded shape in cut paper (see p. 25) would be harmonious.

Both natural and man-made subjects can involve similar shapes. Circular motifs are inherent in many flower-heads and fruit, as well as appearing as manufactured wheels, coins or plates. In considering shapes in relation to embroidery design, remember that the background is also part of the design. When drawing or arranging pieces of cut paper or fabric, look carefully at their distribution and make sure that the areas of background also form satisfactory and harmonious shapes.

The theme of filling spaces in a decorative fashion constitutes a major part of many embroidery methods. Filling stitches, as their name implies, cover the surface material in a fairly solid way. Those such as satin stitch, Roumanian and Bokhara couching, can cover the ground completely; others, such as wave and cloud filling and trellis couching, will leave some of the material showing. Single unit stitches such as seeding, detached chain and fly stitch can be sprinkled lightly over an area or the outlined shape, producing delicate pattern and texture, whilst band stitches, if worked closely together in rows, will fill a solid shape.

Appliqué is a method that uses cut-out

shapes. They make a bold impact, so it is important to plan out the original design carefully. The various motifs must be complemented by the intervening spaces.

English quilting should be composed of well-chosen and defined spaces, as these will constitute the raised areas between the lines of stitching. These shapes should not be too small or the effect of the padding will be lost. In cutwork designs, it is the spaces between the elements that form the design, so the main motifs must be carefully placed with this in mind.

In metal thread embroidery shapes are often filled with closely worked lines of

Appliqué is primarily concerned with the use of shapes, which make a bold statement in an embroidery design. Combined with machine work in this embroidered panel, it is easy to see how the harmonious composition of the design, based on flower borders in a garden, relies on the successful use of lines and shapes. The large appliqué sun motif at the top is echoed in the smaller repeat motifs used as a border round the edges.

EXPERIMENT WITH LINES AND SHAPES

The full potential of embroidery is shown when a pictorial design is successfully worked in a single stitch. Canvaswork done in tent stitch is the most obvious example, but in this picture of the site of a wartime airfield, couching, an essentially linear stitch, is worked vertically in single-strand silk thread down the grain of the fabric. The elements of the scene—the Lancaster plane, the airman, the cows, the clump of trees and the aeroplane flying overhead—are clearly delineated through change of colour. Even quite strong horizontal lines, as well as the subtle formation of a cloudy sky and the colour gradations in the meadow, are all suggested visually.

couched thread, in basket, brick or *or nué*. Some parts of a design can be padded with gold or silver kid, or filled with purls.

All the counted thread techniques, except drawn thread which is mainly made up of lines, are very much concerned with the decorative filling of spaces. The various pulled work stitches will cover an area with patterns containing holes of different sizes and shapes. The decorative nature of blackwork patterns makes it somewhat difficult to achieve realism. However, if outlines are eliminated and tonal values taken into account, a pleasing result can be achieved. Shaded effects can be created by gradually altering the density of a stitch, by changing the thickness of the thread, and by adding or subtracting elements of the pattern.

Both cross stitch and Assisi work are primarily concerned with shape—the regular nature of these techniques relies on the use of harmonious filled-in areas combined with well-proportioned background spaces. In making box charts for these two methods (see p. 29 and p. 102), look carefully at the shapes to ensure that they are immediately recognizable. If not, you may need to accentuate or redefine some outlines.

BORDERS AND EDGINGS
A border is an extension of the linear theme; whether it comprises a repeating motif from the embroidery design itself, a

row of band stitches or a few lines of pulled work or withdrawn threads, the formation is either a single line, four lines or the perimeter of a circle. Some embroidered pieces, such as pictures, require a border or edging to finish them off. Certain types of embroidery, like drawn thread work, virtually incorporate borders within the technique itself.

The border decoration on table and bed linen may well form the total or a major part of the design. Hems, edges or sleeves of garments all offer scope for borders to be worked in a variety of techniques; cushions or panels could have border designs, either as a surround to a central motif or as a series of embroidered stripes. It is essential that borders are worked out at the planning stage rather than added as an afterthought. They should be considered in proportion to the whole; the width, in particular, needs careful consideration.

Items worked in drawn thread, pulled work, cross stitch and Assisi work on evenweave fabric can be greatly enhanced by neatly finished hems and decorative borders. A drawn thread border or edging looks well with any of the counted thread methods; for a sampler in cross stitch it is appropriate to have a border of the same technique or maybe one in Assisi work; some canvaswork embroidery may need a 'frame' to set it off attractively.

For each of these methods, the threads

of canvas or evenweave fabric should be counted and the length of the border measured, marking the centre with a thread. A box or a line chart can then be drawn on graph paper (see p. 29). If you use a repeat motif, always include the surrounding area as part of the unit to ensure that the correct spacing is allowed for.

For a one-edge border, or one in which corners do not have to be considered, divide the length of the edge by the number of threads needed for the unit to ascertain how many units will fit in. A motif pattern can be centred, giving an uneven number of motifs, or spaced from the centre to produce an even number. For drawn thread borders the hemstitching can usually be adjusted. If the number of threads in the total length does not divide exactly, the extra one or two threads can be incorporated within adjacent groups.

The easiest way of making a four-sided border fit a given space is to start by working the corners and gradually move toward the centre of each edge. This will give a mirrored design which, when the midway point is reached, can be adapted to form a central motif; or a few compensating stitches can end the pattern.

Border designs can sometimes be taken out of their original context and used to form geometric patterns in themselves—they can be arranged as stripes, diagonals or in a trellis.

Blackwork designs are based on regular shapes decoratively filled with stitches. Blackwork relies for its effectiveness on tonal contrasts between blocks of stitching, some being worked densely and others to form more lacy, openwork patterns. Borders and edgings based on geometric motifs are characteristically worked into the design.

Blackwork combines well with other counted thread techniques, especially pulled and drawn thread work. In this embroidery the border of the left-hand panel is created with pulled work. The same technique has been used for the flower heads and the pale crosses and diagonals in the right-hand panel.

CONSIDER COLOUR

Before embarking on any embroidery project you need to give careful thought to the colours you will use. The colour theme may even be your starting point, if you are designing a cushion or a chair seat or even a picture to complement a particular room scheme. Many people have an intuitive sense of colour, and indeed everyone expresses their personality in the colours they wear and with which they decorate their homes. Becoming more colour conscious will, however, enhance your abilities as a designer. To this end it's worth knowing the essentials of colour theory. Understanding the principles will enable you to develop more successful colour schemes and to create tonally well-balanced embroideries.

THE COLOUR WHEEL
In the graphic device known as the colour wheel, the colours of the rainbow are depicted arranged in a circle; the colours appear in the same order as in the spectrum but the red and violet from each end are joined up.

The basic colour wheel shows only hues, but each segment of the wheel in fact represents a vast range of shades. The hue gives a particular colour its name (such as brown, purple, orange) and defines its position on the wheel, but shades of colour are scientifically defined by two other characteristics. Its value, or lightness, tells you how much white or black a colour contains, or whether it is light or dark. A tint is pale, i.e. the colour mixed with white, and a shade is dark, i.e. the colour mixed with black. Finally, a colour's saturation is a measure of its purity or intensity. For example, a pinky, dove-grey is low in saturation, high in value, whereas crimson is highly saturated, medium in value.

When planning any colour scheme, all three elements play a part, and it is important to understand their relationship. The tonal value, that is, the lightness and saturation of the colours you choose, is as important as the actual hue in achieving the harmony or calculated contrast that you want. A colour that is subtly greyed, for example, may be discredited next to a clear, bright tone, whereas it could look perfect with other colours of similar value.

As a general rule, related colours, that is, those which appear next to each other on the colour wheel, will blend together well and create a harmonious scheme. Contrasting colours, which appear opposite each other, are known as complementaries. Thus red is complementary to green, yellow to purple and blue to orange. Black and white are of course contrasting. Contrast can also be achieved by using wide tonal differences in a monochromatic design, for example a dark or strong pure colour like royal blue placed next to a tint or muted shade such as a pale sky blue. Using contrasting colours together will produce vibrant, exciting designs. The palest pastels all blend harmoniously, even those derived from opposites on the colour wheel.

In embroidery design the warm, advancing colours (reds, oranges, yellows) are best placed in the foreground, or in some way used as a focal point, while the muted or cool colours (blues, greens, purples) lend themselves to achieving an effect of distance or depth in a design.

Colours can also be considered to have 'personalities'. Reds, for instance, are bold, warm and friendly, sometimes provocative, while browns are homely and restful. Yellows are cheerful and sunny, as compared to greens which can be crisp, cool and fresh. Blues usually evoke calm and serenity. Packaging designers exploit these characteristics to the full, using, for example, pale, clear greens to convey freshness and browns for a nostalgic country style.

How can you apply these colour principles to embroidery? First of all, *use* the colour wheel. Test out your proposed colour choices against the theories of harmonious and contrasting combinations.

To increase your awareness of colour,

The colour wheel, embroidered here in satin stitch, shows the relationship of colour families: which are harmonious and which are contrasting. Use it to explore tonal values also: the inner ring shows tints, with 50 per cent white added to the basic hues, while the outer ring is made up of shades, with 50 per cent black added.

The primary colours are the pure hues of red, yellow and blue from which, with black and white, all other colours derive. The primaries are equidistant on the colour wheel and divide it into three.

The secondary colours are achieved by mixing two primaries together in equal amounts. Thus red

and yellow make orange, yellow and blue make green, and blue and red make purple. These appear between the primaries on the colour wheel; each secondary colour is the complement of the one primary not used in its make-up and appears opposite it on the wheel. Further colours are interspersed. These tertiary colours are mixtures of each primary colour and its adjoining secondary.

Achromatic colours, which do not appear on the wheel, are those made from a mixture of black and white, i.e. greys and neutrals. Mixing all three primaries, plus black and white, in different proportions will produce a range of greys and browns.

start to look at the colour combinations used by professionally trained people: textile designers, window dressers, florists and interior designers, and analyse what makes for a successful scheme.

Make your own colour collection, starting with colour charts from paint shops, colour swatches of fabric and sample cards of threads; these are usually arranged in colour families which blend well together. Collect tearsheets from magazines, commercial packaging, photographs, postcards and scraps of material and wallpaper. You might also include natural objects which are attractive to you purely for their colour, such as shells, pebbles, leaves or dried flowers.

Keep your collection on a pinboard or in an old shoe box and study them. This will teach you a lot about how colour works. It will show the dynamic range of the main colour groups and the unexpected shades and hues within each one.

It's worth doing a few embroidery-related colour exercises before you begin a specific project, particularly if you are a beginner at design. Several are outlined on the following pages. Experimenting in this way brings new possibilities and combinations to mind, and makes you more aware of the way colours react. You will need a wide selection of scraps of different coloured fabric and thread, as well as paint, paintbrush and some white card.

CONSIDER COLOUR

TONAL VALUE

The importance of tone in a composition is paramount. Bear in mind that darker tones will recede and lighter ones advance.

These basic monochromatic exercises use paint, threads and fabric.
1 Start with paint of a pure hue, such as blue, and add different amounts of black to produce five gradated shades; then add different amounts of the blue to white to produce at least five gradated tints.
2 From your selection of threads, choose those of one colour family, in this case blue, and grade them from palest sky blue to deepest navy.
3 Alter the tone of a blue piece of fabric by overlaying it with organza or net, first white, then grey, then black.

A further tonal exercise (not illustrated) is to dye several lengths of white cotton threads, taking them out of the dyebath at intervals for a gradation of tone (see p. 52).

HARMONY

Harmonious colours, that is those in close proximity on the colour wheel, are easy on the eye and generally work well together.
1 Paint several squares in a group of harmonious colours—say orange, orange-yellow and yellow. Do not add any black or white as this will alter the tonal value.
2 Make a harmonious scheme, using threads in the same oranges and yellows (or, say, red, pink and lilac). First of all use equal amounts of each colour, then try to make it more interesting by varying the proportions of each colour used.
3 Make a collection of wallpapers or printed fabrics which employ basically harmonious colours. Notice how the additional contrast (blue-grey) adds interest to the middle fabric, while the splashes of bright orange pep up the colour scheme in the top fabric.

CONTRAST

Contrasting colour schemes employ the complementaries; they are strong, lively and make for vivid and interesting designs.
1 Using primary colours, either in fabric, paint or coloured paper, make several contrasting schemes by trying them in differing proportions.
2 Make a complementary colour scheme with threads in, say, red and green. Notice how vibrant and cheerful it is. Try using different amounts of each colour and analyse your reactions to the result, then add some grey threads and see how the vibrant contrast is subdued.
3 In a strongly contrasting scheme using fabric, add an achromatic colour. Notice how the vividness is subdued; the achromatic shade has a neutralizing effect and reduces the contrast.

COLOUR IN NATURE

Interesting schemes can develop from observing natural objects. Take a ready-made colour scheme from nature, using a shell (or else a leaf, a piece of mineral or bark, or a flower).

1 Examine the colours of the shell and choose threads of stranded cotton or wool in exactly the same shades. Wind them around a piece of card in similar proportions.

2 Using the same colour threads, make a second and a third sample, altering the amount and proportion of each colour or shade. Study the differences and see which you prefer as the starting point for an embroidery design.

Working through some of the exercises opposite and above will provide further insights into the subject of colour. You then have to consider the practical ways to use colour.

Some embroidery techniques, by their very nature, will be best carried out in monochrome—many of the counted thread methods, such as whitework and black-work, look best in one colour. Quilting, which relies for its effect on light playing on the uneven surface, is often stitched in a thread that tones with the fabric. Broderie anglaise and cutwork are traditionally carried out in monochromatic colour schemes, since the effectiveness of those techniques relies on the pattern and position of the holes and spaces in the design.

Colour in embroidery can be applied in several ways; stitching with coloured yarns is the most obvious, but you can also make coloured areas by adding fabrics, by painting and by the use of ribbons or beads. You can create areas of vibrancy with solid stitches in bright colours, or pastel delicacy with lacy threads and a more open stitch. In addition, colour and tonal changes can be varied by interspersing threads in stranded cotton or wool; by placing stitches closer together or farther apart or by shading threads from dark to light. Shading can also be achieved by 'optical mixing' in which two different coloured threads are interspersed to make a new colour. This is a useful device when only a limited colour range is available.

Coloured or patterned pieces of fabric applied to a background will make immediate impact—appliquéed children's wear in bright colours is extremely eye-catching. Transparent fabrics used on an embroidered panel will give infinite

varieties of tone, as shown in the Tonal Value exercise opposite.

The background of an embroidery is a vital part of the design. It should be chosen in conjunction with the proposed threads and fabrics. If you have already selected these, try them out on different backgrounds. When the background colour is already dictated by other factors, such as its position in a room setting, experiment with different tones of that colour to achieve the best effect.

Fabric paints can be applied to background fabrics of any fibre, creating colour without additional texture. Dyeing your fabric to harmonize or tone with threads in exactly the way you wish is another possibility. The practicalities of both these are explained further on pages 30–33.

Ideas for subject matter may strongly influence your choice of colour, but don't feel too constrained by naturalistic representation. Your observation of natural objects such as butterflies, gems or shells may well be a starting point for an embroidery design, but the work itself can be carried out either by reproducing the natural colours exactly, or altering them in some way to suit your purpose.

A reassuring aspect of taking your design idea from nature—whether it is flowers, or a landscape or a piece of bark —is that colours in nature are always harmonious. But this may not always ensure a sufficiently lively or exciting colour scheme for an embroidery. You might need to introduce deliberate areas of contrast.

Once you have the initial inspiration, be prepared to develop the idea: an apple does not necessarily have to be depicted in red or green, it could be worked in gold metal thread. Equally, a tree could be

stitched in purple and a design of shells on a waistcoat could be appliquéed in black and white satin.

Your choice of colour for an embroidery may well be dictated by the intended use of the proposed work. Cushions, for example, will be planned to match, harmonize or contrast with the other soft furnishings in the room, and the colour of an embroidered belt for a ready-made dress will have to balance the overall effect of the garment. For an embroidered panel or wallhanging, these criteria may not be of prime importance, so your choice of colours is more open.

For many, choosing the colours for such a project is the easiest part of the design process. You may have already been inspired by the purchase of a beautiful background fabric or some appealing yarns. Then you need simply choose a colour scheme which you find interesting and with which you feel at ease. This does not mean that you should play safe and use only neutral or harmonizing colours— some areas of contrast could possibly enliven the whole embroidery.

When designing, try to keep an open mind about colour. Consider all the aspects of tone, harmony and contrast at the planning stage, but always be prepared to alter and rearrange some colours as the design progresses.

EXPERIMENT WITH TEXTURE

Texture is an integral aspect of all embroidery, not least because the application of stitches to a surface immediately adds a further textural dimension to it. The appeal of the different embroidery techniques varies from the smoothness of satin stitch worked in silk to the rough chunkiness of tweed and hessians incorporated into a piece of appliqué.

Contemporary designs, particularly those for embroidered panels and wall-hangings, are unlikely to restrict the embroiderer in terms of texture, nor are there usually any implicit practical limitations, except on items of clothing. Threads can be twisted, plaited and superimposed on one another; additional components such as beads, glass or shells can be stitched to the surface; fabrics can be added, padded, manipulated; or the background fabric can be removed to form decorative holes.

Texture is enhanced by contrast, that is, when any rough area is juxtaposed with a smooth one. Imagine, for example, the tactile quality of tweed next to cotton, velvet juxtaposed with silk, or a cluster of beads surrounded by the silk finish of long and short stitch. A mixture of techniques in a simple design is another way of introducing contrast in texture. Try leather appliqué with crewel embroidered canvaswork, for example. Change of texture on dress and household items can also provide exciting possibilities. A plain knitted sweater could be transformed to a luxury evening garment with the addition of beads, sequins or satin or appliqué motifs; a chintz-covered armchair could be complemented by a monochrome cushion worked using an interesting texture such as quilting or canvaswork in pearl cotton.

CREATING TEXTURE WITH STITCHES

The textural effect created by an area of stitching depends on the stitch and on the type of thread used. Satin stitch, for example, is usually worked in a smooth thread, but the same stitch worked in a hairy wool yarn produces an entirely different texture. As a rule, flat stitches, when used in an orthodox way, create a smooth texture. Such stitches include split, stem, back, long and short stitch, as well as couching and satin stitch. By contrast, all the knotted stitches — including French and bullion knots, coral, twisted chain, raised chain band, spider's web and rosette chain — produce knobbly effects.

One of the simplest ways of adding an unusual texture is by using thick thread — bouclé, chenille and chunky knitting yarns will all produce effective results, almost regardless of stitch. A textured area can also be built up by superimposing one layer of stitches on top of another, using a variety of thick and thin yarns.

A change of texture can be achieved by contrasting solid areas of filling stitches with the more open, lacy type of stitch; Roumanian or Bokhara couching would contrast well with wave filling; closely worked line stitches such as stem or chain could be combined with trellis couching.

The texture of conventional machine embroidery is mostly rather flat; the automatic patterns of this technique result in a smooth satiny finish. Incorporating a thick, contrasting thread is a means of adding extra textural diversity; bouclé or slubbed knitting and weaving yarns can also be couched down, using the normal zigzag stitch. Delicate, lacy patterns can be created by using one of the dissolvable methods of machine embroidery, such as vanishing muslin. These methods allow areas of open work to be added as decoration on garments, or can form back-

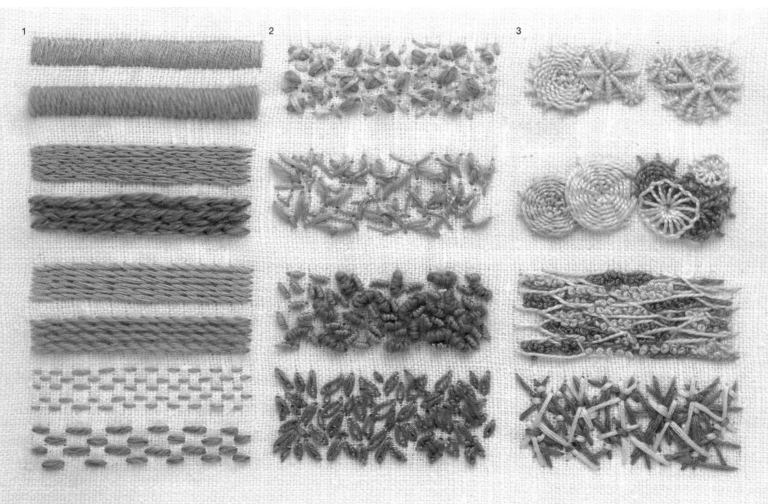

grounds in themselves for filmy hangings and similar embroideries. You can use them to produce freestanding motifs such as butterflies or skeleton leaf shapes.

Goldwork (see pp. 96-7) has an extravagant appeal which can be exploited in a design in combination with the texture of the threads themselves. When gold threads are applied over string as a padding, for example, it forms a bumpy woven surface; gold plate can be crinkled over a screw to reflect the light; rough, smooth and check purls are all in themselves highly textured and, if padded or stitched in loops, create a 'crunchy' effect.

ADDING ON
The addition of beads and/or sequins to embroidery is both decorative and textural. Such additions are made to evening garments and bags or used on embroidered pictures. As well as these conventional additions you can also use a wide range of 'found' objects to create exciting textural effects. These could include washers, curtain rings, plastic and wooden tubing, dowels, coils of wire; or natural objects such as shells, bark, minerals, pebbles, feathers, dried flowers, dried leaves and driftwood.

Any of these objects, if incorporated into an appropriate design with suitably chosen threads and fabrics, could give your embroidery new scope. To work effectively they must, however, integrate well with the surrounding areas of texture. For a more subtle approach, many are best covered in some way or stitched with decorative threads. Those with an inherently attractive appearance can be attached unobtrusively with invisible thread and a spot of glue.

Beads may be sewn on to an embroidery individually, or couched down on a connecting thread. To provide more prominent texture, thread several beads on to previously waxed thread and reinsert the needle into almost the same spot on the fabric from which it emerged. This will result in a loop of beads that stands away from the background. Repeat this process for a thickly encrusted texture.

Shisha glass, which has for centuries decorated Indian mirror embroidery, needs to be sewn on in a special way with crossed stitches, firmly buttonholed, to hold it securely in place. Jewels and small stones or pebbles can be attached in a similar fashion. A spot of glue will help to hold these in place while stitching.

A variety of textural effects, based on contrast, is created by stitches alone or with additional decorations. A selection is shown in the embroidered sample below.

1 Satin stitch and line stitches (split, stem and running) worked first in stranded cotton for a smooth effect, then in angora wool for a rough, more textured result.

2 Filling stitches worked in a combination of contrasting yarns (crewel wool and pearl cotton): seeding, fly, bullion knots, detached chain.

3 Overlapping stitches worked in pearl cotton: spider's webs and buttonhole and woven wheels; Cretan stitch and French knots; seeding and herringbone stitch.

4 Solid stitching combined with open, lacy stitches: Roumanian stitch with wave filling; closely worked chain stitch and trellis couching.

5 Shiny sequins create a brittle texture; they are attached in a diversity of decorative ways, including beads and French knots.

6 Beads and bugles attached singly and in groups for delicate or denser effects.

7 A three-dimensional, highly textured flower motif is created with shells, pearl beads, shisha glass (simulated here by foil-covered card), beads covered with needleweaving, plus buttonhole and detached chain stitch.

8 The goldwork includes padding over felt and string; a variety of smooth purl and pearl purl; Russia braid; and circular couching with rough purl.

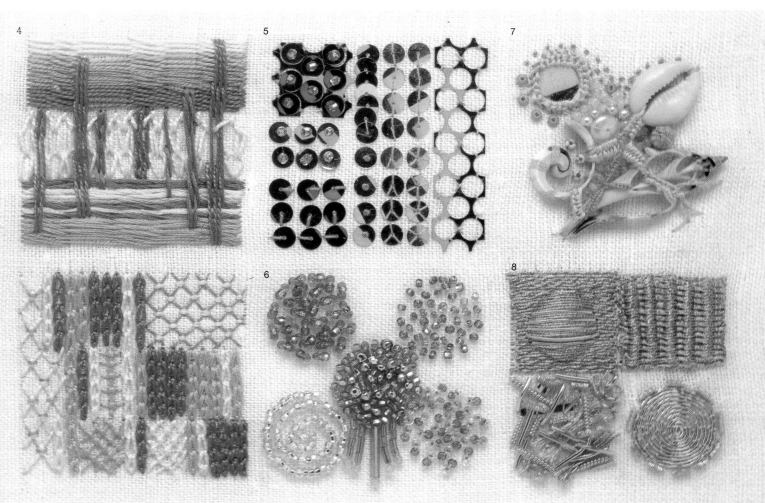

4

5

7

6

8

EXPERIMENT WITH TEXTURE

Texture is an element of every environment. Using a similar approach to the subject of colour (see pp.38–41), start by becoming aware of the textural qualities of natural and domestic objects. Look at the roughness of a wooden fence, the bricks of a wall or house, the bark of trees. Compare the smoothness of the front of a leaf with the ridged effect on the back.

When designing your own embroideries, think about how you might recreate some of these textures, in terms of the fabric and thread you might use, as well as the stitches themselves. The garden wall, for example, might be translated into a design using thick wool yarn on a rough-textured fabric; a collection of smooth pebbles might be the basis for a picture worked in quilted satin with areas enhanced by fabric paint and silk stitchery; a carving might evoke a three-dimensional soft sculpture in padded appliqué and manipulated fabrics.

A practical exercise that will heighten your awareness of texture is to make some rubbings, using wax crayons and thin paper. Select a surface which you think might be interesting, such as the weave of a basket or the ridges on frosted glass. Rubbings of the backs of leaves, with their prominent vein formations, could inspire a composition which might decorate an appliquéed garment, with the addition of Vandyke, fishbone or fly stitches depicting the ridges.

MANIPULATING FABRICS

Altering the existing texture of a fabric can add a new dimension to your work. It is possible to exploit the inherent textural qualities of the fibres and the weave by manipulating the fabric in a number of ways. Soft fabrics such as georgette, chiffon, and crepe will ruche and gather well, but would be difficult to pleat, except in unpressed folds. Crisp fabrics, such as poplin, linen, silk organza and cotton organdie, do not drape satisfactorily, but they can be tucked and pleated precisely. Gathered and ruched fabrics could be incorporated in a garment or could add an area of texture to an appliqué panel. A ruched, scalloped hem can be made by gathering a row of tiny stitches in zigzag formation, producing an unusual edging to lingerie or babywear. Ribbon or narrow lengths of fabric can be similarly treated.

Smocking is a traditional technique which involves gathering fabric into regular folds and subsequently decorating it with stitches. Although most frequently used for dress decoration, the method can be adapted successfully to more sculptural effect.

Pleats and tucks are dressmaking techniques that impart a linear or geometric aspect to a piece of work. Lines of tucks or pleats can be interspersed with

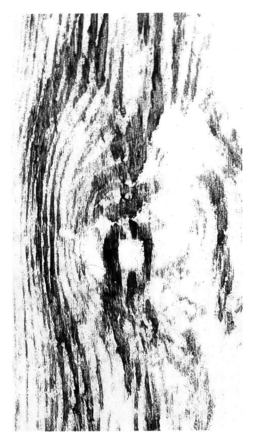

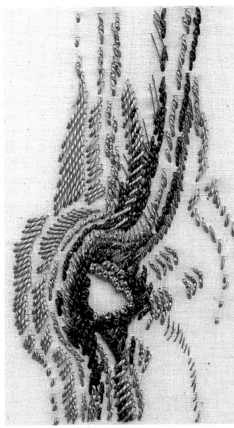

Wood's rough texture is recorded in a rubbing (above) and depicted in pearl and stranded cotton, used in six- and single-strands. The stitches include stem, satin, fly, Cretan and French knots. Alternatively it could be developed into an Italian quilting design.

A plain fabric can be tucked or pleated by machine to add textural interest, or the tucks can be used as a grid, with embroidered motifs decorating the spaces.

rows of automatic machine embroidery, or hand embroidered band and border stitches. In an embroidered picture, these linear effects could be used to interpret architectural features or the natural lines of a landscape.

Quilting methods involve the manipulation of the surface by padding, and usually without additional colour. The all-over padded effect of English quilting relies for its visual impact on the play of light and shade on the surface. It is therefore essential to choose a fabric that is able to create this effect and to avoid dull, dark colours as these will absorb the light and the quality of texture will be lost.

The characteristic channels of Italian quilting can add lines of texture, either in the traditional coiling and interlaced quilting patterns or by reinforcing a linear aspect of the design such as an outline. The padding of trapunto quilting will throw some areas of a design into high relief. This will create focal points or simply strengthen the overall textural quality.

Appliqué is an embroidery method which concerns itself with the addition of texture. Padded and three-dimensional appliqué, in particular, can vary the surface of a design in a way that will produce exciting results. Using wadding will create a soft, squashy texture compared with the firmer effect of felt.

ALTERING THE BACKGROUND SURFACE

To create textural interest, the actual background fabric can be cut, slashed, pulled apart or have threads withdrawn.

The traditional techniques of reverse appliqué, cutwork and broderie anglaise rely on holes and spaces to emphasize the design. These techniques all require firm, closely woven fabrics that will not fray. The first involves slashing the top layers to reveal those underneath. For cutwork methods, the spaces between the main elements of the design are first surrounded with buttonhole stitch, then the enclosed area is cut away carefully with sharp scissors. In broderie anglaise designs, the holes are overcast.

Pulled and drawn thread work also create holes and spaces. A loosely woven, evenweave fabric such as linen is traditionally used but you can experiment with any material whose weave allows the threads to be appropriately manipulated. For pulled work, the weave is pulled apart and stitched, usually in matching thread, to form decorative filling patterns, borders or abstract designs. By using fabrics such as furnishing sheers or linen scrims, you can create much less rigid textural effects.

Withdrawing threads, as in drawn thread work, produces horizontal and vertical openwork stripes. These can be bound together with needleweaving or decorated with hemstitched patterns.

Suffolk puffs (left) are made by gathering around the outer edge of small circles of soft fabric and pulling up the thread (see p. 89). They can simulate circular objects, or be used in an abstract way.

Vanishing muslin allows the creation of lacy effects by machine. The stitching is worked freely and the muslin later 'burnt out' with a hot iron or dissolved in water.

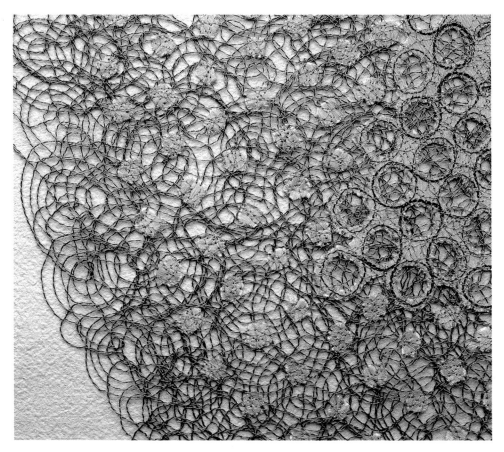

EXPERIMENT WITH FABRICS

Using fabrics in a creative way is one of the most challenging and exciting aspects of embroidery. Fabrics may be patterned or plain, shiny or dull, rough or smooth and made of any kind of fibre. To the embroiderer, all fabrics have both tactile and visual appeal, from the pile of velvet and the flimsiness of chiffon to the profusion of pattern and colour in everyday dress materials. Whatever the project, the fabrics need to be carefully chosen. You need to consider their visual impact, in terms of both colour and texture, as well as practicalities such as wear and washability.

The way a fabric behaves is also an important factor in embroidery design, and the properties of woven and non-woven, natural and synthetic fabrics are discussed fully on pages 14–15. Ideas for embroidery can often be inspired by the pattern or weave of a material—a woven tweed may be suitable for depicting buildings or architectural features in appliqué. In addition, the fabric structure may suggest a technique, particularly if it is suitable for cutting, fraying or withdrawing threads.

The motifs on a printed fabric can be used in appliqué and quilting. In simple, wadded quilting (above, left) the main lines are hand quilted for an overall textural effect. The penguin motif is recreated (above, right) in white satin and black leather; it is appliquéed on to a felt background and embellished with surface stitchery. The edges of the satin are oversewn with blanket stitch and the feet and beak worked in satin stitch.

A bonding web is used to stick rearranged, cut-out motifs on to the felt background (left, top); without bonding, the raw edges will have to be turned under or oversewn with blanket stitch (left, below). Trapunto quilting is used (far left) to pad out the front of the penguin: wadding is inserted from behind and the outlines hand quilted.

PRINTED MATERIALS

One of the simplest ways of using patterned fabric is to cut out motifs or areas of the design and appliqué them to a background. The quickest method is to use a double-sided bonding material (such as Bondaweb) which will stick the motif to the background and will stand up to washing and a good deal of wear, particularly if the edges are sewn down firmly or satin stitched by machine. When positioning the pieces, make sure that the spaces between the cut-out shapes are harmonious and that the size of the motif is in proportion to its surrounding area. It is a good idea to spend some time cutting up a number of shapes, moving them about, overlapping some and studying the relationship between them and the background.

A simple use of this method would be to decorate a tablecloth and napkins, cutting out, for example, large flowers or other motifs from a patterned fabric. Very often motifs of different sizes appear in a printed design, which would be suitable for this type of project. The idea could also be used in reverse, appliquéing shapes of a plain fabric on to a decorative background. Similarly, motifs can be stitched to children's wear, such as sweatshirts and dungarees, or incorporated in an embroidered picture.

Do not overlook the possibility of using the back of a fabric in contrast or preference to the front. The reverse side of printed material is usually paler in tone than the right side and this could well be exploited in an appliqué landscape, to soften the tone and achieve an effect of receding into the distance. Patterned, mainly geometric fabrics, such as striped or check silks and cottons, can be used to provide direction or atmosphere in an appliqué design. Stripes could be used in a realistic way to portray awnings in a market scene or deck chairs on the beach, for example. (The natural weave of wool or tweed can be exploited in a similar way.)

Altering the pattern of a printed fabric with the addition of stitches can be an interesting experiment. Choose a fabric with a simple design, such as spots or widely-spaced repeating motifs, and add stitches to transform the pattern—spots can be enlarged, turned into different shapes, such as stars, triangles or flowers, or can be embroidered so as to join up with each other.

You can achieve interesting results through smocking a printed fabric. Some of the design will disappear in the folds, so that with a degree of forethought during the gathering process, you can plan for particular effects. If you use checked gingham, take care that it is smocked with flair and sensitivity, or it can look out-of-date or ordinary.

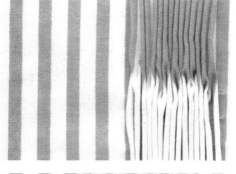
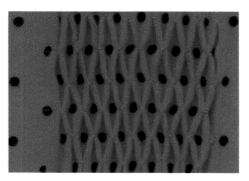
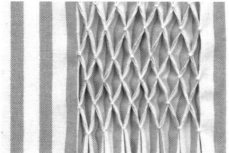
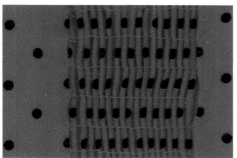

WOVEN FABRICS

Fabrics in which the weave is an important characteristic will give plenty of opportunity for experimentation. Loosely woven evenweave materials, such as the specialist embroidery linens and cottons shown on page 15 are suitable for the traditional counted thread techniques of pulled and drawn thread work. The regular warp and weft make it easy to count the threads, thereby leading to the many patterns and designs which are a feature of these methods. The stitches, usually worked in thread to match the background, will alter the surface of the fabric in different ways.

In pulled work the stitches pull the weave apart, creating a pattern of holes. Traditionally this would have been done only in regular geometric designs but today a freer approach, using less rigid and regular stitches, can produce exciting results. Drawn thread work is less easy to use in a contemporary style, but both these methods can be adapted in a more experimental approach if you use non-traditional fabrics such as loosely-woven furnishing sheers.

Frayed and fringed effects made by unravelling woven materials can be incorporated in all kinds of embroidery. For example, you can finish a set of linen table napkins with a simple fringed border, or make a decorative edge to an embroidered wrap or cape. Frayed fabrics can also provide a textural feature in an embroidered panel to give feathery or wispy effects—frayed silk could suggest feathers or ferns, for example.

Shot fabrics are usually in shiny silk or synthetic fibres simulating silk, the warp

Striped fabric can be tucked, pleated or folded to eliminate one colour or to accentuate another (top left). Spots and stripes can also be smocked to good effect by manipulating the fabric in a particular way when gathering and when smocking.

threads being in one colour, the weft in another. Thus an orange fabric will be made up of a combination of red and yellow, a lilac one from pink and blue. This property can be exploited by using the fabric in such a way that the light playing on the fibres accentuates the irridescent effect.

In an appliqué design, place some pieces of fabric with the warp running horizontally and others with the warp running vertically, to produce a distinct change of colour. Shot fabric will produce a fringe of one colour if frayed horizontally and the other colour if the fraying is done vertically.

The colour of pile fabrics such as velvet, velveteen or corduroy will alter depending on the way the fabric is placed. If the pile runs upward on a garment or hanging, the effect is darker and richer than if it runs downward. On some fabrics the back may be entirely different from the front, both in colour and texture—some dupion curtainings have a pale, very shiny reverse side compared with the darker, more matt right side. You can choose which is the more suitable or combine both in a design.

The characteristics of a firm, closely woven fabric will invite experimentation by means of cutting through the surface, for such techniques as cutwork, broderie anglaise, inlay and reverse appliqué. The effects created in cutwork and broderie anglaise (both whitework techniques) are opposites. In cutwork, the holes cut in the fabric are part of the background area between the main elements of the composition, while in broderie anglaise the pattern of holes actually forms the design. Both these techniques are suitable for lingerie, for babywear, such as christening robes, and for traditional bed and table linen. They can be updated and used in conjunction with surface stitchery.

Reverse appliqué requires a fine, closely woven fabric such as lawn, in order that the various layers can be cut away and hemmed satisfactorily. A much less difficult way of achieving a similar effect to reverse appliqué is to use layers of felt or leather which will not need to be turned under.

Transparent fabrics offer scope for new dimensions in embroidery, both in technique and design. Chiffon, georgette, organdie, organza, fine muslins and net are some of the materials with which you can experiment to create subtle effects of water, skies and dark shadows in an appliqué or mixed-technique panel. Overlay other fabrics with them to alter the tonal value or to change a colour completely. Grey organza, for example, will darken an area for the effect of shadow; red chiffon placed on top of yellow satin will produce orange.

Shadow work, a technique that probably orginated in India, makes use of transparent fabric. Double back stitch (see p. 73), is worked on the reverse side of the fabric to produce the desired shadow effect. The thread chosen needs to be much brighter than the intended finished colour, since the fabric overlay will soften the tones considerably. The same applies to the coloured yarns and fabrics used for shadow quilting (see p. 95), a technique which produces a most delicate result.

An experimental sample of drawn thread work on a loosely woven furnishing sheer combines hand and free machine embroidery (top right). The hand embroidery includes hem stitch and herringbone stitch as well as needleweaving, whipping, buttonhole wrapping and interlacing. The eyelets are worked by machine to create a more solid effect.

Exploit the inherent characteristics of individual fabrics in embroidery as shown in the panel on the right. Try juxtaposing contrasting weights (top left); varying the direction of the grain so that the light plays on a shiny fabric in different ways (bottom left); withdrawing the warp threads and fringing both warp and weft of a shot silk fabric, to reveal its two-colour composition (top right); using the back as well as the front of a fabric to achieve both variety and continuity (bottom right).

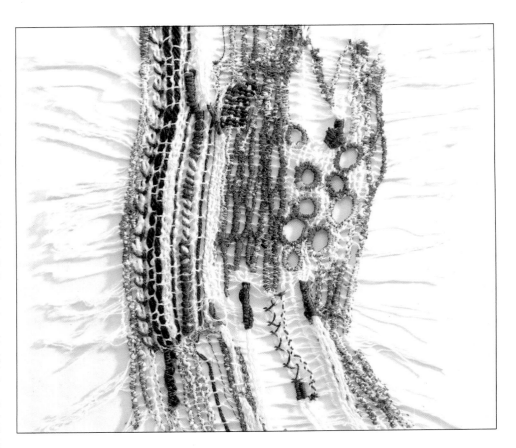

NON-WOVEN FABRICS

Materials such as felt, leather, suede and interfacings, which are not woven, can play an interesting part in your experiments, mainly in appliqué. Their virtue is that, when cut into shapes, they do not become distorted and do not fray.

Felt is often used in appliqué for this reason, but you should choose it as much for its matt textural quality or its colour as for its ease of application. It could give an otherwise sophisticated piece of work an unwanted naïvety. However, for some designs requiring bold areas of flat colour, felt may well fit the bill: an embroidered panel for a child's room, for example.

Leather and suede, unlike felt, can add a touch of luxury to a design if the shapes are applied to garments or accessories using stitches that suit the subject. Double-sided, padded, three-dimensional shapes such as leaves and flowers in one of the non-woven fabrics can also be incorporated in a decorative wallhanging. Gold and silver kid have a strong brilliance and are often used in association with metal thread embroidery. It is conventional to pad this type of work, either with layers of felt, or with wadding for a softer effect.

An unusual application for bonded sew-in interfacing is to treat it as a fabric in its own right. It can be painted or dyed and used for padded or three-dimensional work in the same way as felt or leather. A soft flimsy type can be used for flower petals; the stiff pelmet quality to depict something more rigid and freestanding.

Modern decorative and experimental techniques also employ paper and plastic in combination with embroidery, particularly machine embroidery. Paper of all types and thicknesses can be tried; polythene sheeting of different grades, though not durable, can offer scope for experimentation. Automatic patterns (see p. 116) work well on typing, tissue and cartridge papers as well as on the more unusual and expensive hand-made varieties. Free machining techniques (see p. 119), with the paper or plastic held firmly in a frame, can also be used, but take care not to machine too thickly or it will tear.

Some of the subtle and varied effects in the use of transparent and semi-transparent fabrics are demonstrated in this panel on white silk.

In the Italian quilting (top) the wool is revealed at intervals to show how the strong colours are muted by the silk.

In the examples below, the techniques of reverse appliqué, shadow appliqué and cutwork are combined with machine stitching using layers of felt, organza and silk.

Layers of chiffon in different shades are placed on top of one another and cut away to produce subtle colour variations.

A thick tissue paper forms the experimental 'fabric' in this example of hand quilting and hand embroidery.

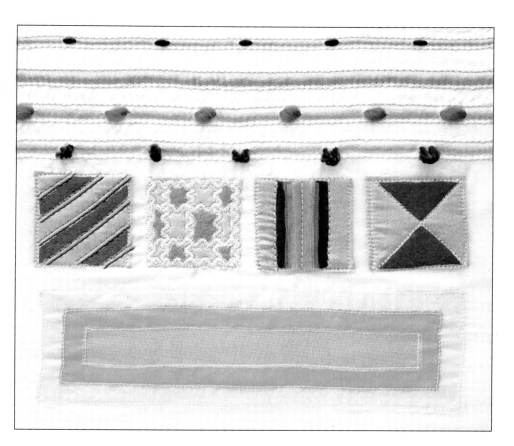

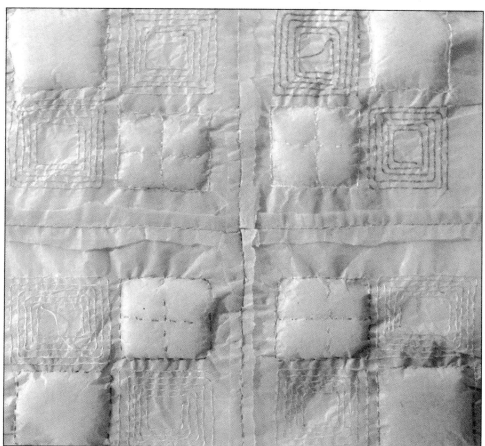

EXPERIMENT WITH THREADS

To anyone interested in textiles, a basket containing hanks of colourful wools tumbling in profusion or of skeins of embroidery cotton lying neatly in serried ranks in a box have an intrinsic attraction. This attraction can often lead to a purchase which will, in turn, spark off inspiration for an embroidery. Buying some balls of unusually textured knitting yarn in autumn colours could develop into an idea for an embroidered panel depicting harvest-time; a skein of silver thread could be the inspiration for decorating the yoke or hem of an evening dress.

Although by tradition certain threads are deemed correct for specific embroidery techniques, the modern view of the craft allows plenty of room for experimentation—as techniques are adapted in scale and form, so the accompanying threads can be altered to suit the aesthetic quality or the practical needs of the design. It is essential to experiment with different qualities, colours and textures of yarn to provide the widest possible choice —ideas will then develop for their use.

If the intended project has a practical use, such as clothes, accessories or table linen that would need to be washed, then the fibre content and the thickness of the yarn should be taken into consideration in planning and executing the design. For example, the yarns traditionally used for canvaswork have been crewel or Persian wools; these were chosen particularly for their hardwearing qualities, appropriate for uses such as for chair seats, kneelers and footstools. Today this tradition still holds good, but if canvaswork is used for pictures and other decorative pieces, these materials can be supplemented with any other yarn which will pass through the canvas without distorting it and which will cover it. This means that textured knitting yarns, as well as ribbons, raffia, tape, string, strips of leather and fabric can all be incorporated if you wish.

Surface stitchery is usually worked in conventional embroidery threads, as well as those manufactured for knitting and crochet. But almost anything that can be threaded through the weave of the back-

ground fabric can also be incorporated, provided the practical use allows. Very coarse threads may have to be couched down to the surface (see p. 71).

TEXTURED THREADS
The thickness of the thread can usually be altered to suit your purpose. Some embroidery threads, such as stranded cotton and wool, are manufactured with this in mind, allowing the strands to be divided and used individually or as a combination of any number together. Some yarns, such as pearl cotton and carpet thrums, will not divide satisfactorily, however, since they rely for their strength on being twisted.

For a subtle change of colour, two lengths of yarn of different hue can be split and reformed to produce a range of tones. Using a six-stranded cotton in yellow, for example, remove one strand and replace it with another in, say, blue; twist them together slightly, if appropriate. Take another length, remove two strands of yellow and replace them with two of blue.

Continue in this way until you have replaced all the yellow with blue. Stitching with these threads will give subtle gradations of tone to a filled area of embroidery.

Most yarns can be doubled or trebled if a thicker version is needed, though some care may well be needed to make sure the tension of the stitch is satisfactory, and that the yarns do not separate untidily. Threads of different textural qualities can also be combined—a shiny rayon used with a matt wool will add a glint of light to an otherwise dull surface.

Textured threads can be made from most yarns by knotting, plaiting and twisting. These will generally need to be couched to the surface, since the knots and the thickness will prevent the thread penetrating the background fabric, unless the latter is very loosely woven. The simplest textured thread can be made by tying knots in a single or doubled length of yarn, at regular or irregular intervals—the knots themselves can be pulled tight or left loose. Or two contrasting yarns can be knotted together to form a thicker thread.

Simple three-strand plaits can be made with either a single type of yarn or a variety of yarns. Such plaited yarns can be used as a textured line, as a braid to cover an edge, or to make a decorative border. Different thicknesses and types of yarns can be twisted together to form cords suitable for decorating cushions, bags and household items. You may need to make an occasional invisible stitch to maintain the twist.

ALTERNATIVE YARNS

Ribbons, tapes and strips of fabric, suede or leather can be combined with embroidery—as, indeed, can any other material cut or torn into lengths. Ribbon and tape are available in a number of widths from 2mm upward. The narrow type can be threaded through a needle and used exactly as a normal thread, for a variety of stitches from simple running stitch to French knots. In combination with other yarns it will add texture and interest to a piece of canvaswork, or it can replace conventional threads when smocking.

The photograph below shows the experimental diversity possible with threads.
1 French knots using stranded cotton (6, 2 and 4 strands), pearl cotton and tapestry wool.
2 Rows of satin stitch in stranded cotton, colour graded from blue to yellow; satin stitch blocks in different directions, in 1 down to 6 strands; stranded cotton; blocks of satin stitch in matt soft embroidery cotton and shiny pearl cotton.
3 Twisted and plaited threads: twisted cord in soft embroidery and pearl cotton; knotted soft embroidery cotton; plaited pearl cotton; slubbed knitting yarn with knots; twisted cord in pearl cotton with knots; 2-colour, 3-strand plait in pearl cotton; twisted cord in pearl cotton, diagonally couched; soft embroidery cotton, couched in a brick pattern.
4 Wrapped piping cord and thin cardboard, couched down; threads woven through fabric, leaving fringed ends.
5 Ribbons and braid: blue ribbon threaded with cotton tape; 3-colour plaited ribbon; French knots in narrow ribbon; running and back stitch worked in bias binding; nylon string, twisted and couched; knotted ribbon; raffia plaited with yellow soft embroidery cotton and blue wool; crocheted ribbon couched down.
Interwoven strips of shot silk with frayed edges; ribbon weaving.

EXPERIMENT WITH THREADS

By tradition, ribbons are threaded through whitework edgings for babywear and lingerie. Drawn thread work, cutwork and broderie anglaise all incorporate holes through which either traditional or more innovative threads can be woven.

Ribbon weaving is currently popular for articles such as pincushions, spectacle and needle cases as well as decoration on dress. This technique can also combine the use of fabric strips, lace and braid for a more varied texture.

DYEING THREADS

It is well worth experimenting with dyeing threads, since this will add both scope and individuality to your work. Some embroidery threads are produced in a limited range of colours, in which case dyeing is the only way of extending the tonal range within a piece of work. Threads can be dyed at the same time as a background fabric, in order to match it exactly, can be shaded to achieve a range of tones, or can be space-dyed in different colours.

Yarns of natural fibres—cotton, wool and linen—as well as some mixtures, accept both hot- or cold-water dyes satisfactorily. Follow the manufacturer's instructions on the packet of dye to prepare the dyebath. You will not need to use all the dye powder unless dyeing large quantities of yarn, so adjust the amount of dye, fixative and water accordingly.

Wind the threads into a skein or cut them into manageable lengths before dyeing, otherwise they will tend to become entangled in the dyebath. Secure each skein at the top with a long thread which can be used for lowering it into the dye and can be tied to the handle of the dyebath or looped over its edge. If the skeins are left in the dye for different lengths of time, they will take up the dye accordingly and you will achieve a wide range of tones.

Remember that after rinsing and drying the depth of any dye colour will be considerably reduced. If dissimilar yarns of different fibres are placed together in the dyebath, they will accept the dye to a different extent, giving a variety of shades. Used in and embroidery, these will produce an inherently harmonious colour scheme.

Space dyeing is a tie-dye method (see pp. 32-3). This method produces a two-coloured thread. The process can be repeated by retying and redyeing in another shade for a multi-colour result.

As well as threads, ribbons and tapes can also be space-dyed; fine fabrics such as chiffon, muslin and even nylon tights, cut or torn into narrow strips, can be treated in the same way.

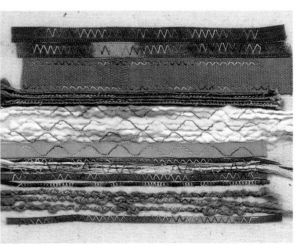

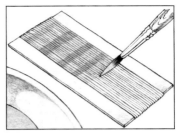

To apply fabric paint, wind the thread around stiff card. Then paint on both sides with a fine, soft-haired brush. Fix the colour by ironing across the threads when dry. **Left** Hand-painted, multi-coloured threads (silk twist, wool, pearl and stranded cotton).

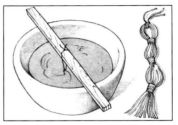

For space dyeing, the skeins of thread are bound or knotted firmly with string or cotton at even or random intervals, then put into the dyebath. The dye will not penetrate the bound areas.
Left Multi-shaded lengths of thread in one colour, dyed for different periods of time; wool and soft embroidery cotton treated in the same dyebath for the same duration.

Dyed threads and alternative yarns (below left) couched down by machine using space-dyed thread.

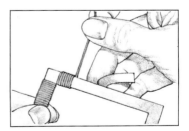

To bind a mount Apply double-sided adhesive tape to the back of the mounting board. Peel 2cm from the backing of the tape, then fasten the end of the binding thread to the sticky side. Continue binding in this way, peeling off the backing as you go. The corners can be painted or left uncovered.

WRAPPED THREADS

Wrapping is a technique traditionally used to bind the warp ends of woven garments and rugs, or is used for making the decorated tassels that edge ethnic embroideries. Wrapped threads can be incorporated in modern embroidery in exactly the same way, or the method can be adapted for more unusual possibilities.

Simple binding involves winding another yarn around a central core of string or cord. The ends can be knotted and taken through under the binding when completed. If you are using fabric, the ends can be sewn invisibly. Apart from changing its colour and texture, binding a piece of string or cord with yarn will cause it to become much more rigid.

Wrapped effects can also be produced with a sewing machine. The easiest method involves the use of an embroidery, or, better still, a braiding foot. Thread the yarn to be wrapped through the hole in the base of this foot, and set the stitch width to coincide with the thickness of the yarn. Ordinary zigzag and decorative automatic stitches can be used to cover the yarn with differing effects. If you do not have these particular machine attachments, the yarn would have to be fed by hand: hold it taut both behind and in front of the machine needle.

Wrapped frames and inserts or mounts can add an individual finishing touch to an embroidered panel (see left). The threads can be chosen to match or contrast with those used in the embroidery. These frames and mounts can then be glued on, to surround the whole embroidery or to enhance a particular area or focal point.

MAKING FRINGES

Textured or knotted threads or cords can be made into a fringe to complement the design of a wallhanging, household item or garment. Attach them by looping them through the edge of the embroidery on, for example, a woollen shawl or canvas-work cushion. On a hanging, you might need to sew them to the lower edge. They can hang freely or be formed into loops.

Ribbons and tapes can be manipulated to twist or curl; wind them around a piece of dowel and spray them with a fabric stiffener such as that sold for use on roller blinds. For a slightly gathered effect, you can machine a line of stitching either along one edge or down the centre of a length of ribbon. The edges of cut or torn bias strips of fabric can be zigzagged to make a fringe for a wallhanging, or rouleaux loops of silk will make a frothy edge for a luxury garment. Strips of shot silk will produce a two-colour fringe if some are frayed horizontally and some vertically. Such finishing touches can lend embroidery of all kinds an individuality absent from manufactured articles.

A variety of **decorative fringes**, incorporating knots and wrapped threads. The 'fabric' is made of threads, laid on vanishing muslin (see p. 121) and machine embroidered. Textured linen threads (left) have a tuft of blue silk threads bound into each tassel.

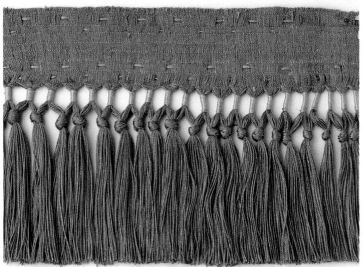

Smooth blue silk threads are tightly bound into tassels with yellow silk thread; each tassel is then divided into two and each half knotted together with the adjacent tassel to form a fringe.

A combination of silk, **linen, slubbed and other threads** has an elaborate fringed edge; each tassel is held in a bound tube like a bead. To make such 'beads', wrap a small piece of paper around a pencil, then bind it tightly with coloured threads. Remove the pencil, cut away any excess paper and push a bundle of threads through each wrapped bead.

EXPERIMENT WITH STITCHES

Stitches are the very essence of embroidery. They can decorate almost any textile from simple garments, cushions and table linen to elaborate wallhangings intricately stitched with textured yarns. If you are prepared to experiment, there are effects which imaginative stitchery can create, irrespective of colour and texture. Embroidery stitches can delineate shapes, make patterns, fill in areas and introduce mood and individuality. They direct the eye of the viewer and give movement and rhythm to a design.

The scope of stitchery is infinite: meticulously worked formal stitchery can have a quality of precision and order. Uneven, haphazard work will produce a livelier, less formal effect.

Surface stitches can be categorized in many ways—some form lines, for example, while others produce a single unit. Yet others are categorized as border stitches or as filling stitches. Stitches that produce lines, including running, back, stem, chain, broad chain, coral and couching are essential for outlining or emphasizing a shape; single unit stitches, like tête de boeuf, detached chain, detached twisted chain, seeding and fly, can create an overall texture or pattern. Some stitches are ideal for circular motifs and dots. Examples include French knots, buttonhole and woven wheels, spiders' webs and circular couching. Openwork stitches that will still reveal the background fabric include wave and cloud filling, trellis couching and buttonhole stitch.

Border and band stitches, such as chevron, herringbone, feather and raised chain band, lend themselves to edgings and striped designs. However, although a stitch may be put into a certain category, these groups are always arbitrary, and should not prevent you from using a stitch as you please. A chain stitch will make a line, but it can also fill a solid space, form an openwork lacy pattern, or be worked as individual detached chain stitches.

Instructions and illustrations for working stitches are usually given for the orthodox method. This is fine if you want to create a precise, regular effect, but you will find, if you experiment, that most stitches can be adapted or modified. Try altering the scale and direction of a stitch, work it unevenly or use varying thicknesses and types of yarn. The textural variations created by using unusual or improvized yarns are explored in the sections on Texture (pp.42-5) and Threads (pp.50-3).

MAKING A SAMPLER

A useful way to start experimenting with stitches is to make a one-stitch sampler. Choose buttonhole stitch, for example, and work it in as many ways as possible. Initially, do not include any additional distractions such as change of colour or thread; you can move on to these variations later.

1 Using stranded wool or cotton, work a neat, even row conventionally, with each stitch the same size and evenly spaced.
2 Now make the effect more random. Still maintaining the essential method of stitching, make some stitches large, some small, some upright, some slanting.
3 Try to create a change in tonal value in the following way. Stitch one row with the stitches close together, trying to cover the background completely. Space the stitches of the second row a little farther apart, and with each subsequent row gradually increase the amount of background fabric showing.
4 Allow the stitches to encroach upon each other; they can overlap or be worked on top of each other. Try building up a highly textured area in this way.
5 Experiment further to make twists, spirals and circular motifs.

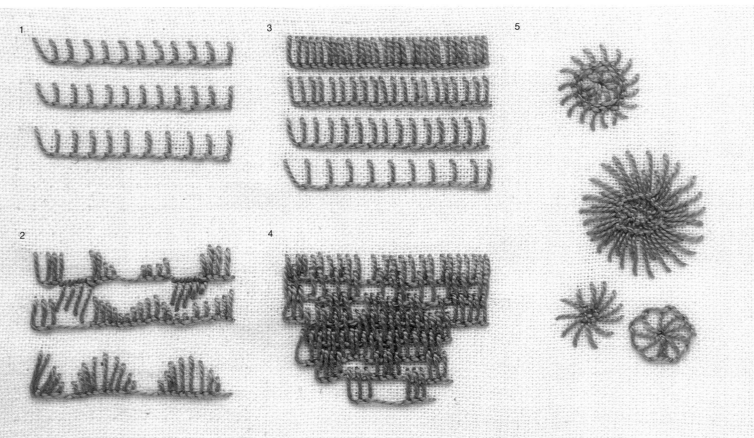

COUNTED THREAD EMBROIDERY

Experimentation with any of the counted thread methods usually involves a change of scale or direction of stitching. Florentine embroidery, for example, can be worked in different directions (see four-way Florentine design, p.128), or a more random approach could be adopted with uneven lines of varying length stitches meandering over the surface.

Instructions for most techniques worked conventionally state that a stitch should cover a specific number of threads and be executed in a certain direction. However, a little trial and error will prove that many stitches can be modified to suit your design. Thus, in canvaswork, cushion stitch can be made to cover a larger or smaller square. The direction of stitching can also be altered and extra stitches can cover those already worked. Of course, not all canvaswork stitches can be altered in this way, so try them out on a spare piece of canvas or fabric, bearing in mind any practical considerations, such as the need to totally cover the canvas.

If experimenting with the scale of drawn thread and pulled work, particularly for table linen, remember that washing and ironing will tend to weaken the ground fabric. For this reason, do not withdraw too many threads or make large stitches which might catch when in use or being ironed. Traditional blackwork can also be altered in scale, and the tonal values of the design can be diminished by gradually omitting parts of the pattern.

All counted thread methods can incorporate the use of surface stitches if you so desire. These can add another texture—French knots combine well with pictorial canvaswork for example. Surface stitches can also establish or emphasize lines – adding a row of whipped chain or couching to pulled work or blackwork, for instance, can reinforce a curve that is otherwise difficult to distinguish.

TRADITIONAL TECHNIQUES

Never feel restricted to a precise stitch. Even an embroidery method such as cutwork, which employs traditional stitches for legitimate practical reasons, may be open to freer interpretations. Buttonhole stitch undoubtedly secures the cut edge satisfactorily, but you could experiment with one of the variations of buttonhole stitch such as tailor's or up-and-down, working them either precisely or to uneven lengths.

Smocking traditionally incorporates those stitches which will best hold the gathers in place—stem, cable, honeycomb or chevron. Besides using these orthodox stitches in regular formation, try a more random approach with uneven curving lines of other stitches such as feather and double feather, and by adding some surface stitches such as French and bullion knots in between the pleats.

Using wool yarn gives an embroidery an exciting, unusual quality. This sample (above), worked on linen scrim, uses conventional line stitches but some are pulled tight and others worked more loosely. This variation in the tension creates a swirling effect and gives the work a sense of movement.

Samplers of buttonhole stitch (below left) and Cretan stitch (below right) worked in no.5 pearl cotton show the diversity possible within a single stitch.

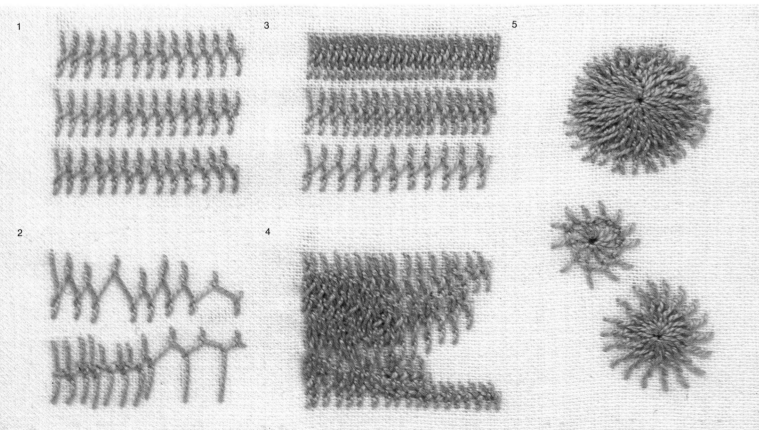

EXPERIMENT WITH STITCHES

Cretan stitch used as an outline

Blocks of satin stitch worked in different directions to catch the light

Cretan stitch superimposed with fly stitch

Detached buttonhole stitch worked in a 'ladder'

Encroaching Cretan stitch, with fly stitch interspersed

Roumanian stitch

Surface stitchery lends itself readily to being worked freely. The detail of the above picture depicted in surface stitchery has a lively quality that comes from the imaginative use of stitches. The stranded cotton is used in varying thicknesses; going down to a single strand and allowing more fabric to show through toward the right conveys the impression of receding into the distance. Juxtaposing the direction of stitches, and allowing stitches to encroach densely, builds up an interesting surface texture.

SURFACE STITCHES

To depict	Suggested stitches
Circular motifs, including flower centres, flower heads etc.	Buttonhole wheels, spider's webs, woven wheels, French knots with tails, bullion knots in rose formation and with tails, circular couching, radiating fly stitches, straight stitches in star formation, Turkey work for a fluffy centre, Cretan and rosette chain in circular formation.
Leaves	Detached chain, buttonhole (several variations), close herringbone, Cretan, Vandyke, raised chain band, quill, feather, fly, long and short, satin, tied satin.
Petals	Smaller versions of leaf stitches.

To depict	Suggested stitches
Grasses	Straight, Cretan, herringbone, fly.
Outlines, including stems	Line stitches including chain, back, stem, broad chain, coral.
Trees and bushes	French knots, bullion knots, rosette chain, herringbone, satin stitch, fly, feather, buttonhole.
Sky or water	Line stitches—split, stem, chain, wave, couching; Cretan.
Architectural features, paths and walls	Brick, satin stitch blocks, couching, laid work, Bokhara and Roumanian couching, cloud filling. Raised chain band, herringbone, chevron.

Two shades of grey stranded together for a speckled effect

Jacquard stitch

French knots worked in two colours

Mosaic stitch

Tent stitch in two colours

Long and short slanting satin stitch

Cross stitch

Diagonal satin stitch

Alternating oblong cross stitch

Lighter grey thread for highlights

Small chequer stitch

Tent stitch worked in reverse direction

Canvaswork is a technique which imposes certain restrictions through the regular canvas grid, but a great variety of different stitches can successfully be incorporated in a single picture, as seen above. An impression of texture is created by varying the number of threads over which a stitch is worked, by changing the direction of stitching and by the use of French knots. Juxtaposing different stitched areas creates a patchwork effect in the background. Stranding colours together adds to its subtle complexity.

CANVASWORK STITCHES

To depict	Suggested stitches
Flowers and leaves	Leaf (altering direction and scale); Gobelin in different directions; eyelets, diamond eyelets, rice.
Skies	Tent, slanted Gobelin, fan, fern.
Clouds	Tent, velvet.
Architectural features	Cushion, brick, Scottish, Brighton, Parisian, Moorish, Byzantine, rice, Hungarian, upright Gobelin.
Backgrounds	Tent, diagonal, mosaic, Gobelin, Hungarian.
Geometric	Square stitches: Rhodes, Smyrna, rice, leviathan, Scottish, cushion.

BORDERS, MOTIFS AND ALPHABETS

Borders and motifs have always been an important feature of embroidery designs. Borders effectively 'frame' a piece of embroidery. Whether the border elaborates a simple design or creates a neat edging to a more intricate one, it must be in scale with the composition as a whole; it should not overwhelm the central design.

A border can be basically linear and continuous – sometimes split up into sections to add interest – or made up of repeating motifs. The motifs may be geometric or pictorial and worked as a straight, reversed or mirror-image repeat. A mirror can help to resolve the corners of a border (see p.29), or the border can be interrupted and a suitable motif used to fill the angle of the corner.

Lettering has also played a historic part in embroideries, either in the form of samplers, in which the whole alphabet was worked as a stitching exercise, or as initials and dates on household linen. Embroidered initials can still turn an everyday item or garment into something personal and special. Letters and numbers can be arranged to form a design in their own right, as in overlapped or interlocking monograms. You can adapt a non-embroidered alphabet for an original approach: look at magazine and television graphics for inspiration.

It is essential to use a smooth thread and to select an embroidery stitch that will make well-defined letters; satin stitch is the most popular in surface stitchery, though chain and stem stitch lend themselves to curved letter forms, the latter being especially good for script lettering.

This page shows an alphabet and several motifs and border patterns suitable for surface stitchery. Those on the facing page are all designed on a regular grid for counted thread methods of embroidery. They may all be traced off and either used actual size or enlarged or reduced (see p.21).

58

ADAPTING A DESIGN THEME

Eight embroideries: interpretations of a simple design theme using different techniques

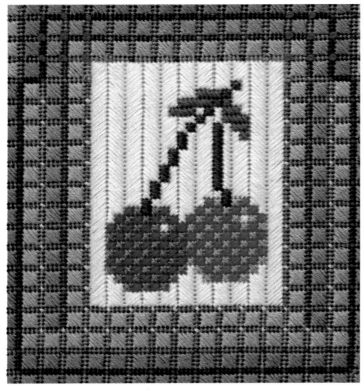

Canvaswork, using tent stitch, diagonal satin stitch, Scottish stitch, mosaic stitch, cross stitch and French knots

Cross stitch and Assisi work (counted thread techniques)

Shadow quilting, using fabric paint to enhance the effect

Appliqué, using bonding web, with the embellishment of surface stitchery

Pulled work, using mock faggot filling for the background and needle-weaving for the stalks; the solid cherries are stitched on the back to create slight padding

Surface stitchery, using satin stitch, stem stitch, back stitch, leaf stitch and split stitch

Cutwork, using buttonhole stitch

Free machine embroidery, using layers of straight stitch

EMBROIDERY BASICS

The amazing diversity of modern embroidery design is made possible by an equally varied range of techniques. Some of these techniques are centuries old: the metal thread embroiderer, for example, uses methods that have not changed significantly since the Middle Ages. Others, such as experimental smocking, are modern adaptations of traditional techniques. A few are recent innovations—an example being machine-embroidered lace worked on dissolvable fabric. Imaginative embroiderers are continually inventing new stitches and new ways to use the rich variety of materials at their disposal.

In the past mastery of embroidery techniques was often considered an end in itself. Young girls spent long hours learning to stitch correctly. Precision was of paramount importance; experimentation was not encouraged. Today, a more relaxed attitude prevails. Embroidery is taken up as a satisfying pastime, a means of self-expression and is an art form in its own right. The techniques you choose to acquire are mainly a matter of following your inclinations. Those who like to work methodically may be attracted to counted thread techniques, such as cross stitch or blackwork. For those who most enjoy working with fabrics, appliqué will have a strong appeal. Canvaswork has tactile qualities and a pleasant rhythm which help to give it wide appeal. Embroiders with less patience may prefer the speed and the impromptu nature of free machining. Some techniques lend themselves to both meticulous and spontaneous ways of working: surface stitchery, for example, can be as precise or as bold and free as you like.

Whatever type of embroidery you choose, it is important to acquire a thorough understanding of its materials and methods and to be able to use them effectively. In some cases experts disagree on the best method of working a particular stitch or achieving a certain effect; try different methods and decide which you prefer. You might even devise a new method of executing a stitch that works best for you.

Do not be afraid to branch out and try different types of embroidery. The more techniques you have at your disposal, the more scope you will have in interpreting your design ideas. And the greater your mastery of those techniques, the more successful your original designs are likely to be.

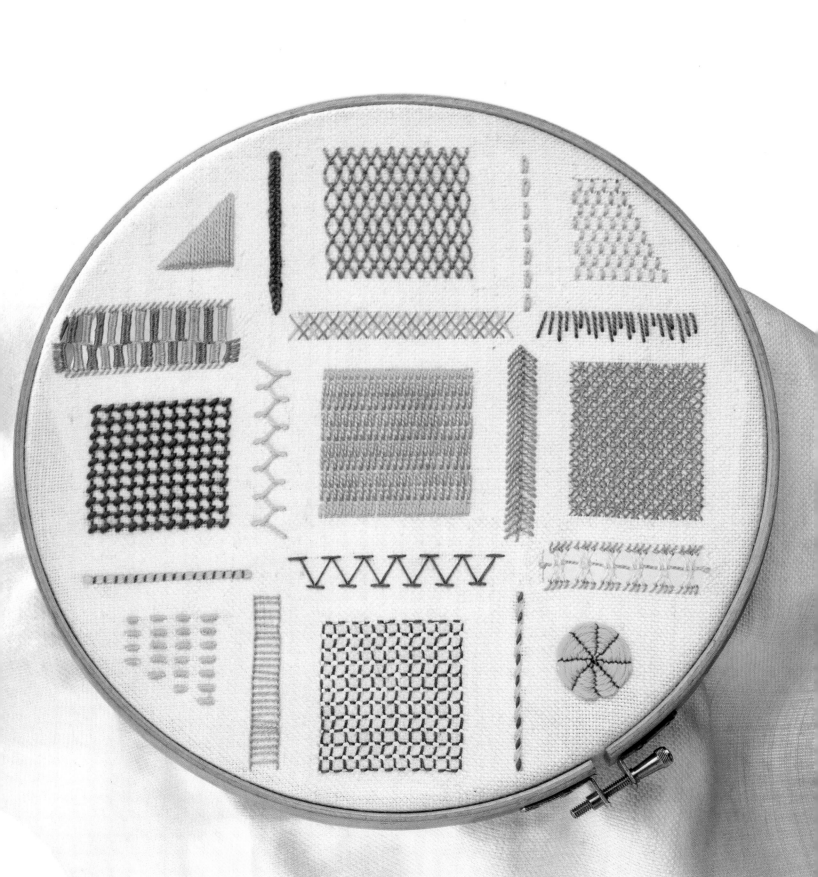

The success of any piece of embroidery depends not only on the skill with which you work the stitches (and, of course, the quality of the design) but also on your preparation. The design must be transferred to the fabric in the most appropriate way, and the fabric must be mounted in a suitable frame. There are several methods of transferring the design, explained below.

Before cutting the fabric for the embroidery, make sure – if the item is to be washable – that the fabric is pre-shrunk. If you are in any doubt, immerse it for a few minutes in hand-hot water, then let it dry naturally and press it.

Cut the fabric at least 5cm larger than it will be after making up to allow for seams and/or hems. (Depending on the type of frame you are using, you may need to increase these margins.)

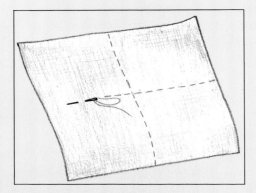

Positioning the design is normally a simple matter and can be done by eye – especially on tracing paper. But in some cases, such as working a motif in the centre of a tablecloth, it may be necessary to position the design precisely.
1 Mark the centre of the fabric by folding it into quarters, pressing after each fold; or use tacking.

2 Similarly, mark the centre of the design with two pencilled lines. When transferring the design, superimpose the marks.

DRESSMAKER'S CARBON

This method can be used on any smooth-textured fabric and is suitable for fairly complex designs, as well as simple ones. On rough-textured fabric the lines tend to be distorted.

Dressmaker's carbon can be purchased in haberdashery departments and usually comes in a packet containing several colours, suitable for different fabrics. Do *not* use office carbon paper, which would leave indelible marks on the fabric. Even better than dressmaker's carbon (which may leave a faint smudge on some fabrics) is artist's tracing-down paper; this can be obtained from some art shops. You will also need a ballpoint pen (a worn-out one will do). Positioning the design is easier if it is on tracing paper, as shown here, although this is not essential.

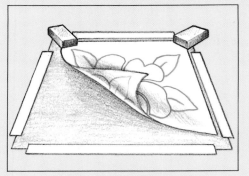

1 Tape the fabric to a smooth, hard surface (or fix it with drawing pins). Place the design, right side up, on top of the fabric, making sure that it is positioned correctly. Secure it with weights or masking tape.

2 Slip the dressmaker's carbon between fabric and tracing, coloured side down. Using the ballpoint pen, go over the lines of the design firmly. Carefully lift the paper and carbon to check that you are pressing firmly enough.

DIRECT TRACING

This method is best suited to sheer or translucent fabrics, although it can be used on a light-coloured, medium-weight fabric provided the design is fairly simple.

You will need a fabric-marking pen or dressmaker's marking pen, available in haberdashery departments, which makes a mark that should wash out with water (test it on your fabric first). One word of warning: some experts fear that these pens can in fact rot the fabric. If the item will not be washed, a hard pencil can be used.

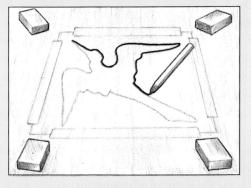

Tape the design to a flat surface. Place the fabric over it, right side up, and tape or weight the fabric to secure it. Trace the design with the fabric-marking pen or pencil.

If the design is not easily visible through the fabric, attach it and the fabric to a window with masking tape, making sure there is enough natural light coming through. Then trace the outline on to the fabric.

Going over the lines on the paper first with a heavy black felt-tip pen may also help to make the design more easily visible through the fabric.

If you like the tracing method you may want to invest in a light box. Available from graphic designers' suppliers, it consists of a shallow box containing fluorescent tubes, covered with frosted glass.

TRANSFER PENCIL

Make sure that the transfer pencil you buy is of the non-smudge type. There are various transfer pencils on the market, and they differ considerably in quality. The best type resembles an ordinary lead pencil; others have a waxy texture and must be applied with a very light hand in order not to leave a thick line. Before using any transfer pencil for your design, test it on a scrap of the fabric.

You will also need some tracing paper and an iron.

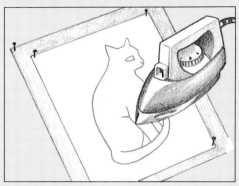

1 Trace the design on to tracing paper with an ordinary pencil. Turn the paper wrong side up so that the design is reversed, and retrace the design on the back, using the transfer pencil.

2 Pin the fabric to the ironing-board or another flat, heatproof surface, and position the tracing, right side up, on top. Using a dry iron, at a temperature appropriate for the fabric, iron over the paper to transfer the design.

THE PRICKING METHOD

This transfer method is well suited to any kind of design and can be used with any fabrics except highly textured ones. It is a particularly good method to use if you need to repeat a motif, since the tracing can be reused several times.

You will need: fairly stiff tracing paper, a medium-size, sharp-pointed needle, a cork, a small piece of felt, pounce powder (see p.11) or tailor's chalk, and either a fabric-marking pen or a fine brush and watercolour paint in a shade slightly darker or lighter than the fabric.

To speed up this process, you could use a sewing machine to make the holes, if the design permits. Remove top and bobbin threads and, using the longest stitch length, stitch along the design lines.

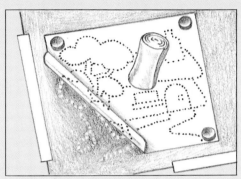

1 Trace the design and turn the tracing wrong side up to reverse it. Place it on a padded surface, such as a folded towel. Use the needle to prick holes along the lines. Make the holes about 1cm apart – or closer for a complex design. The needle is easier to handle if the blunt end is first inserted into a cork.

2 Lay the tracing right side up on the fabric and secure it in place. Fold the felt into a small pad, dip it into the powder and rub the powder through the holes with a circular movement.

Then carefully remove the tracing. Using the fabric-marking pen or brush and watercolour, connect the powder dots.

TACKING

This is the method to use on highly textured fabric. It is also ideal if you want to work the embroidery freely and spontaneously. The tacked lines serve as a guide for positioning the main lines and shapes, and you can then add details or build up textures without being restricted to a permanently marked line.

You need lightweight tracing paper (greaseproof paper is ideal) and ordinary sewing thread in a shade slightly darker than the fabric.

Before transferring the design, mount the fabric in the appropriate frame (see pp. 66-7).

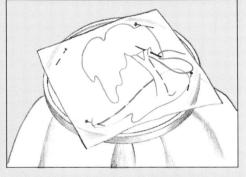

1 Trace the design and pin the tracing, right side up, to the fabric. Using the sewing thread, work running stitches (see p. 69) along the lines through both paper and fabric. Secure the thread at beginning and end with a couple of back stitches (see p. 69).

2 When the tacking is completed, run the point of a needle along the tacked lines to score the paper then gently pull the paper off the fabric.

Depending on the embroidery technique you are using, you can either cover the tacking completely or remove it as you go.

Some kinds of embroidery can be worked without a frame, but, for most kinds, a frame is essential. A frame not only keeps the fabric smooth but also helps to ensure that the thread is kept at the correct tension – neither so tight that it puckers the fabric nor so loose that the stitches lack definition.

Several different kinds of frame can be used for surface stitchery. A ring frame, also called a hoop, is the most common. A simple ring frame is useful for practising stitches and is easily portable. The disadvantage of a ring frame is that, unless the project is fairly small or the embroidery well scattered, you will need to move the fabric in order to reach all the areas of the design, which may entail pressing the ring over

previously worked stitches and possibly flattening or damaging them. In some cases this can be prevented by placing tissue paper or muslin over the fabric before fixing the outer ring, then tearing the paper or cutting the muslin away to reveal the working area.

A better solution, if the work is too large for a ring frame, is to use a slate frame or stretcher frame of a size to accommodate the work. Such a frame not only avoids damaging the embroidery; it also permits you to see the whole area at once – enabling you to make adjustments in the design, if necessary.

Dressing each type of frame, that is, mounting the fabric in it correctly, is explained below.

BACKING THE FABRIC

Many pieces of embroidery benefit from the use of a backing fabric. If the embroidery fabric is lightweight or loosely woven, it should be backed to give it body and to prevent the underside of the stitches and threads from showing on the right side. In some cases – where an extra layer is not wanted but stitches need to be strengthened – it may be desirable to use a backing fabric, then carefully cut it away around the stitching when the work is completed.

Choose a natural fibre fabric for the backing. Lawn, muslin and organdie are suitable for backing a lightweight fabric. If you need a heavier backing, choose calico or curtain lining.

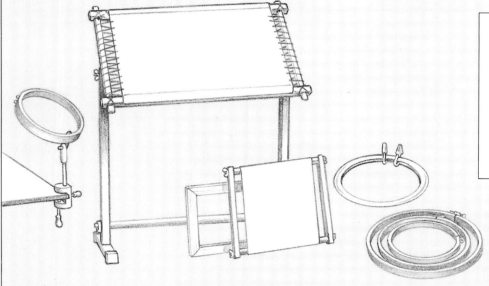

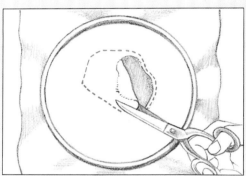

If the work is smaller than the frame available, or if it is an awkward shape, first stitch it on to a backing of the necessary size. Then either work through both layers, or cut the backing away under the embroidery fabric from inside the frame before you begin stitching, as shown here.

DRESSING A RING FRAME

Ring frames come in various sizes and styles. Whatever size you get (and you may want to have several), make sure that it has a screw for adjusting the tightness of the outer ring for a snug fit. There is also a new spring-type ring frame whose inner ring automatically grips the fabric against the outer ring. The portable ring frame, though convenient, will not permit you to stitch with both hands (see p. 68). But other models of ring frame are designed to stand on a table or on the floor, to clamp on to a chair arm or table, or to rest on a chair seat, held in place by the embroiderer's body. All of these do allow you to work with both hands.

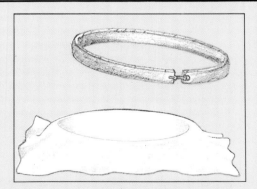

Adjust the screw so that the outer ring fits easily, but not loosely, over the inner ring. Remove the outer ring, without loosening the screw, and place the fabric over the inner ring. Binding the inner ring will protect a delicate fabric and give a better grip (see p.118).

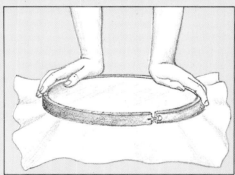

Press the outer ring firmly and evenly down over the fabric. The grain should be straight and the fabric should be as taut as a drumskin; if it is not, remove the outer ring, tighten it slightly and try again. Do not attempt to tauten the fabric by adjusting the screw or pulling on the fabric once it is mounted; this will distort the weave.

DRESSING A STRETCHER FRAME

A stretcher frame consists of four wooden strips with mitred corners. To assemble the frame you simply slot the corners together. You may want to sand the frame slightly if it is rough to the touch, but this is not usually necessary. The stretchers can be purchased at art shops and come in a wide range of sizes, enabling you to form whatever shape you need. Remember, however, that the width of the stretchers will reduce the size of the stitching area. If your design measures 30cm square, for example, the assembled frame should measure at least 40cm square on its outer edges. The fabric should be cut slightly larger than this to allow for attaching the edges to the frame.

To work on a stretcher frame, prop it against the edge of a table or other firm support, with the lower edge in your lap.

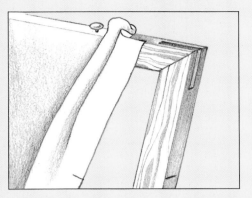

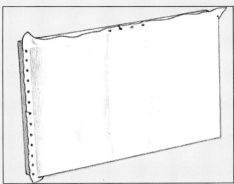

1 Mark the centre point of each side of the frame and the fabric with a pen or pencil.
2 Align the centre marks of the top edges of fabric and frame, and fasten the fabric to the top edge of the frame with a drawing pin.
3 Fasten the rest of the top edge, inserting the drawing pins at 2-3cm intervals.

4 Fasten the opposite edge in the same way, pulling the fabric very taut.
5 Fasten the centre marks on the side edges.
6 Fasten the side edges alternately, inserting a pin on one side, then fastening the corresponding point on the opposite side, working outward to the corners.

DRESSING A SLATE FRAME

The main advantage of a slate frame – also called a square or scroll frame – is that the fabric can be retautened while the work is in progress. The frame consists of two adjustable rollers held together by battens. The top and bottom edges of the work are sewn to strips of webbing attached to the rollers; the sides are laced to the battens.

Slate frames come in various sizes, and some are designed to fit on to a floor stand, which makes them especially convenient to use. The maximum width of the embroidery is limited by the length of the webbing on the rollers, but the length can exceed the length of the battens, if necessary. The excess length is simply rolled on to one of the rollers, then unrolled and rolled on ' to the other as the work progresses.

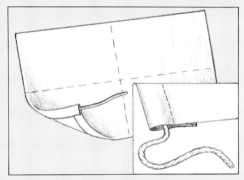

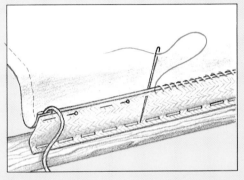

1 Tack along the vertical and horizontal centre lines of the backing. Press under a 2cm hem on the top and bottom, then the side edges.
2 Cut two fairly long lengths of string; place each inside a side hem and machine stitch to form a casing over the string.

3 Mark the centre of each strip of webbing. Pin the bottom edge of the fabric to one webbing strip, matching centres, and oversew them together, using double button thread. Work from the centre to one side, then to the other. Join the top edge to the other strip of webbing in the same way.

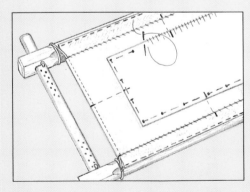

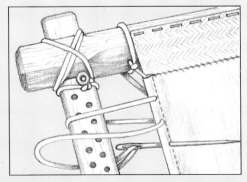

4 Slip the battens through the rollers and fasten them with the pegs so that the fabric is fairly taut. Tie the string ends around the rollers.
5 Mark the centre of each edge of the embroidery fabric. Pin it to the backing, matching centres, and oversew it as shown, alternating long and short stitches to distribute the tension.

6 Using a large-eyed needle and string, sew the side edges of the backing to the sides of the frame, taking the string over the battens and sewing through the fabric over the side strings, at 3cm intervals. Pull firmly to tauten the fabric, and tie the string ends around battens and rollers.

The term 'surface stitchery' embraces a great variety of embroidery styles. The simple floral motifs often worked on table linen, the swirling, fantastic forms of Jacobean crewel work, and the rich, delicate silk embroideries that decorated eighteenth-century costume are some types of traditional surface stitchery. Modern surface embroidery uses many of the same stitches but uses them in new, experimental ways, producing highly individual effects.

The one thing that all types of surface stitchery have in common is that the stitches' formation is independent of the fabric weave – unlike counted thread types of embroidery, such as blackwork and pulled work. Because surface stitchery can be worked in any direction, it is sometimes called free stitchery or free embroidery.

MATERIALS AND EQUIPMENT

As a general rule, the fabric should be firmly woven and opaque; sheer fabrics can be used – and in fact are required for shadow work (p. 73) – but keeping the wrong side sufficiently neat can be difficult. And until you gain some experience, it is best to stick to fabrics made mainly of natural fibres, which are easier to work on than most synthetics.

Another general rule is to match the weight of the fabric to the weight of the threads. Embroidery worked mainly in fine cotton thread, for example, would not be effective on hessian. Threads for surface stitchery include the whole range of embroidery threads (see p. 13) and many more besides. The best needles are crewels and chenilles, both of which have sharp points. The eyes of chenilles are larger, to accommodate thicker threads.

STITCHING TECHNIQUES

To achieve the best results with hand embroidery, you need to learn to use both hands properly and to manipulate the needle in a specific way to create each stitch. In the following illustrations showing how to work the stitches, the needle is often shown as if it is used horizontally, as in ordinary sewing; but this is simply to make the construction of each stitch clear.

When you work on a frame you should stab the needle vertically through the fabric, using both hands if possible. In some cases the 'underneath' hand must be brought to the top of the work – for example, when one hand holds a loop of thread in place while the other one stitches.

For embroidery stitches that are worked partly through each other, so that the needle does not penetrate the fabric, it helps to take the needle through eye first.

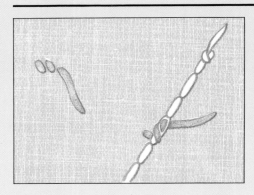

To begin work you can either make a small, neat knot at the end of the thread or take it under some existing stitches on the wrong side, then work a back stitch over them before bringing the needle to the right side. Back stitches can simply be worked into a backing fabric, taking care not to catch in the main fabric.

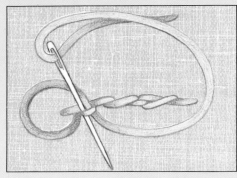

To end a line of stitching, take the needle through some stitches on the underside and anchor the thread with a back stitch.

Fastening the thread is also greatly facilitated if a backing fabric is used.

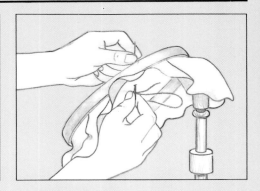

Using both hands may seem awkward at first, but it will become easy with practice. Using your right hand under the fabric (or your left, if you are left-handed) will facilitate the work. A thimble is normally unnecessary unless the fabric is very thick.

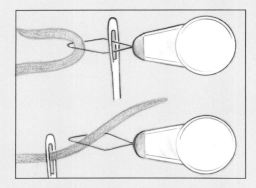

Threading the needle Various techniques can be used to make needle-threading easier. Moistening the thread will smooth it; a cotton thread can be flattened slightly with your teeth. Or a needle-threader can be inserted through the eye and used to pull the thread through as shown.

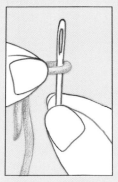 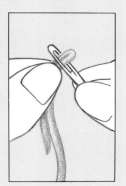

Wool threads are often easier to thread if you first loop the end around the needle, then pinch the loop tightly between thumb and forefinger and press the eye of the needle down over it.

A NOTE TO LEFT-HANDED READERS

Some of the stitches shown in this book are naturally worked (by a right-handed person) from left to right or from right to left, and are illustrated accordingly. In some cases, a left-handed embroiderer will find it easy enough to work in the same direction, provided the two-handed method of stitching is used. If this is not possible, the direction of working should be reversed. (The finished effect will be the same.) Holding the illustration up to a mirror may help to make the method of working clear.

References to 'right' and 'left' in the text have been kept to a minimum. Where they do occur, left-handed readers may prefer to reverse the directions.

LINE STITCHES

When worked in the simplest way, stitches designated 'line stitches' produce the effect of a thin line. Between pages 72 and 75 you will find stitches that characteristically form bands or narrow motifs; between pages 76 and 81, those used for round motifs or to fill larger areas of a design.

These distinctions are, however, somewhat arbitrary, since most surface embroidery stitches can be used in a variety of ways. Lines of chain stitch worked close together make an attractive texture for depicting leaves, flower petals and other objects.

Many of the basic stitches also have variations, some of which appear quite different from the 'parent' stitch. Chain stitch is again a good example: five variations of chain are described here and others can be found among band and filling stitches.

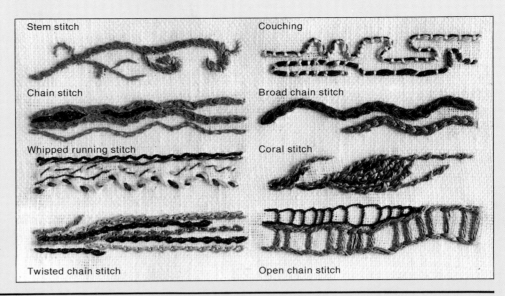

Stem stitch   Couching

Chain stitch   Broad chain stitch

Whipped running stitch   Coral stitch

Twisted chain stitch   Open chain stitch

RUNNING STITCH

This is the simplest of all stitches, used for outlining and for hand quilting. Take the needle in and out of the fabric at regular intervals, working several small stitches at a time.

Running stitch is a surprisingly versatile stitch. It can be worked in rows in a regular pattern to form a solid filling stitch (see Darning, p. 78), or less regularly to form textured areas within a design.

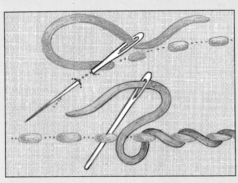

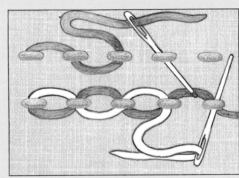

Whipped running stitch Work a line of simple running stitch. Then, using a tapestry needle and contrasting thread, take the thread under the stitches (not through the fabric). Do not pull it tightly.

Interlaced running stitch Work a line of even running stitches. Then, using a tapestry needle, take another thread – contrasting, matching or toning – alternately up and down under the stitches.

Take a third thread under the stitches in alternating directions as shown.

BACK STITCH

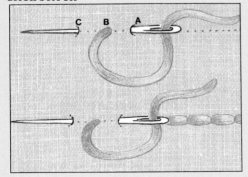

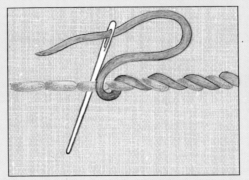

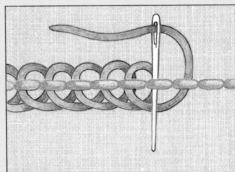

Back stitch This is useful for thin lines, as in lettering. Bring the needle up at B, a short distance from the starting point (A), then take it down at the starting point. Bring it up the same distance ahead of A, at C.

Whipped back stitch Work a line of back stitch. Then, using a tapestry needle and contrasting thread, work under each stitch as shown, without going through the fabric.

Pekinese stitch Work a line of back stitch. Then, using a tapestry needle and contrasting thread, if desired, work loops under the stitches, without going through the fabric. The loops may be worked tightly or loosely, depending on the desired effect.

STEM STITCH

This is arguably the most useful of all line stitches. It forms a smooth, ropelike line which can be thin or thick, depending on the angle at which the needle is inserted. Thin lines of stem stitch are ideal for flower stems or lettering. They may also be worked close together to fill a shape and produce a satiny texture.

It is important always to bring the needle up on the same side of the stitching line. When working around a curve, bring the needle up on the inside. Shorten the stitches slightly when working sharp curves.

Bring the needle up at A. Take it down at B, then bring it up halfway between at (C). Take it down at D, forming the same length stitch.
For a thicker line, work the stitches across the stitching line, rather than along it. The two methods may be combined to produce a line varying in thickness – useful in script lettering.

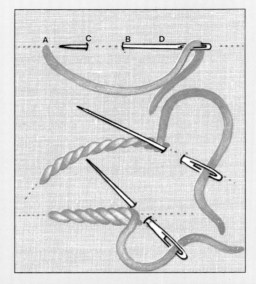

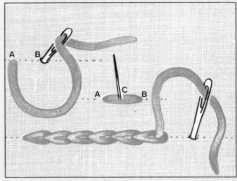

Split stitch This stitch produces a thin line. It can also be used to fill a shape with a matt texture. Bring the needle up at the beginning of the line (A), take it down at B, then bring it up halfway between these points (C), splitting the thread. Repeat.

CHAIN STITCH

Basic chain stitch produces a medium-thick line consisting of a series of loops shaped like teardrops. The thickness can be adjusted, to some extent, by drawing the thread loosely or firmly; however, it should not be pulled so tightly that the chain effect is lost.

If the lines are long, fasten off at the end of each line; if they are short, take the thread back under the wrong sides of the stitches to the starting point.

Variations of chain stitch can be used for different effects. For a thick, solid line, use broad chain stitch; for a more textured line, use twisted chain. Many other decorative effects can be produced with the stitches shown here and with other forms of chain (see pp. 75 and 77).

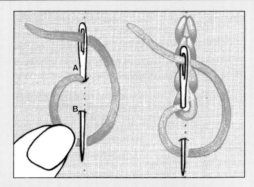

Bring the needle up at the beginning of the line (A) and take it down at the same point, forming a loop (hold the loop in place with your thumb or forefinger). Bring the needle up at B and take it over the loop, to form the first stitch. Repeat.

When using chain stitch to fill a shape, work all the lines in the same direction to achieve a smooth effect.

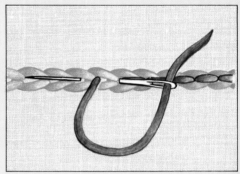

Back-stitched chain stitch First, work a line of chain stitch. Then, using contrasting thread, work back stitch (see p. 69) through the centre of the chain.

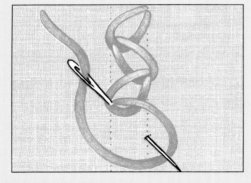

Zigzag chain stitch Work as for basic chain stitch, but with the stitches placed diagonally between two parallel lines. (These can be marked with tacking first.) On the second and following stitches, insert the needle through the centre of the thread to hold the loop firmly in position.

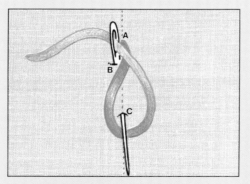

Twisted chain stitch
1 Bring the needle up at A, on the stitching line. Form a loop, as for basic chain, but take the needle down at B, crossing over the loop. Bring it up at C, and then down again over the loop.

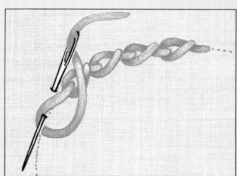

2 Work the following stitches in the same way, always inserting the needle to the left of the stitching line, slightly below the point where the thread emerges. (When practising this stitch, it may be helpful to mark the stitching line on the fabric.)

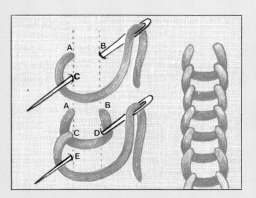

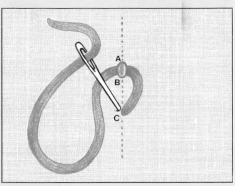

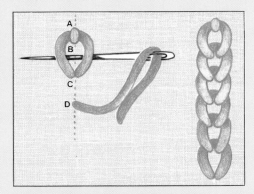

Open chain stitch
1 Bring the needle up at A, take it down at B, and bring it out at C, just below A.
2 Pull the thread through, but leave a wide loop. Take the needle down at D, inside the loop on the opposite side, then bring it out at E, forming the next loop in the chain.

Broad chain stitch
1 Work a single small running stitch (A – B) at the beginning of the stitching line.
2 Bring the needle up a short distance below (C) and take it back up and under the running stitch (not through the fabric) then bring it down again at C.

3 Bring the needle up at D, slightly below the first chain. Take it back under the chain and down again at the same place. Repeat step 3 until the chain is the desired length.
  For a thick, plaited effect, use a thick or double thread and keep the chains fairly short.

CORAL STITCH
Coral stitch consists of a line of small knots, which can be placed close together or farther apart as desired.
  Lines of the stitch worked close together make an interesting rough-textured filling. Stagger the positions of the knots on alternate rows.
  Coral stitch is most effective if worked in double thread.

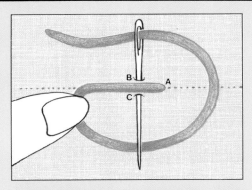

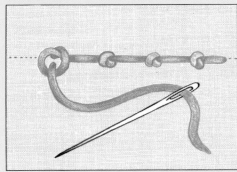

1 Bring the needle up at the beginning of the stitching line (A). Lay the thread along the line and hold it with your thumb or forefinger. Take a small vertical stitch under it (B – C), and loop the thread under the needle.

2 Pull the thread through, forming a knot, as shown.

SIMPLE COUCHING
Couching is a means of attaching a thread to the surface of the fabric by working a series of small stitches over it, using another thread. Here, couching is shown in its simplest form, as a line stitch, but the basic technique can be varied to produce some interesting filling stitches (see pp. 80-81).
  Couching is used mainly for attaching threads that are too thick, too highly textured, or too expensive (such as gold threads) to be stitched through the fabric in the usual way. It greatly expands the range of threads you can incorporate in your work.
  For the couching stitches themselves, you can use a fine thread in a matching colour for an almost unbroken line; or you can use a thicker, contrasting thread to make a feature of the stitches, perhaps working them in a pattern as shown right.

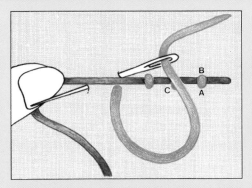

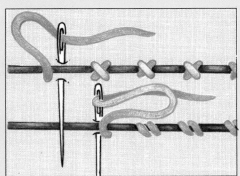

1 Bring up the thread to be couched (called the 'laid thread') to the right side of the fabric; remove the needle and hold the thread in place with your thumb or forefinger. Thread another needle with the couching thread and bring it up on the stitching line (A). Take it down over the laid thread (B), and bring it up again at C.
2 Work another stitch a short way along the line. Repeat to the end of the stitching line; fasten off.

3 Rethread the laid thread into a needle and take it to the wrong side. Secure it with a few stitches worked in a fine thread.
  Varied effects can be produced by using different stitches to work the couching and by making them larger. Pairs of diagonal stitches, worked side by side or to form a cross, are two of the many possibilities.

BAND STITCHES

When worked in the conventional way, the band stitches shown on the next four pages form relatively wide bands. These stitches are also extremely versatile. Many can be used effectively as filling stitches, others for small oval shapes such as leaves.

Buttonhole stitch is one of the most useful of all embroidery stitches, and can be varied in many ways to produce quite different effects (see the worked sample on p. 54). If the stitches are worked a short distance apart the effect is like that of the edging on a blanket, but when worked close together, the stitches make a solid band with a firm lower edge, a form most often used for cutwork (see p. 100). Buttonhole stitch can also be worked in a circle to make small wheels (see p. 77).

When embroidering band stitches, it may help to work between marked lines.

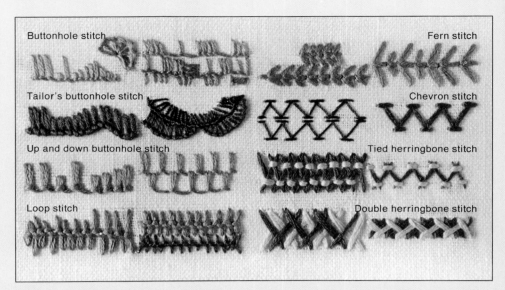

Buttonhole stitch
Tailor's buttonhole stitch
Up and down buttonhole stitch
Loop stitch
Fern stitch
Chevron stitch
Tied herringbone stitch
Double herringbone stitch

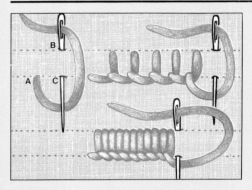

Buttonhole/blanket stitch Bring the needle out on the lower stitching line (A). Insert it on the upper stitching line a short distance to one side (B), then bring it out on the lower line (C) and pull it through, over the thread. Finish by taking the needle down on the lower line.

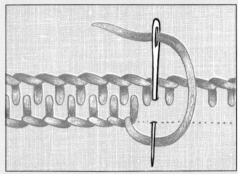

Double buttonhole stitch This makes an attractive border for the cuff of a sleeve or the hem of a child's dress. Work a line of blanket stitch, then turn the fabric and work another line, interspersing the new stitches between the first ones as shown.

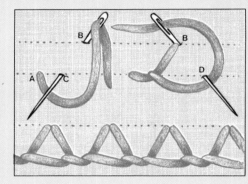

Closed buttonhole stitch
1 Work a narrow buttonhole stitch (A–B–C), but place it diagonally as shown.
2 Work a second diagonal stitch, inserting the needle at the top of the first stitch (B) and bringing it out on the bottom line, over the thread (D).
   Repeat steps 1 and 2 to form a row of interlocking triangles.

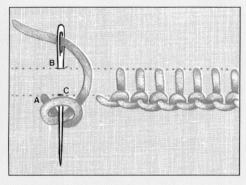

Tailor's buttonhole stitch
1 Bring the needle up on the lower line and form a small loop. Holding the loop in place with your forefinger, insert the needle on the upper line.
2 Bring the needle up through the loop and draw the thread through gently, forming a small knot at the base of each stitch.

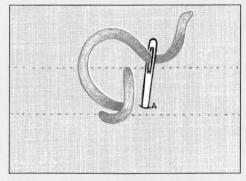

Up and down buttonhole stitch
1 Work an ordinary buttonhole stitch but do not pull the stitches tightly.
2 Take the needle down opposite the point where it emerged, but do not pull the thread through.

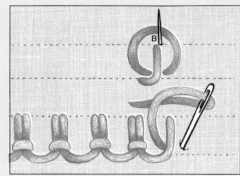

3 Bring the needle up alongside the first stitch and pull the thread through the loop.
   Repeat steps 1–3.
   Up and down buttonhole makes a pretty border, but it is even more effective as a filling, with each row overlapping the one above.

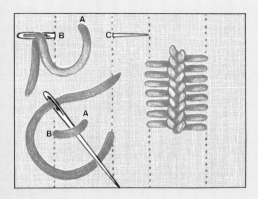

Loop stitch
1 Bring the needle up at A.
2 Insert it at B and bring it up at C.
3 Take the needle under the diagonal stitch thus formed and over the working thread and draw it through gently, easing the knot into place with your free hand. Repeat steps 2-3

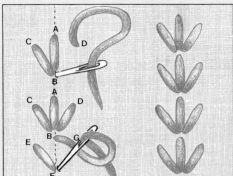

Fern stitch As its name implies, this stitch is useful for suggesting fernlike foliage.
1 Work three straight stitches, bringing the needle up first at A, then C and then D, and taking it back down at B each time.
2 Make a straight stitch from E to F, another from just below B to F, and a third from G to F.
Repeat step 2 as required.

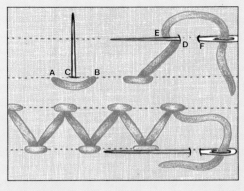

Chevron stitch This stitch is most effective when worked evenly as a decorative border.
1 Make a small stitch from A to B. Bring the needle up at C, between A and B.
2 Take the thread to the upper stitching line at an angle. Take it down at D and bring it up at E. Now take it down at F and up again at D.
Repeat step 2 on alternate lines.

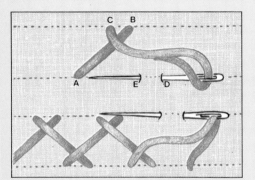

Herringbone stitch This is most commonly used for edgings and fillings.
1 Bring the needle up on the lower stitching line at A, take it up diagonally to B and bring it out again at C, making a small back stitch.
2 Take the thread diagonally down to the lower line and work a back stitch (D–E) as before.
Repeat steps 1 and 2.

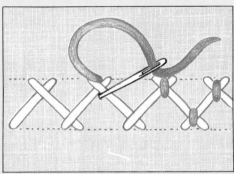

Tied herringbone stitch This is a simple way of embellishing the basic herringbone stitch. The tying stitches are normally worked in a contrasting colour.
Work a row of herringbone, then make a small stitch over the crossing points, taking the needle up on the outside and down on the inside.

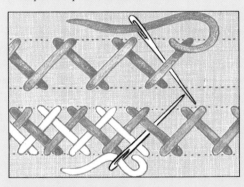

Double herringbone stitch
1 Work a row of herringbone, but take each downward diagonal stitch under the upward one rather than over it.
2 Using contrasting thread, work another row as in step 1, but, when taking the thread up, take it under the downward stitch of the first row; use the blunt end of the needle if preferred.

SHADOW WORK

This type of stitchery, in which the stitches are seen through a sheer fabric, makes use of herringbone stitch. In this context it is also called shadow or double back stitch. The stitches are worked closely on the underside of the fabric to create a more or less solid band of stitching that shows through on the right side.

The stitching may be worked in the same colour as the fabric, but more interesting effects can be created by using a coloured thread on a white fabric. The thread colour will be softened by the fabric, except at the edges, where it forms the back stitch.

There are two alternative ways of working shadow stitches. For method 1, transfer the design to the wrong side of the fabric, using the direct tracing method (see p.64). For method 2, simply trace the design on to the right side of the fabric.

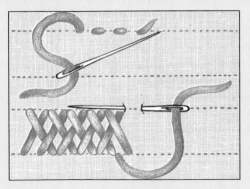

Method 1 On the wrong side of the fabric, work a few running stitches on the stitching line to fasten the thread. Then work herringbone stitch between the marked lines, working the stitches close together for a solid effect, and making sure that each back stitch touches the one before it.

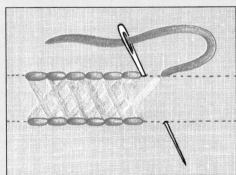

Method 2 On the right side of the fabric, work back stitches as shown, working on alternate stitching lines to form the herringbone stitches underneath.

CRETAN STITCH

This versatile stitch is used extensively by modern embroiderers, since it can create many varied and interesting textures. Its simplest form, open Cretan stitch, looks like a more graceful version of herringbone. When worked irregularly, in overlapping rows, this stitch makes an attractive filling, ideally suited to depicting grasses; it is also useful to create areas of abstract texture. The use of threads of different thickness, different colours, or both, offers even more possibilities. If worked vertically, the stitch is excellent for suggesting water.

Closed Cretan stitch looks completely different from the open, spiky version, but it is formed in basically the same way. This version is well suited to stylized leaves and other motifs, but can also be worked to form a solid band.

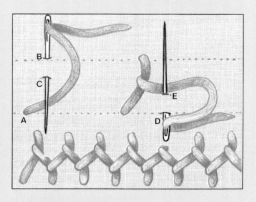

Open Cretan stitch
1 Bring the needle up at A, take it down at a slight angle, at B, and bring it up directly below, at C.
2 Pull the thread through, but not too tightly. Take it over the first stitch, and insert it at D, bringing it up at E. Pull the thread through and take it over the stitch as before.

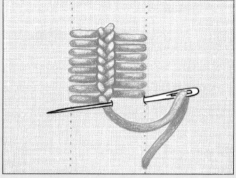

Closed Cretan stitch The stitches are formed in basically the same way as for open Cretan, but are usually worked vertically and with the central crossed area proportionately smaller. To fill a shape evenly, mark both the edges and the centre line where the stitches will cross with tacking or with a hard pencil.

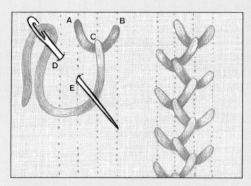

Feather stitch This stitch makes an attractive border for clothing. Mark four evenly spaced stitching lines, as shown.
1 Bring the needle up at A and take it down at B. Bring the needle up above the loop at C.
2 Take the needle down at D and bring it up again at E, keeping the thread under the needle.
3 Work the third stitch to the right and work alternately to right and left in this way.

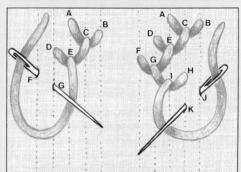

Double feather stitch This variation forms more pronounced zigzags, by working two or more stitches to the right and left alternately. Mark five stitching lines on the fabric.
1–2 Work as for steps 1–2 of feather stitch.
3 Take the needle down at F; bring it up at G.
4 Take the needle down at H and bring it up at I.
5 Take it down at J and bring it up at K.
Repeat steps 2–5.

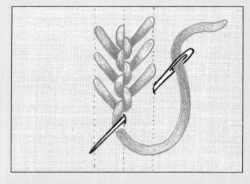

Quill stitch This variation of feather stitch has a spiky appearance that is useful for depicting certain kinds of foliage, such as pine branches.
The stitch is worked as for feather stitch, but you must change the spacing and proportions of the stitches as shown.

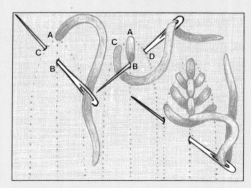

Closed fly stitch This stitch is ideal for leaves. Before working it, mark the centre line.
1 Bring the needle up at A, then take it down at B and bring it up at C.
2 Insert the needle at D, bring it up at B, holding the loop down with the finger or thumb, and take it over the working thread.

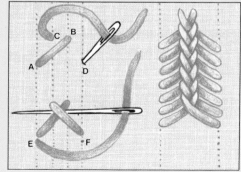

Vandyke stitch This stitch is used for foliage.
1 Bring the needle out at A, take it up diagonally and insert it at B; bring it up at C, and down at D.
2 Bring the needle up at E, take it up diagonally and slide it under the crossed threads (eye first if this is easier). Take it down at F.
Repeat step 2, always sliding the needle under the last pair of crossed threads, and taking care not to pull the thread too tightly.

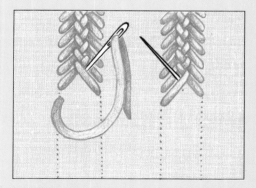

Flat Vandyke In this variation of Vandyke the centre plait is worked right through the fabric, not merely through the crossed threads, which makes it easier to maintain the V-angle on a curve. The texture is slightly flatter than ordinary Vandyke stitch.
Work throughout as in step 1 of Vandyke stitch, taking care not to split the stitches.

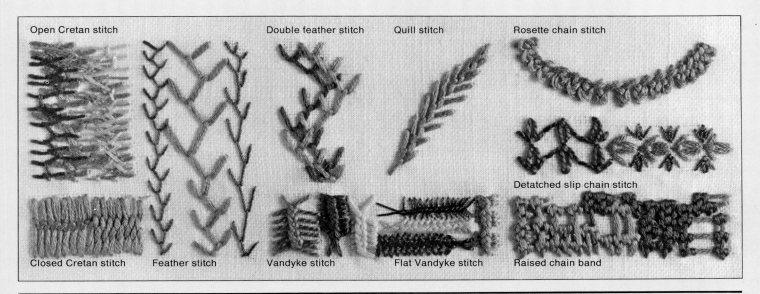

Open Cretan stitch   Double feather stitch   Quill stitch   Rosette chain stitch

Detatched slip chain stitch

Closed Cretan stitch   Feather stitch   Vandyke stitch   Flat Vandyke stitch   Raised chain band

CHAIN BANDS

Many of the chain stitch variations form attractive, textured bands. One of the prettiest, rosette chain, makes an attractive edging on clothing, and can also be worked in a ring, with the rosettes pointing outward. It is less complicated than it looks, but always take care to space the rosettes evenly. Marking the stitching lines will help to keep each one the same size. Avoid pulling the thread tightly.

Detached slip chain stitch is ideal for a vertical border, worked down the front of a blouse, for example.

Raised chain band is extremely versatile. It can be worked evenly or freely. Several lines together create a pleasing 'crunchy' texture. A foundation of cross threads of varying lengths can be worked at random to create an interesting pattern, as shown above.

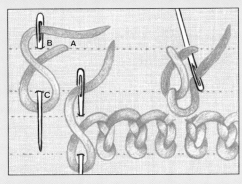

Rosette chain
1 Bring the needle up at A, take it down at B and bring it up at C, looping the thread under the needle as shown.
2 Keeping the needle inside the loop, pull the thread through gently.
3 Slide the needle under the upper strand of thread, ready for the next stitch.

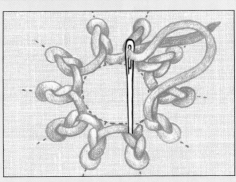

To work rosettes in a ring First mark the inner circle on the fabric, then indicate the positions of the rosettes with short radiating lines. After working the last rosette, take the needle down into the first one, as shown.

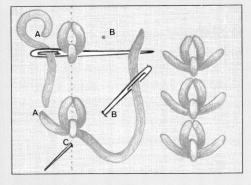

Detached slip chain stitch
1 Work an ordinary chain stitch (see p.70) and anchor the loop with a small vertical stitch.
2 Bring the needle up to the left of the chain loop at A, and slide it under the vertical stitch without piercing the fabric. Take the needle down at B.
3 Bring the needle up at C to work the next chain.

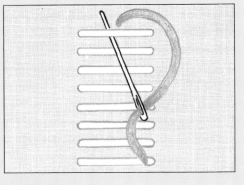

Raised chain band
1 Work horizontal stitches down the length of the stitching line.
2 Thread a tapestry needle with contrasting thread, and bring it up just above the centre of the top stitch.
3 Bring the thread over and slide the needle up, under the horizontal stitch to the left.

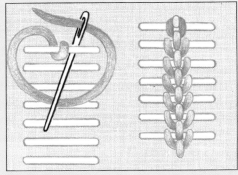

4 Pass the needle down under the horizontal stitch to the right of the thread, forming a loop stitch, and pull the needle through the loop.
Repeat steps 3 and 4, taking care to keep the tension even and not too tight. Do not pierce the fabric.

FILLING STITCHES

Stitches that are ideal for filling areas of embroidery fall into several groups: detached stitches, which are scattered or clustered on the fabric to create texture or shading; small round motifs, which can be used individually or massed together; solid filling stitches, which cover the fabric completely or almost completely; and patterned fillings, which cover relatively large areas with a network of threads.

Detached fillings include some of the most useful stitches: French knots, seeding and straight stitch, for example. The single French knot is commonly used as a flower centre or the eye of a bird, but massed French knots have a wonderfully tactile quality. Both seeding and French knots combine well with beads. Straight stitches, the simplest of all fillings, can be used for cross-hatching as in a drawing.

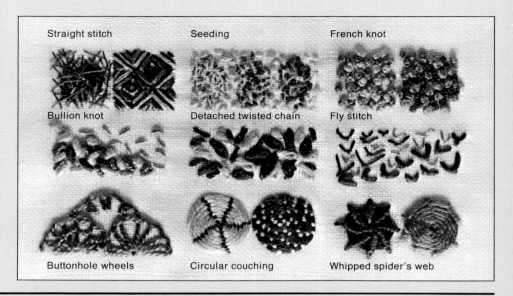

Straight stitch   Seeding   French knot

Bullion knot   Detached twisted chain   Fly stitch

Buttonhole wheels   Circular couching   Whipped spider's web

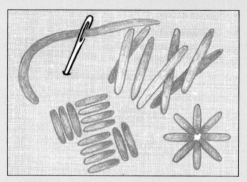

Straight stitch To work a straight stitch, simply bring the needle up where required, and take it down the desired distance away. Use long stitches for tall grass, blocks of short ones for cross-hatching or basketweave effects. To make a simple star or flower motif, work the stitches around a central point.

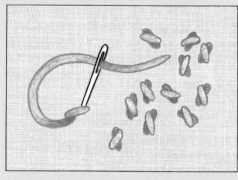

Seeding Worked in graduated density, seeding creates interesting speckled effects of shading and texture.

Work a small straight stitch, then work another stitch diagonally over the first one. If a thick thread is used, more or less the same effect can be achieved with only one stitch. Beads can be sewn on individually to echo and contrast with the texture of the stitches.

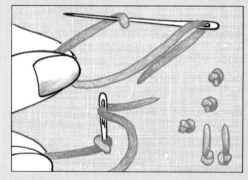

French knot
1 Bring the needle up at the chosen position. Wind the working thread once around the needle. (For a larger knot, use thicker thread.)
2 Holding the thread taut, but not too tight, insert the needle close to the starting point, and draw the thread smoothly through the loop.

For knots on stalks, take the needle down a short distance away.

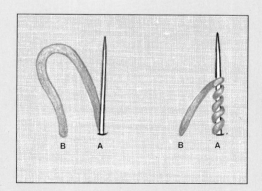

Bullion knot These knots make a curly, textured effect.
1 Bring the needle up at A and take it down at B, leaving a loop of thread, then bring just the point back through at A.
2 Wind the loop of thread around the needle point until the closed-up coil measures the same as the distance from A to B.

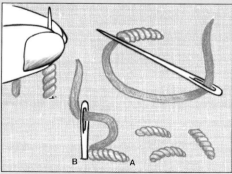

3 Gently holding the coil in place, bring the needle and thread up through it. Pull the knot toward B, and continue pulling on the thread so that the knot rests on the fabric. Use the needle to adjust the coil and smooth it if necessary.
4 Take the needle down at B.

Detached chain stitch This stitch is often used to make leaf or flower shapes. Work individual chain stitches (see p.70) as desired over the fabric, fastening each loop with a small tying stitch. Or work them in a circle to make 'lazy daisy' stitch.

Free chain loops can be produced by working the anchoring stitch at the top of the chain rather than over the loop.

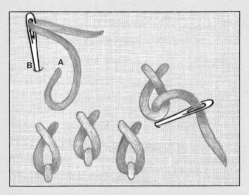

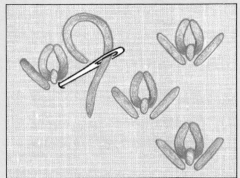

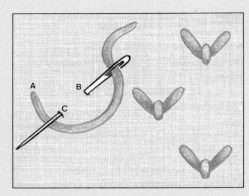

Detached twisted chain stitch This variation can be worked in patterns or scattered over the fabric.

Bring the needle up at A, hold the thread to the left and take it down at B, forming a loop, as shown. Then work a small stitch at the bottom of the loop to hold it in place.

Tête de boeuf These 'bull's head' stitches make charming miniature flowers.
1 Work a single detached chain stitch (see p.76).
2 Then work two diagonal straight stitches to either side of the chain.

Fly stitch This stitch can be used realistically to suggest distant birds, or in an abstract way to create a rough-looking texture. Equally, fly stitch can be joined up to form a band or border.

Bring the needle up at A, take it down at B, holding the loop down, and bring it out at C, making a small stitch to anchor the loop.

ROUND MOTIFS

Circular motifs are obviously ideal for stylized flowers and fruit, cartwheels and other round objects. Here are several, both flat and three-dimensional, which can be used for different effects.

To practise these motifs, first draw a circle on the fabric, using a coin or circular piece of card as a template if you like. When you become more adept at working the stitches, you may want to dispense with this step and work the motifs more freely.

Another stitch often used for small round shapes is padded satin stitch (see p.78).

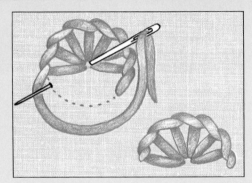

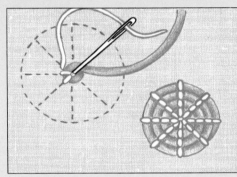

Buttonhole wheels First draw a circle on the fabric. Then bring the needle up at some point on the outer edge and work buttonhole stitches (see p.72) all around the circle, working each one into the centre.

Semicircles and fan shapes can be made in the same way.

Circular couching For this variation of simple couching (see p.71), first draw a circle, then mark the lines for the couching stitches. Bring up the main thread at the centre, then bring up the couching thread and work stitches over the main thread in the chosen pattern.

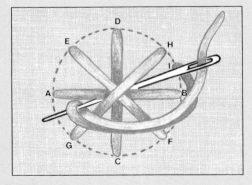

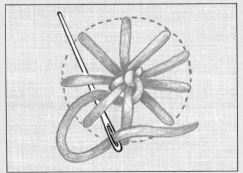

Whipped spider's web
1 Draw a circle on the fabric. Using a tapestry needle and a thread at least 50cm long, cross the circle with four diagonal stitches (A–B, C–D, E–F, G–H). Place point H closer to D than to B in order to leave room for the ninth 'spoke' between them. Bring the needle up at I, slide it under all threads where they intersect, and loop the working thread over the needle.

2 Pull the thread through to tie the stitches together at the centre.
3 Working from the centre outward, slide the needle under two threads, pull the thread through firmly, then take the needle back over the second thread and then under both it and the next one.

Repeat step 3 all around the circle, as often as necessary to cover the threads (or leave them partly uncovered if you prefer), loosening the tension gradually toward the edges.

For a woven spider's web, take the needle under and over the threads alternately, as though weaving.

77

SATIN STITCH

Apparently one of the simplest of all embroidery stitches, satin stitch is also one of the most difficult. You can learn the basics of how to work it in no time at all, but you will need a great deal of practice before you can work it well, so that the stitches lie side by side in perfect parallel lines.

Keeping the edge smooth can also be a problem. To make this easier, first work a line of split stitch (see p.70) along the edges of the area to be filled. This will serve as a guide for your needle and will also give the work a well-defined edge.

Wherever possible, satin stitch should be worked at an angle to the edges of the shape being filled. This makes it easier to work the stitch evenly. The stitches should not be too long. About 1.5cm is the limit on an item that will be handled frequently, otherwise the threads are likely to catch.

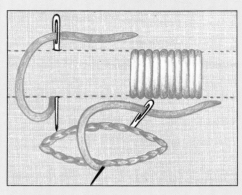

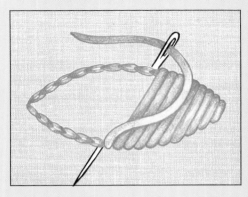

For basic satin stitch, bring the needle up on one edge, take it down on the opposite edge, then back up on the first one again.

To fill a shape:
1 Work a line of split stitch around the edges.
2 Work a straight stitch diagonally across the shape, somewhere around the middle, to establish the slant.

3 Work satin stitch to the nearer end, working over the split stitch but very close to it for a smooth edge.
4 Take the thread under the stitches on the wrong side and work in the other direction. To prevent the angle from flattening out, exaggerate it slightly toward the end.

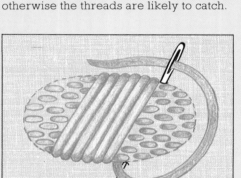

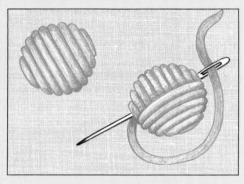

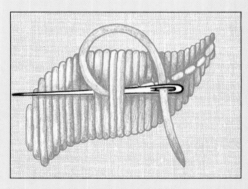

Padded satin stitch
1 Work lines of running stitch (see p.69) across the shape to be filled. For a gently sloped effect, work the stitches more thickly on one side of the shape than on the other.
2 Fill the shape with satin stitch.

Alternative method of padded satin stitch
1 Fill the shape with satin stitch, running the stitches in the opposite direction from that intended for the finished work.
2 Work a second layer over the first, at right angles to it. More than two layers may be worked, if desired, but take care to keep the edges neat.

Satin stitch tied with back stitch Satin stitches should not be too long or they may become damaged. Anchoring them with a line of back stitch is one way around the problem.
1 Work satin stitch in the usual way.
2 Work one or more lines of back stitch across the satin stitches.

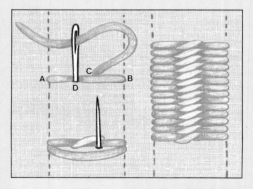

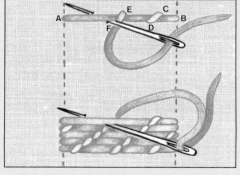

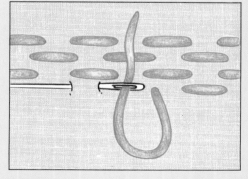

Roumanian stitch This is sometimes called Roumanian couching.
1 Bring the needle up at A, take it down at B, then work a stitch diagonally over the long stitch from C–D.
2 Work another long stitch just below the first, as in step 1, but bring the needle up for the diagonal stitch before pulling the thread through.

Bokhara couching This is similar to Roumanian stitch, but has more tying stitches.
1 Work a long stitch from A–B across the shape.
2 Work short diagonal stitches (C–D, E–F, etc.) at regular intervals over the long stitch.
Repeat steps 1 and 2, arranging the short couching stitches in a diagonal pattern.

Darning This is a simple way of filling an area with smooth lines of stitching while allowing the fabric to show through.
Simply work lines of running stitch (see p.69) to fill the shape. The stitches may be worked evenly, perhaps to form a pattern, or at random.

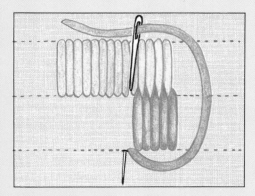

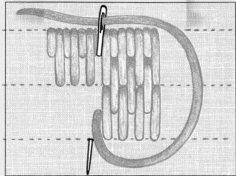

Encroaching satin stitch This is also known as block shading, since it is often used with thread in graduated shades of a single color.
1 Work a row of vertical satin stitches.
2 Work a row below, bringing the needle up on the lower line and taking it down between the ends of the stitches in the row above.

Brick stitch This stitch is named for the brick-like pattern it produces.
1 Work vertical satin stitches along the top edge, making them alternately long and short.
2 On following rows make all the stitches the same length, as shown. Fill in the gaps in the last row with short stitches.

Satin stitch   Padded satin stitch   Satin stitch tied with back stitch   Encroaching satin stitch

Roumanian stitch   Bokhara couching   Darning   Brick stitch

LONG AND SHORT STITCH

This stitch figures prominently in some types of traditional embroidery, such as crewel work, and is used to achieve subtle effects of shading in flower petals, leaves and other motifs. Like satin stitch, it is basically simple but is difficult to execute well. The rows of different colors must seem to flow into each other as in a realistic painting, and the stitches must lie smoothly. This is relatively easy to achieve if the area to be filled is rectangular. But more often it is curved, and angling the stitches correctly involves occasionally working a "wedge" stitch (see p.80), which is not worked into in the next row.

When practicing long and short stitch, begin by working the stitches regularly, as shown. As you become more skilled, you can vary the length of the stitches more freely.

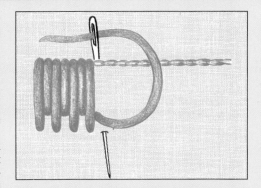

Long and short stitch in straight lines
1 Work a line of split stitch (see p.70) along the upper edge.
2 Work vertical stitches down from this edge, taking the needle over it, and making every alternate stitch about three-quarters the length of its predecessor. The longer stitches should be at least ⅜in long.

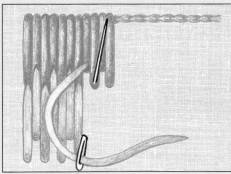

3 Using thread a shade or two lighter or darker than the first, work another row of stitches, all the same length, below the first. Bring the needle up through the corresponding upper stitch, splitting the thread, as shown.

Repeat step 3 as required.

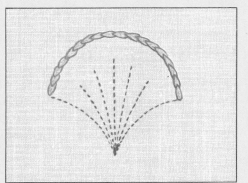

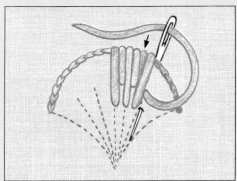

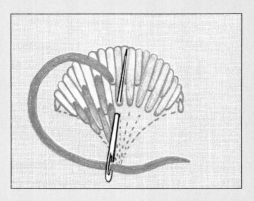

Long and short stitch in a curved shape
1 Mark guidelines within the shape to help you slant the stitches correctly.
2 Outline the shape with split stitch.

3 Starting at the centre of the shape, work long and short stitches alternately to one side, then return to the centre and work to the other side. Slant the stitches as indicated by the guidelines, working a short 'wedge' stitch (see arrow) where necessary.

4 Work subsequent rows in graduated shades, working into the upper stitches as in step 3 of straight long and short stitch. Keep the stitches fairly long for a satiny effect. Some practice is needed to cover the split stitch at the sides without distorting the angle of the long and short stitches.

LAID WORK
If a large area needs to be filled with a flat, solid stitch, laid work can be a good choice. Unlike satin stitch, which it superficially resembles, laid work covers only the right side of the fabric, and thus is more economical of thread, a factor worth considering if the area is large.

Because the laid stitches are usually long, they must be held in place by 'holding' stitches. Lines of split stitch, stem stitch, chain stitch or couching (see pp.70–71) are all suitable choices for this. The stitching can simply be worked in lines perpendicular to the laid threads or it can form more elaborate patterns.

Subtle effects of shading can be achieved in laid work by using two colours of stranded cotton in the needle and altering their proportions as illustrated on page 50.

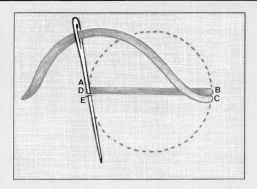

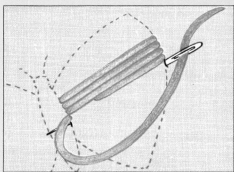

For basic laid work, bring the needle up at A and take it across the shape and down at B. Bring it up at C, as close as possible to B, then down at D, and up again at E. Continue filling the shape, working first out to one side and then to the other. Avoid pulling the stitches tightly or they may be distorted by the holding stitches.

To change the direction of the threads, if the shape requires it, work a shorter stitch occasionally, taking the needle down a little before the edge, then bringing it up on the edge, close to the last stitch but one, and continuing as before.

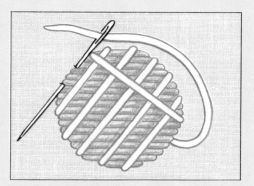

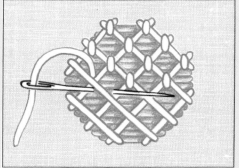

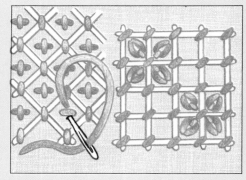

Laid threads tied with crossbars
1 Work a row of long holding stitches diagonally across the laid stitches, as shown, starting at the widest point and spacing them 7–8mm apart.
2 Work another layer of holding stitches across the first at the opposite angle and the same distance apart.

3 Anchor the diagonal stitches by working a small stitch over each intersection. These stitches, and the long holding stitches, may be worked in a contrasting thread. For a simpler pattern, work only one set of diagonal stitches and couch them down at regular intervals.

Squared filling
1 Work a crossbar pattern directly on the fabric, as in steps 1–3 of Laid threads tied with crossbars.
2 Embellish this trellis with other stitches as desired, worked between or over the original stitches. The basic pattern may be worked horizontally and vertically instead of diagonally.

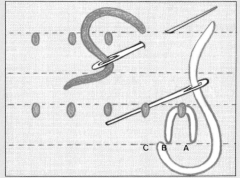

Wave filling

1 At the upper edge of the area to be filled, work a series of short, evenly spaced stitches.
2 Using a tapestry needle, bring the thread up at A, take it through the first straight stitch, then down again at B. Bring the needle up again at C, close to B, and continue in the same way.

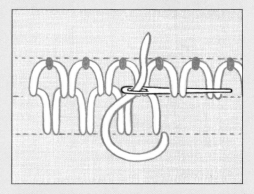

3 Work back, as for step 2 but in the opposite direction, taking the needle under each pair of stitches, as shown, and taking care not to pull the thread tightly.

To help keep the stitches even, draw horizontal guidelines on the fabric.

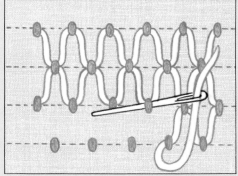

Cloud filling

1 Work straight stitches as in step 1 of Wave filling, but over several rows, staggering them.
2 Using a tapestry needle, take the thread up and down under the straight stitches to form a series of loops. Fasten the thread under the last straight stitch before beginning the next row.

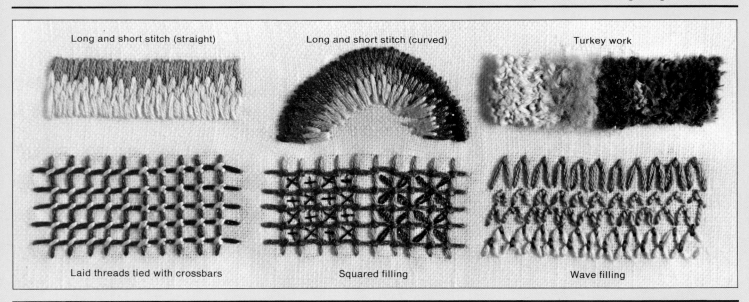

Long and short stitch (straight)

Long and short stitch (curved)

Turkey work

Laid threads tied with crossbars

Squared filling

Wave filling

TURKEY WORK

This stitch can be used to give a raised, velvety texture similar to that of a carpet, which gives it its name. Basically it consists of lines of back stitch (see p.69), in which every alternate stitch is not pulled through but left as a small loop. When the work is completed, the loops can either be trimmed closely and evenly for a pile effect, or left uncut for a looped texture.

Cut Turkey work is best worked closely in straight lines, as shown. (Incidentally, this is one stitch that is best worked with a 'sewing' movement, as illustrated, rather than up and down.) If the loops are to be left uncut they can be worked in curved lines – for example, in concentric circles to suggest a flower.

The loops or pile will slant backward slightly, so allow for this by turning the work in the appropriate direction before beginning to stitch.

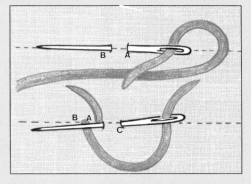

1 Take the needle down at A and bring it up at B, leaving a short end free.
2 Take the needle down at C and up at A, leaving the working thread below the needle. Pull the thread through, holding the free end in place with the thumb or forefinger.

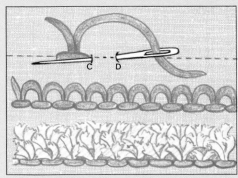

3 Work another back stitch, from D to C, but this time keep the thread above the needle. Pull the thread through, leaving a loop.

Repeat steps 2 and 3, making small stitches and placing the rows close together.

When the work is complete, snip through and trim the loops, or leave them uncut.

At its most simple, appliqué consists of stitching one piece of fabric on top of another. One of the most versatile types of needlework, it can take many forms, from a simple monogram or crest machine-stitched on to a jacket to a detailed pattern of tiny leaves and blossoms applied by hand and embellished with surface embroidery. Appliqué can be worked on the underside of a sheer fabric to create a subtle, shadowy effect; it can be padded, stuffed or quilted; it can even be worked in reverse, with the background fabric placed on top and cut away to form the motifs.

Appliqué is best suited to designs featuring strong, relatively large shapes, rather than intricate patterns of line and texture which are better interpreted in surface stitchery, since this is ideal for fine detail. However, if your design was based

on a bowl of fruit, for example, appliqué could be an excellent medium in which to convey the solidity and well-defined shapes of the various fruits and the bowl itself. It would be easy to find fabrics in the appropriate colors, and their textures might even suggest the textures of the fruits too—red satin for an apple, perhaps, and coarse-weave orange linen for the rough surface of an orange. The finished work would make a bold statement about shape and color, with a fresh, spontaneous quality similar to that of a paper cut-out.

In a more sophisticated form, appliqué can benefit from the addition of some stitchery. In some appliqué methods the motifs are attached with embroidery, which can be used to soften or accentuate the edge of a shape, depending on the type of stitch and the color of the thread.

Stitchery can be used on the motifs themselves, too, to suggest texture. For example, instead of choosing a textured fabric for the orange, you could use a piece of smooth cotton or lightweight wool, then work a few seeding stitches (see p. 76) near the edges to suggest both the texture and the special contours of the fruit.

Embroidery can also be used to provide detail. A picture or panel depicting an urban scene might use appliqué for the buildings themselves, to create a solid look, then embroidery for the windows, doors and other architectural features.

The following pages describe several methods of working appliqué, suitable for different types of project and design as well as for different fabrics.

FABRICS FOR APPLIQUÉ

Virtually any fabric can be used for appliqué, indeed this is much of the craft's appeal. The wide variety of materials available can inspire all sorts of design ideas. Blue moiré taffeta or shot silk might suggest water; gray velvet the fur of a cat; dark brown tweed the bark of a tree. Layers of chiffon could be placed on top of each other to depict the sky at sunset, while leather or suede could be used realistically for a pair of boots; or as abstract shapes to provide textural interest.

However, although the choice is wide in theory, it may be more limited in reality, at least for practical items. In this case, you will have to consider whether the fabrics will stand up to a degree of wear, and whether or not they are washable. Felt, for example, is an easy fabric to appliqué,

since its edges do not fray, but it cannot be washed. For any appliqué that will be washed, such as a child's jacket, all the fabrics, including the background, must be compatible in terms of their care. So do not mix rayon with linen, for example, as they will not only need washing, but also ironing, at different temperatures.

Another consideration is the chosen method of appliqué. If you are using the turned-edge method shown on page 85, you should avoid thick, springy fabrics unless you are an experienced embroiderer. A lightweight, closely woven cotton is ideal, although it should not be so fine that the turnings will show through on the right side. Slippery fabrics, or those that fray badly, can be made easier to handle either by applying iron-on interfacing to the wrong side or by applying them to the background fabric with bonding web, as

shown opposite. Both methods will arrest fraying, and interfacing will give a flimsy fabric the necessary body.

On any item that will receive wear, always appliqué motifs with the fabric grain matching that of the background. Ideally, the warp threads (those parallel to the selvage) should be aligned, but if you are using scraps without a selvage this may be impossible to ascertain. In this case, make sure that the grains cross at right angles. Even if the work is purely decorative, the shapes will be easier to apply if the grains match.

TRANSFERRING THE DESIGN

The shapes to be appliquéed must first be transferred to the appliqué fabrics. This is normally done by means of templates.

If the design is simple, the motifs can usually be positioned on the background fabric by eye. If centring them is important, mark the background fabric with lines of tacking to serve as guides.

Even a fairly complex design can usually be assembled by numbering the shapes on the master design and referring to this as you work.

If you prefer to mark the positions of the shapes on the background fabric, you can do so using dressmaker's carbon paper or tacking (see pp. 64–5).

If you have used the cut-paper method of planning your design (see p. 24), you will already have templates, but otherwise you must make them, unless you are using the interfacing method shown opposite.

Making the templates
1 To make the templates, first number each shape in the master design. (If the design is very simple, this step can be omitted.)
2 Trace each motif from the design, using fairly stiff tracing paper. If you intend to use the motifs for a repeating design, you could use the tracing to cut a more durable template from thin cardboard.

3 Mark each template with the number corresponding to that in the design. Mark a small arrow indicating the shape's vertical alignment, so that you cut the motif with the grain running correctly.
4 Cut around the traced lines to make the templates.

USING IRON-ON INTERFACING

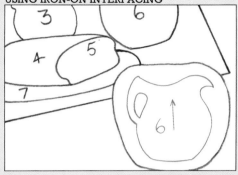

1 Place the interfacing, shiny (adhesive) side up, on the design, and trace the shape, using a pencil or waterproof fabric-marking pen. Cut around the tracing, leaving a small margin (about 1–2 cm) all around which will be cut off later. Mark the grain line and the number on the non-adhesive side.

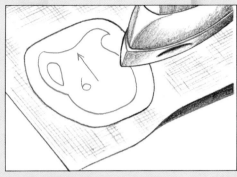

2 Place the interfacing, shiny side down, on the wrong side of the fabric, aligning the grain line with the fabric grain. Using the point of the iron, fix the interfacing to the fabric at one point to hold it in place. Cover the motif with a damp pressing cloth and press with a dry or steam iron.

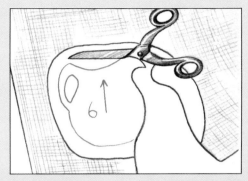

3 Cut around the shape, on the marked line. The motif is now ready to be applied to the background by machine or by hand, as shown in the following pages.

USING BONDING WEB

1 Place the template, wrong side up, on the non-adhesive (paper) side of the bonding web and draw around it with a pencil. This will produce a mirror image of the original shape. Mark the grain line and the number on the bonding web.
2 Cut around the pencil line, leaving a margin all around.

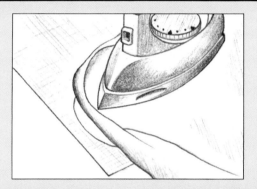

3 Place the bonding web motif, adhesive side down, on the wrong side of the fabric. Using the point of the iron, fix the bonding at one point to secure it, then cover the work with a damp cloth and press with a hot, dry iron.
4 Allow the fabric to cool, then cut around the outline through both fabric and bonding.

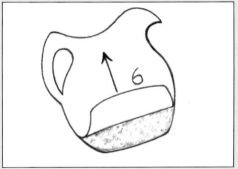

5 When you are ready to apply the motif, simply peel away the paper backing. Position the motif on the background fabric, secure it with the point of the iron and then press, using a damp cloth and a hot iron.
Note When using either iron-on interfacing or bonding web, always test it first on a spare piece of fabric.

PERSIAN APPLIQUÉ

Also called appliqué perse, this is one of the simplest ways of decorating fabric. It consists of cutting a whole motif, such as a flower, from a printed fabric and applying it to another (usually plain) one. As the edges are not turned under, it is a good idea to use either the interfacing or the bonding web method.

There is no need to trace the motif on to the interfacing or bonding web; simply cut a piece slightly larger than the motif and iron it on to the wrong side of the fabric. Then cut out the motif and apply it to the background fabric either by bonding or by a suitable hand or machine method (see pp. 84–6). If bonding is used, the edges can then be secured with some decorative stitching, such as buttonhole or Cretan stitch, as shown right.

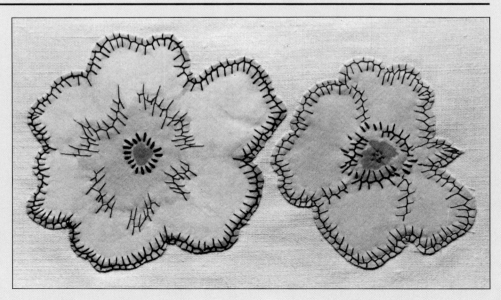

HAND APPLIQUÉ

There are several different methods of hand appliqué. Fabrics that do not fray, such as felt and leather, can be cut to the finished size and applied flat with stab stitch. Woven fabrics that do not fray easily, or fabrics that have been interfaced or backed with bonding web (see p. 83), can also be applied without turnings.

If a fabric is thin or sheer, so that turnings would be visible through the right side, it can be applied using the stitch and cut method shown below. Another way of handling such fabrics is to cut a piece of iron-on interfacing, apply it to the fabric, then cut out and apply the motif using the turned-edge method (see p. 85).

Before tacking a motif to the fabric, it is best to mount the background fabric on a frame (see pp. 66–7). This will ensure that the fabrics lie smoothly together.

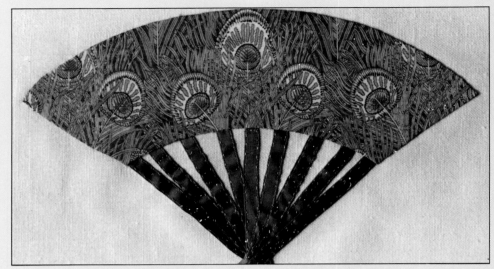

The fan is hand appliquéed using the turned-edge method and invisible stitching.

NON-FRAY FABRICS

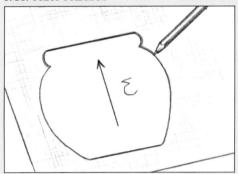

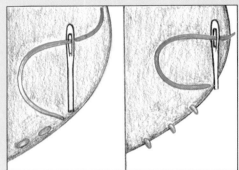

1 Place the template, right side down, on the wrong side of the fabric and draw around it. Cut out the motif on the marked line.

2 Mount the background fabric on a frame, then position the motif and secure it with a few pins. Tack it in place with lines of diagonal tacking.

3 Using matching sewing or embroidery thread, stitch the motif in place with stab stitch —tiny running stitches. Work close to the edge.

Alternatively, work the stab stitches over the edge, as shown on the right.

FRAY-RESISTANT WOVEN FABRICS

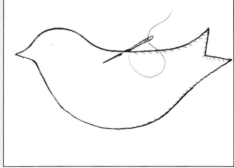

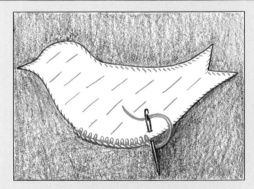

1 Mark and cut out the motif as in step 1 above or as described on page 83 for interfaced or bonded motifs. If the fabric is not interfaced or backed with bonding, work small oversewing stitches around the edges with matching thread.

2 Pin and tack the motif to the background fabric.

3 Work buttonhole stitch (see p. 72) around the edges, using matching or contrasting embroidery thread and spacing the stitches as desired. A different stitch, such as Cretan or herringbone (pp. 73 and 74), may be used if preferred.

STITCH AND CUT METHOD

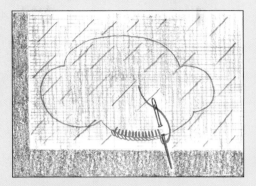
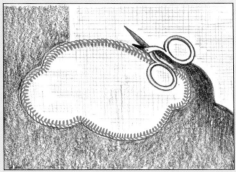

This method is well suited to thin fabrics, including those that fray easily.
1 Place the template right side up on the right side of the fabric and mark around it. Cut roughly around the shape, leaving a generous margin.

2 Pin and tack the motif to the background fabric, working the tacking over the whole area.
3 Work close buttonhole stitch over the marked line, through both fabrics.

4 Using sharp-pointed embroidery scissors, carefully cut away the excess fabric just outside the stitching line.

TURNED-EDGE METHOD

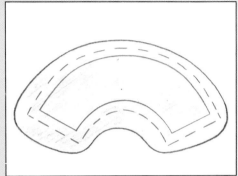
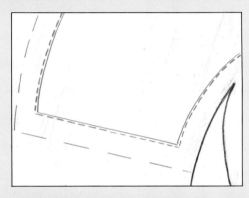
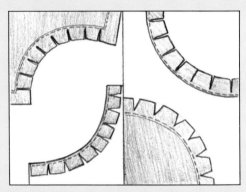

1 Place the template, right side up, on the right side of the fabric and mark around the edge with a fabric-marking pen or tailor's chalk.
2 Mark a turning allowance 5–7 mm outside the marked line.
3 Cut out the shape, leaving a generous margin outside the turning allowance.

4 Stay stitch (machine straight stitch) just outside the inner marked line. This step is not strictly essential, but makes it easier to turn the edges under.
5 Cut away the excess fabric, leaving just the turning allowance.

On curved edges Clip or notch the turning allowance up to the stay stitching.
   For an inner curve (left), clip the edge so that it will fan out when turned under.
   For an outer curve (right), notch the edge to prevent excess bulk when turned.

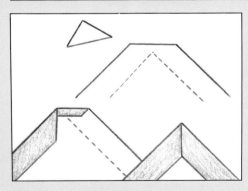
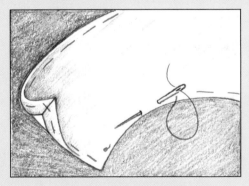
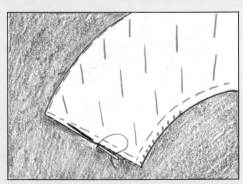

Mitring corners For an outer corner, mitre the turnings as follows. Cut across the corner to eliminate excess bulk, turn down the corner, then turn down the two adjacent sides.
   For an inner corner, make one clip into the stay stitching.

6 Turn the seam allowance under and tack it in place. If you are experienced, this step may be omitted, and the allowance turned under as you stitch (see below); but it is recommended for beginners. Make any knots on the right side of the motif for easy removal of tacking stitches.

7 Pin and tack the motif to the background fabric using diagonal tacking.
8 Using matching sewing thread and slip stitch, sew the motif in place. Make the stitches as nearly invisible as possible and space them about 3–5 mm apart.
   If the edges have not been tacked turn them under as you stitch. The point of a seam ripper is useful to help turn under the edges.

MACHINE APPLIQUÉ

The obvious advantage of machine appliqué is speed, but it has other advantages too. Machine stitching, being stronger than most hand stitching, is ideal for any item that will be subjected to hard wear or frequent laundering.

Some machine appliqué can be done with a straight stitch only, but a machine that will also do zigzag stitch expands the range of possible effects. An open zigzag stitch, perhaps in a contrasting colour, will provide a decorative edge, while close zigzag, or satin stitch, will cover raw edges completely. Machine embroidery thread, which is finer and glossier than ordinary thread, will enhance the satiny effect, but for most purposes an ordinary sewing thread is suitable. Cotton-covered polyester thread is ideal, since it is both strong and compatible with all fabrics.

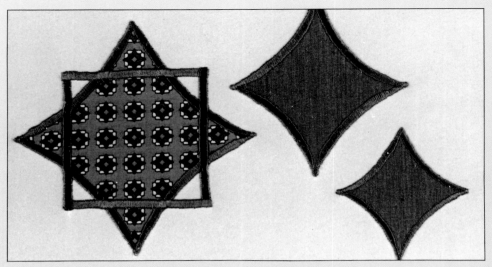

Zigzag machine stitch is used to appliqué this geometric motif.

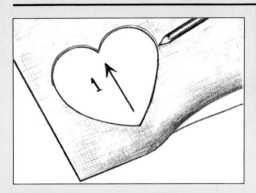

1 Place the template right side up on the right side of the fabric and mark around it with a waterproof fabric-marking pen or pencil.
2 Cut around the motif, leaving a margin of 1–2 cm.

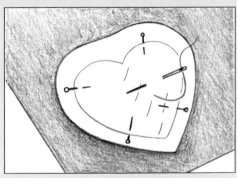

3 Pin the motif to the background fabric, placing the pins perpendicular to the edge, as shown. Tack it in place using diagonal tacking, making sure that both layers lie smoothly against each other.

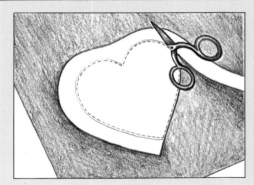

4 Work straight stitch around the marked outline.
5 Using sharp-pointed embroidery scissors, cut away the excess fabric close to the stitching. Depending on the fabric and the effect desired, the appliqué could be left as it is, but if the edges need to be covered, proceed to step 6.

6 Work zigzag stitch over the edges, covering the first line of stitching. Page 118 includes detailed instructions on working zigzag stitch.

If an open zigzag stitch is to be used, it is better to bond the motif (see p. 83) in place, then work the zigzag, omitting the straight stitch.

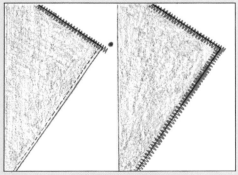

To work a corner Stitch slightly beyond the edge of the first side to the width the new line of stitching will cover. Remove the work and take the threads to the wrong side. Reposition the needle just inside the first line of stitching and continue stitching in the new direction.
To work around tight curves Pivot the work every few stitches: stop the machine with the needle in the fabric on the inside of the curve;

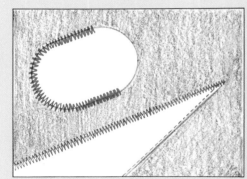

raise the foot, turn the fabric slightly, then lower the foot, and work two or three more stitches. Repeat.
To work sharp points Narrow the stitch width gradually, starting about 2–3 cm from the point, until the stitch just covers the edges. Pivot, as described for curves, and resume stitching, gradually widening the zigzag.

SHADOW APPLIQUÉ

In this form of appliqué the motifs are applied to the underside of a sheer fabric such as organdie, organza, fine linen or lawn. The appliqué fabric is usually fairly thin also. It is normally a solid colour, which may be the same as the main fabric or contrasting. Any contrasting colour will be softened by the top layer.

The motifs are applied using a variation of the stitch and cut method shown on page 85. This lends itself to more intricate designs than are possible with most other appliqué techniques.

A variety of stitches can be used for shadow appliqué. Back stitch produces a thin line and combines well with shadow stitch (see p. 73). Another stitch often used is point de Paris, or pin stitch, a type of pulled thread work which forms tiny holes along the stitching line.

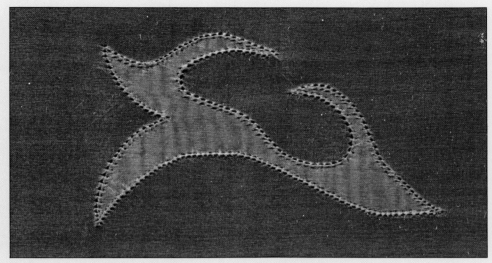

The sinuous curves of this abstract motif in shadow appliqué are outlined in point de Paris.

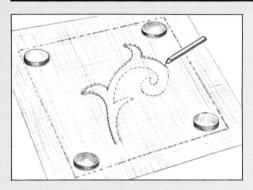

1 Place the main fabric right side up over the design (having darkened the lines first if necessary). Hold it in place with weights or tape, making sure that the grain runs straight, and trace the design using tailor's chalk or pencil.

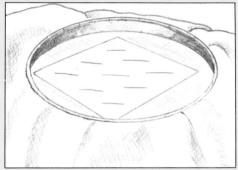

2 Mount the main fabric on a frame (see pp. 66–7).
3 Cut a piece of the appliqué fabric slightly larger than the motif and pin it, right side down, to the wrong side of the main fabric.
4 Tack it in place using diagonal tacking.

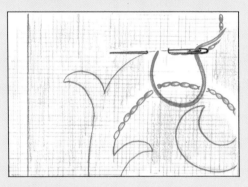

5 Work back stitch (see p. 69) or another embroidery stitch of your choice over the design outlines. Secure the thread at the beginning by making one or two back stitches in the appliqué fabric. When fastening off or starting a new thread, secure the thread by working it into existing stitches.

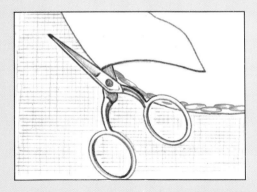

6 Using sharp embroidery scissors, carefully cut away the excess appliqué fabric outside the stitching.

Remove the work from the frame.

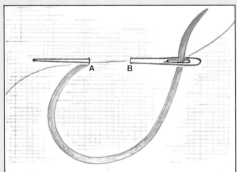

Point de Paris Transfer the design, mount the main fabric in a frame, and tack the appliqué fabric in place as described above. Then, using a tapestry needle and ordinary sewing thread in a matching colour, work the stitching as follows:
1 Work a back stitch from A to B, bringing the needle up again at A in the same hole.

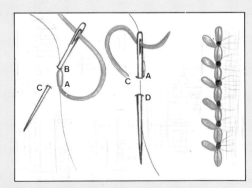

2 Work another back stitch, bringing the needle up at C, just inside the design outline.
3 Take the needle down again at A and bring it up at D.

Repeat steps 1–3, pulling the thread tightly on each stitch, especially in step 2, to form the holes.

REVERSE APPLIQUÉ

In most forms of appliqué, the design is formed by applying motifs to the surface of the main fabric. Reverse appliqué, by contrast, is worked by cutting away one or more layers of superimposed fabric to expose the fabric underneath.

The traditional method of reverse appliqué, sometimes called San Blas appliqué, is a complex procedure in which the design is built up from the bottom layer of fabric.

The simpler version of reverse appliqué, shown here, called cut-through appliqué, involves working from the top downward. The basic method can be varied to create many different effects within the same piece of work, especially if four or five layers of fabric are used.

Choose fabrics that are opaque, lightweight and closely woven, so that the edges will not fray.

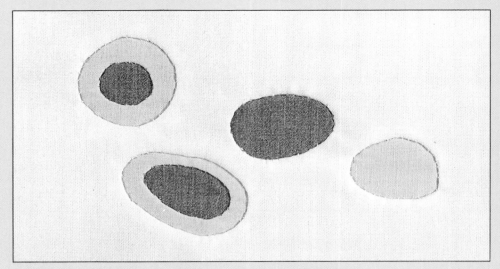

Reverse appliqué, showing the permutations using three layers of fabric

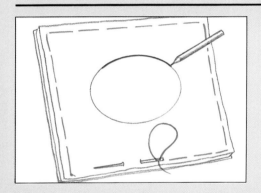

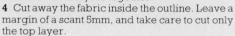

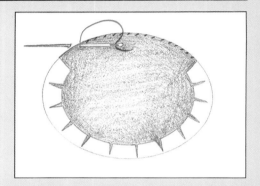

1 Cut all the fabric layers to the required size, allowing extra for finishing. (Three layers are used in the illustrations.) Pin them together over the whole surface and tack around the edges.
2 Make templates (see p. 82) for the outer shapes—those that will be cut from the top fabric. Position these on the top fabric and trace around them lightly with pencil or tailor's chalk.

3 Tack all around, 1.5 to 2cm from the outline, to hold the fabric layers together.
4 Cut away the fabric inside the outline. Leave a margin of a scant 5mm, and take care to cut only the top layer.

5 Using matching thread and slip stitch, stitch the edges of the cut-out shape to the layer below, turning under the edges as you work. Take an occasional stitch through all layers to hold them in place permanently. Clip the edges where necessary so that they will lie smoothly.

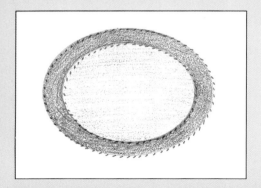

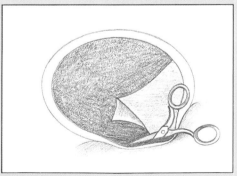

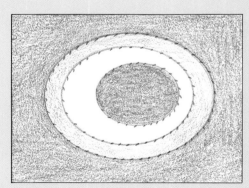

6 Repeat steps 4 and 5 to reveal lower layers of fabric, reducing the size of the cut-out shape as you work downward. It is not usually necessary to draw another outline; simply cut free-hand, remembering to allow a little fabric for turning under.

To miss a layer and reveal the one below it, cut away the top layer as described in step 4, then cut away the next layer, taking it back well under the top fabric. Turn under the edges of the top fabric and stitch them to the third layer.

Shapes can be added within the cut-away spaces for additional interest. Simply prepare the shapes and stitch them in place as for turned-edge appliqué (see p. 85), or use another appliqué method if you prefer.

PADDED APPLIQUÉ

Many interesting three-dimensional effects can be achieved with appliqué by padding or raising shapes. A useful padding technique consists of sewing layers of felt to the background fabric to build up a smoothly rounded shape, then applying the motif over them. This technique is used extensively in metal thread work (see p. 99) to enhance the sheen of the metal thread and fabrics. It performs a similar function for shiny fabrics such as satin but can be used with almost any fabric.

A softer effect can be achieved by using layers of thin polyester wadding instead of felt. For a stiff effect, well suited to architectural forms or hard-edged designs, a motif can be reinforced with cardboard.

Small, freestanding motifs can be made and sewn to the background fabric at one point only so that they project out from it.

Satin fabric accentuates the roundness of the shapes in padded appliqué

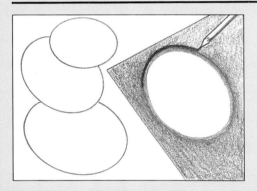

1 Using a template (see p. 82), trace the motif on to felt and cut it out. Then cut one or more smaller shapes (a total of three to six is normally used), making each about 5mm smaller all around than the previous one.
2 Cut the appliqué slightly larger than the template to allow for the space taken up by the layers of padding.

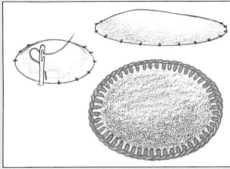

3 Pin and stitch the felt pieces to the background. Use stab stitch and work upward from the smallest to the largest. For an asymmetrical effect, pad unevenly as shown above, top right.
4 Stitch the appliqué motif to the fabric using one of the methods given on pages 82–3.

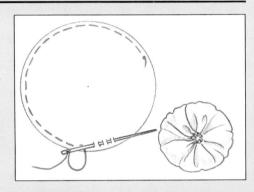

Suffolk puffs These small circular motifs can suggest flowers or other round shapes.
1 Cut a circle of fabric twice the desired diameter.
2 Work running stitch close to a folded or turned edge.
3 Pull up the stitches and fasten the thread securely on the underside. The motif is then ready to be sewn into place.

Padding with cardboard
1 Cut a piece of card (or stiff pelmet interfacing) the size of the finished motif.
2 Cut the appliqué fabric 1–2cm larger.
3 Centre the cardboard on the wrong side of the motif. Spread fabric glue on the outer edges and stick the fabric edges over it.
4 Apply the shape to the background fabric using invisible or decorative stitches.

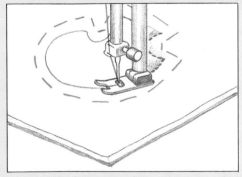

Stuffed freestanding motif
1 Trace the motif on to the top fabric.
2 Place the top and bottom fabrics together, with a piece of lightweight wadding between. Tack them together just outside the outline.
3 Machine stitch along the outline using a small straight stitch.

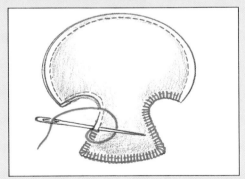

4 Cut out the motif carefully with embroidery scissors. Then work buttonhole stitch around the cut edges by hand.
5 Alternatively, work close zigzag stitch over the first line of stitching, then work around the cut edges once more with zigzag stitch to neaten them.

The simplest and most familiar kind of quilting, sometimes called padded or English quilting, involves working lines of stitching, either by hand or machine, through two layers of fabric with a layer of padding sandwiched in between. Designs for padded quilting have traditionally been of two main types: repeating patterns, which cover the whole surface, and motifs, which may be used singly or in various combinations. Designs for borders often incorporate elements of both types. Modern designs for quilting, however, can take many other forms, both pictorial and abstract. Quilting can also be used to outline or echo a printed or appliqué motif.

The lines of quilting should be distributed fairly evenly over the area. Dense areas of quilting will flatten the work and cause any adjacent unstitched areas to stand up in relief and assume undue importance.

MATERIALS AND EQUIPMENT

Fabrics for quilting should be soft, light- to medium-weight and closely woven to prevent padding fibres pushing through to the surface. Those made from natural fibres, such as cotton, wool and silk, are easiest to sew. Plain, light-coloured fabrics show off the quilting design to best advantage.

If the underside of the quilting will not be seen, as in a cushion cover, the backing fabric is usually a soft, serviceable cotton such as muslin. For a quilt or wallhanging, however, the backing should be of a quality similar to that of the top fabric.

In the past, the padding material, or wadding was usually made of cotton or wool, but today polyester wadding is the usual choice, because it is lightweight, stable and washable. It comes in several thicknesses and widths. Some quilters prefer cotton wadding, which is flatter and denser and thus better suited to traditional, intricate quilting patterns. Pure cotton, however, has a tendency to shift—which may help explain the intricacy of those old designs. A new type of cotton wadding, containing 20 per cent polyester, is more stable, and is hand-washable.

For hand or machine quilting, use a strong thread. Quilting thread, which is a cotton-wrapped polyester with a lustrous finish, is available from some specialist suppliers. Ordinary poly-cotton thread is also suitable, but should be run over a block of beeswax before use to make it tangle and fray resistant. Use silk twist, coton à broder or pearl cotton to make a special feature of the stitching in hand quilting. Choose a thread one or two shades darker than the fabric.

A repeating pattern is the most common type of quilting design. It usually extends over the whole area. Transferring the design is facilitated by using a single template.

Traditional motifs are also familiar in padded quilting. They may be used as a single, central motif or repeated around a border. They are usually based on curved lines.

'Echo' quilting around a Hawaiian appliquéed motif takes the form of contour lines following the basic outline of a symmetrical motif based on a cut paper shape.

TRANSFERRING THE DESIGN

The design is normally transferred to the top fabric before the three layers are assembled. Various different methods can be used, including direct tracing, pricking and tacking (see pp. 64–5). Transfer pencil and dressmaker's carbon paper are not recommended because they leave a permanent mark which cannot be covered by the stitching.

Two other methods are often used for quilting designs. In one, used mainly for repeating patterns, a template is placed on the fabric and its outline traced. Motifs are often transferred by means of a stencil. Both templates and stencils can be purchased at larger needlework shops. For marking the fabric, use tailor's chalk or a dressmaker's marking pencil, both of which rub off, or a silver-coloured pencil specially designed for quilting. This makes an indelible but very faint line.

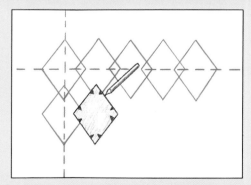

Using a template If you are making your own template, cut it from cardboard. Notch the edges as shown if the pattern is composed of overlapping shapes, and use the notches as guides to positioning. Begin tracing at the centre of the fabric, which you have first marked with tacking, and work outward.

Using a stencil Place the stencil on the fabric and mark through the slits with a quilter's or dressmaker's pencil. The lines of a stencil are necessarily broken; when quilting you simply continue stitching across the breaks where appropriate. The lines of a quilter's pencil are invisible once the quilting is worked.

HAND QUILTING

At its best, hand quilting is worked with tiny, even stitches. Like any hand-worked embroidery, it has slight, barely perceptible irregularities that give it a unique charm.

The stitch traditionally used for hand quilting is running stitch. Back stitch can be used instead, if a solid line is preferred, but only in cases where the wrong side of the work will not be visible. Both stitches can be worked either with a vertical, stabbing movement or with a sewing movement. The first method is only possible if the work is mounted on a frame, while the second is easier if the work is not framed.

The use of a frame will help to hold the layers in position. It also enables you to work the very small running stitches even through thick layers. Extra-large quilting frames are available for making quilts.

A quilting design based on the contour lines of a map, worked in back stitch and running stitch

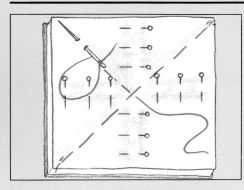

1 Cut the fabrics and wadding slightly larger than the finished size, since extra fabric is taken up by the quilting.
2 Transfer the design to the top fabric.
3 Pin the layers together and tack from the centre to each corner, leaving long thread ends, as shown, to avoid knots at the centre.

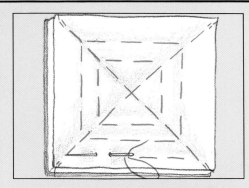

4 Now tack in concentric straight lines from the centre to the edges, placing the lines about 3cm apart. This helps to keep the layers as smooth as possible and prevents excess fabric from bunching up at the centre during the quilting.

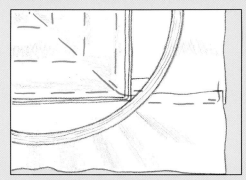

5 Mount the work on the frame if you are using one. If you are using a slate frame, mount the backing fabric first, as shown on page 67, then tack the wadding and top fabric to it. If you are using a ring frame, you may need to tack strips of fabric to the edges to allow you to quilt the corners.

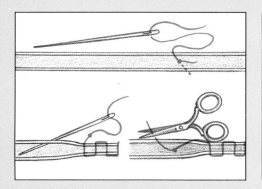

6 To begin stitching Knot the thread, bring it up from the wrong side, and tug gently to bring the knot into the wadding.
To finish off, knot the thread close to the last stitch, take it into the wadding for a short distance then bring the thread out and cut it; the end will disappear into the wadding.

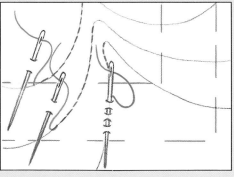

7 Using single thread, work running stitch along the design lines (ideally 5 per cm). It is important that the stitches are even and that they penetrate all three layers of fabric.
If using a sewing movement, always work toward yourself. Where possible, keep several needles in the work and complete the part of each line that runs toward you before turning the work to stitch in another direction.

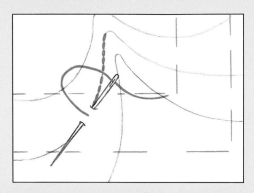

Back stitch can be worked for a solid line if preferred (see p. 69). For a thicker line use stem stitch or chain stitch (see p. 70). Other embroidery stitches can be added if appropriate to the design.

MACHINE QUILTING

A sewing machine can facilitate padded quilting, especially in simple all-over patterns such as lattice designs. It can also be used effectively, after only a little practice, for working 'free-hand' patterns of wavy lines, which have a spontaneous quality.

The machine produces a solid line similar to back stitch; zigzag stitch is also appropriate for quilting. Some machines can be fitted with a twin needle to produce a double line of stitching. A quilting guide is a useful attachment, since it can ensure that the lines remain parallel.

There are, however, several limitations to machine quilting. The technique is not suitable for complex patterns and motifs which would entail turning the work frequently. Also, the size of the project is limited by the amount of fabric and wadding that will fit, rolled up, under the arm of the machine. And when the centre is being quilted, half the work will lie to the right of the needle. So if you wish to work a full-size quilt by machine, you must plan the design in sections that can be quilted separately.

Fabrics suitable for machine quilting are essentially the same as those for hand quilting. For ordinary stitching use quilting or other sewing thread. For a special effect, use embroidery cotton in the bobbin, and work from the wrong side.

It is important to cut the fabric and wadding generously to allow for the extra taken up by the quilting. Because the work is not framed, careful and ample tacking is particularly important. Always test the stitching on a sample made of the same fabric(s) and wadding. You may need to loosen the tension and/or pressure slightly. Use a medium-length stitch (4–5 per cm).

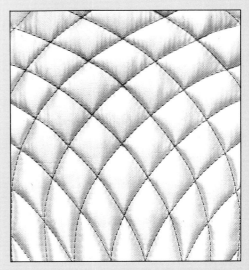

A curved lattice pattern can be machine quilted.

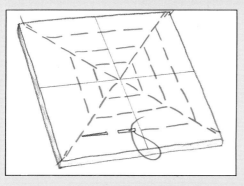

1 Transfer the design to the top fabric using a fabric-marking pencil (see p. 65), and a ruler or template as appropriate. Only the centre lines need be marked if a quilting guide is used.
2 Pin and tack the layers together as for hand quilting (see p. 90), modifying the tacking pattern if necessary to avoid the design lines.

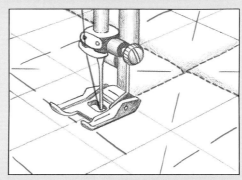

3 Begin quilting at the centre, since this helps to prevent the wadding from slipping to one side or the other. If the design is a grid pattern, work the centre line in each direction, as shown.

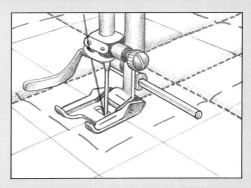

4 Work following lines from the centre out toward one side; use the quilting guide, if you have one, to keep the lines parallel (otherwise, follow the marked lines). Remove the work from the machine and work from the centre to the other side. Work the lines in the other direction in the same way.

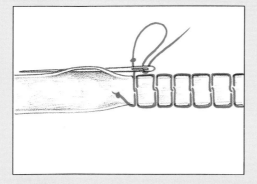

To start or end a line in the middle of the work, do not reverse to secure the thread as in normal machining, but leave long thread ends. Make a small knot and take each thread into the wadding and out again, then cut it close to the surface.

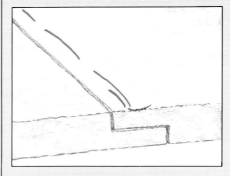

JOINING WADDING
If you need to join two pieces of wadding to make up the required width, cut each edge in a notched shape as shown, then fit them together and join them with large running stitches. This prevents excess bulk. Use the same method when hand quilting.

ITALIAN QUILTING

Also known as corded quilting, Italian quilting is a decorative technique in which two layers of fabric are stitched in parallel lines to form channels, which are then filled with yarn or cord. The result is a pattern of raised lines on a flat background.

The top fabric should be of a plain colour, smooth and closely woven. Unless you are using the shadow technique (see p. 95) it should also be opaque. The bottom layer is a sheer, loosely woven fabric such as muslin or voile, which allows the needle to be brought up and reinserted to take it around curves.

To fill the channels you can use either quilting yarn, a soft, thick yarn made for the purpose, knitting yarn, or piping cord, which gives a firmer effect. (Pre-shrink the cord if the work is to be washed.) Suitable threads are the same as for hand or machine quilting (see pp. 91–2).

The method used to transfer the design depends on whether the stitching is worked from the right or the wrong side. This in turn is determined partly by the choice of stitch. Because the essence of Italian quilting is its linear quality, a solid line of stitching is usually preferred. This can be either hand-worked back stitch or machine straight stitch.

Back stitch must be done from the right side, so the design is transferred to the top fabric. The pricking method (see p. 65) is a good choice if the design is intricate.

If machine stitching is used, the work can be done from either side; transfer the design to the backing fabric by the direct tracing method (see p. 64). The same method can also be used if the design is worked in running stitch.

The intertwined lines of a Celtic motif

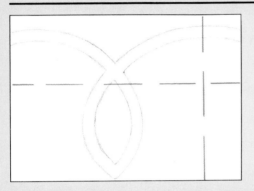

1 Transfer the design to the top fabric or the wrong side, as appropriate. Note that where one line goes over another the outline of the lower line must be interrupted.
2 Tack the two fabrics together thoroughly. (If you are working on a frame, two perpendicular lines of tacking are adequate.)

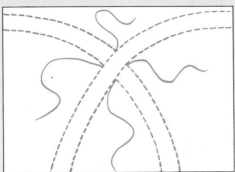

3 Work back stitch along the marked lines; or stitch by machine. Where lines are interrupted, end the machine stitching, without reversing, and leave long thread ends for tying later on the wrong side (see opposite).

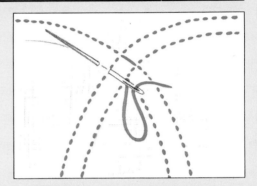

To work from the wrong side Transfer the design to the backing, then tack the fabrics together. Stitch by machine or by hand, using running stitch. Where one line goes under another, simply take the thread across, as shown.

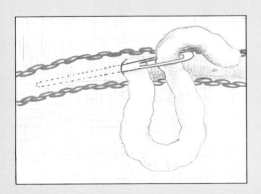

4 Remove the work from the frame, if used, and remove the tacking. Thread the yarn into a large tapestry needle or bodkin and insert the needle into one of the channels from the wrong side, piercing the backing fabric. Slide the needle through the channel, as shown.

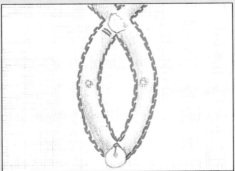

On curves, bring the needle up through the backing every 3cm or so, then reinsert it in the same hole. At corners or sharp curves, leave a small loop of yarn to reduce puckering. Where a line is interrupted, cut the yarn and secure it to the backing with a few stitches.

Work a sample first to determine the best width of channel for the yarn or cord you are using. The yarn should fill the channel well, but not so tightly as to cause puckering around curves.

Running stitch produces a broken line, but if the work is done in a frame, stab stitch can be used for a more solid effect.

When an Italian quilting project is completed, a lining must be added to conceal the wrong side.

TRAPUNTO QUILTING

In essence, trapunto resembles Italian quilting: a design is stitched through two fabrics and sections of the design are then padded. In trapunto quilting, however, shapes rather than lines are filled— usually with stuffing or pieces of wadding. The technique is most frequently used for embroidered panels, to give a three-dimensional quality to certain parts of the design. The hard backing of a panel provides a firm support for the padded sections, making them stand out in relief.

Two different fabrics are normally used for trapunto quilting. The top fabric should be soft and closely woven, so that it is pliable but covers the stuffing thoroughly. The backing fabric should be lightweight but firm. If the shapes are small, choose a fabric, such as organdie, the threads of which can be separated for inserting the stuffing. If the backing must be cut, choose a firm, non-fraying cotton.

Polyester stuffing or wadding can be used to pad the shapes, and the threads used are the same as for other forms of quilting (see pp. 90–92).

Hand-worked trapunto is best mounted on a frame during both the stitching and stuffing processes. Because the mounted fabric is held taut it is easier to see the effect of the stuffing and thus avoid over-padding the shape. If the backing is stiff, however, you may need to remove the work from the frame before cutting the slits.

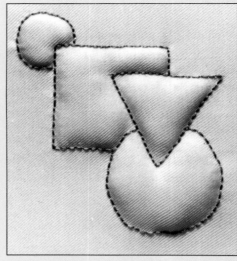

Trapunto shapes are padded with wadding.

HAND-WORKED TRAPUNTO

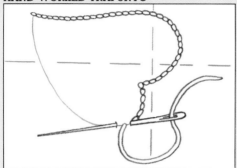

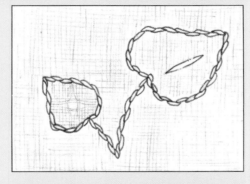

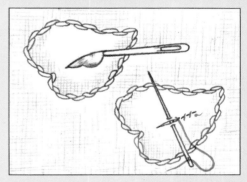

1 Transfer the design to the top fabric by pricking, direct tracing or using a template.
2 Tack the top fabric and the backing together as for Italian quilting (see p. 93) and mount the work on a frame.
3 Stitch along the outlines of the motif using back stitch or stab stitch. Back stitch gives the shape a better definition.

4 With the work still framed, turn it wrong side up. Insert the point of a tapestry needle into the backing fabric in the centre of the shape and separate the threads. On some fabrics it may be necessary to cut one or more slits in the backing, using sharp embroidery scissors.

5 Insert small pieces of stuffing into the shape, using a knitting needle or large tapestry needle to work them into corners. Take care not to overstuff the shape.
6 If a hole has been made, simply push the threads back together. If a slit has been cut, stitch the edges together. Do not pull the stitches too tightly.

MACHINE-WORKED TRAPUNTO

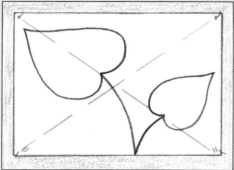

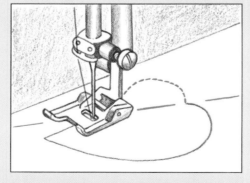

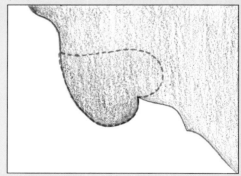

1 Tack the two fabrics together around the edges.
2 Pin the design, which you have first traced on to thin paper, on the top fabric, then tack from the centre out to the four corners. If the area is large, a few more lines of tacking may be necessary.

3 Machine stitch along the design outlines through all layers, using a short straight stitch. At corners, lift the presser foot, with the needle in the work, pivot the fabric, then lower the foot and continue stitching in the new direction.

4 When the stitching is complete, carefully tear away the paper as shown.
5 Open or slit the backing fabric as described in step 4 above.
6 Stuff the motif and close up the hole or slit.

SHADOW QUILTING

Like shadow appliqué (see p. 87), shadow quilting involves the use of two fabrics, the top fabric being sheer. In shadow quilting, however, the design is formed not only by stitching but also by the insertion of other materials between the two fabrics.

Both Italian and trapunto quilting can be adapted to shadow quilting, simply by using coloured yarns for the filling. Another shadow quilting technique is to insert a flat motif, usually made of felt, between the two fabrics. The motif is held in place by stitching worked just outside its edges.

For the top fabric choose organdie, organza, voile or a similar sheer fabric. Normally the backing is a firm, closely woven, opaque fabric, either the same colour as the top fabric or chosen to match that of the felt or other padding materials.

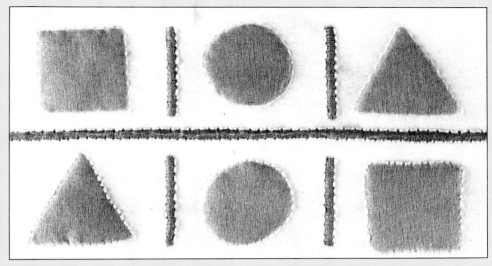

In shadow quilting the flat shapes are stuffed with felt and the lines with lengths of wool.

TRANSFERRING THE DESIGN

Felt motifs Cut a paper template and trace around its edges on to the felt. Cut out the felt shape.

Trapunto and corded motifs Trace the motif(s) on to the backing fabric using dressmaker's pencil, dressmaker's carbon or another suitable method (see pp. 64–5).

APPLYING A FELT MOTIF

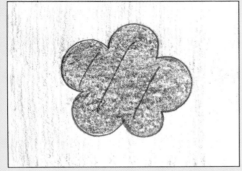

1 Mount the backing fabric on a frame.
2 Tack the motif to the backing. Make sure that the knot is underneath the backing or you will not be able to remove it later.

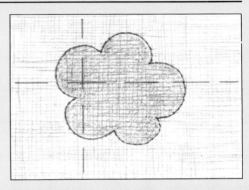

3 Place the top fabric over the work and pin it to the backing, aligning the fabric grains. Tack it in place. Two perpendicular lines are usually sufficient, but if the area is large or the top fabric slippery add lines of diagonal tacking.

4 Work around the motif using the chosen stitch. In this example stem stitch is used, but back stitch, stab stitch, chain or another line stitch are alternatives.

If stitching by machine, use the zipper foot, with the foot positioned away from the motif so that you can stitch close to the edge.

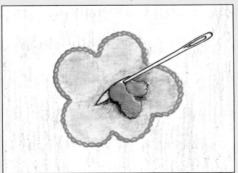

Italian and trapunto shadow quilting
Tack the top fabric to the framed backing as in step 3 above. Work the stitching and insert the yarn in one of the ways described on page 93. For trapunto, cut short lengths of yarn rather than one long length and insert them as shown above. Two or more colours of yarn can be combined in a shape for a subtle blend of colours.

In shadow quilting, the yarn must be dark or bright enough to show through the top fabric. For trapunto choose a soft yarn, such as a loosely twisted Icelandic wool.

Embroidery worked in gold and silver is one of the most highly prized forms of needlework and one of the oldest. There are references to this work in the Bible, and gold threads have been discovered in ancient Egyptian tombs. From early times, metal threads have been used to adorn royal and ecclesiastical vestments, their shimmering, lustrous quality suggesting temporal or divine power.

The costliness, as well as the beauty, of these threads also made them the natural choice for embellishing the court attire of the aristocracy and other 'special occasion' garments for those who could afford such luxury.

Metal thread embroidery is less often seen on modern clothing, except for evening wear, but it is still extensively used on religious vestments, and some of the most valuable examples of twentieth-century metal thread can be seen in churches and synagogues. The subtle effects of the different metal threads are also being imaginatively exploited in panels, wall-hangings and various decorated objects such as boxes, mirror frames and evening bags.

Technically, metal thread embroidery —which is often simply called goldwork since most of it is worked in gold—is a type of surface stitchery, being worked freely on a closely woven fabric. The stitches are, however, almost entirely forms of couching (see p. 71). Most metal threads are either too stiff, too delicate or too expensive to be stitched through the fabric, and thus are couched to the surface with fine silk or other sewing threads. A variety of effects can be created by couching in different patterns, by massing the threads to fill diverse shapes and by padding the work in different ways to accentuate the sheen of the materials.

Gold and silver kid may be applied to the fabric to provide smooth areas complementing the lines of couched threads. Small pieces of coiled wire, called purls, can be sewn on to create a range of interesting textures.

THREADS

In the past, gold threads were made of pure gold, which was beaten into paper-thin strips and coiled around a silk thread. The technique was developed in the east, and the thread was known as Japanese gold. Today, real Japanese gold is no longer available, but a good substitute has been developed which, like the original, is smooth, lustrous and non-tarnishing. Substitute Japanese gold comes in several thicknesses. A silver thread is also made.

Many other metal threads can be used for this work. Some contain a small percentage of gold or silver while others, such as lurex threads, are entirely synthetic. The advantage of lurex is that it is non-tarnishing (most real metal thread will tarnish a little in time), but it is less attractive in colour and texture than real metal threads.

Most metal threads, both real and synthetic, have a twisted structure, which gives them a 'crinkled' appearance, in contrast to the smooth sheen of substitute Japanese gold. In some of the thinner threads, the fineness of the twist produces a matt finish. The finest thread, called tambour, can be stitched through the fabric. At the other extreme are the heavy cords and braids. These are less easy to manoeuvre than the fine threads, but are useful for bold lines and outlining shapes.

Plate is a bright, flat strip of metal that is usually applied in zigzag patterns.

Purls are coiled metal wires that come in several forms and thicknesses; they are usually cut into short lengths and sewn on like beads. Smooth purl has a shiny finish and rough purl a matt finish. Also available are a check purl, which has a crinkly texture, and a pearl purl, with a beaded appearance.

A limited selection of metal threads, cords and braids can be found in the needlework departments of some of the larger stores, while specialist embroidery shops carry a wider range. Some of these will supply, at a small cost, sample cards of metal threads from which the required varieties can be selected, then ordered by post. (See list of suppliers, p. 144.)

Although the metal threads currently available are less expensive than pure Japanese gold, they do cost rather more than wool, cotton or even silk threads. Treat them with care; store them in a plastic or fabric-lined sewing box or wrap them in acid-free tissue and keep them in a cardboard box. Avoid overhandling the threads when working. A selection of metal threads is illustrated on page 15.

For couching the metal threads use fine silk sewing thread in gold or silver-grey.

FABRICS AND EQUIPMENT

The only general requirement of the fabric for goldwork is that it should be firmly woven and unpatterned. It can be a lustrous fabric such as Thai silk or satin, or a matt-finish one such as fine linen. Many furnishing fabrics, both natural and synthetic, are well suited to this work, since they tend to be strong and are often available in a good range of colours. Those with a slubbed texture make an attractive background for goldwork.

Most fabrics need to be backed to prevent them from puckering under the weight of the work. A medium-weight fabric such as calico is generally suitable.

Gold and silver kid are often used for appliqué within a design. Woven gold or silver fabrics can also be applied; these are usually backed with iron-on interfacing (see p. 83) and applied in the same way as the kid, over padding.

Felt is required for the padding itself. If it will be covered by threads, use yellow felt for gold work and pale grey for silver. Other materials used for padding are cardboard—a thin variety that can be pierced by a needle—and string, about 3–5mm in diameter, in yellow or white.

The needles you will need for goldwork include crewel needles for working the couching stitches, large chenille needles for taking the metal threads to the wrong side, a leather needle for applying kid and fine beading needles for applying purls and beads. You will also need some straight-bladed nail scissors for cutting purls.

Beeswax is needed for strengthening the couching thread. Other useful pieces of equipment are a pair of tweezers for picking up beads and purls, a stiletto for opening large holes in the fabric to take thick cords, a small pair of pliers for pulling threads through and a thimble.

FRAMES; TRANSFERRING THE DESIGN

A frame is essential for all metal thread work. The embroidery must be kept absolutely taut so that the threads and other materials can be positioned accurately. Also, because the finished work cannot be blocked with water in the usual way, the tautness is vital to avoid any creases. A slate frame is ideal, because the work can easily be retautened as necessary; on a stretcher frame this is more difficult. A ring frame is suitable only for small pieces; bind the inner ring as shown on page 116 to grip the fabric securely.

Tacking is the best method of transferring the design to the fabric (see p. 65) since it does not permanently mark the fabric and thus allows a measure of flexibility in working the embroidery. For the tacking use a fine thread the same colour as the fabric. This will be concealed by the metal threads.

COUCHING TECHNIQUES

The basic couching stitch is shown on page 71. Goldwork, however, involves special techniques, both practical and decorative, which are shown here. Practise these using string or another cheap material.

Metal threads are usually applied in a double strand. A smoother effect is produced in this way, and it is easier to fill a space. The ends are left on the surface and taken to the wrong side later. If the couched thread is fine and pliable it can be bent double at the starting point.

The thread used for the couching stitches must be strengthened by running it over a block of beeswax, otherwise it will be frayed and weakened by the metal threads. Solid areas of couching are best worked in a brick pattern, to distribute the couching stitches evenly and attractively.

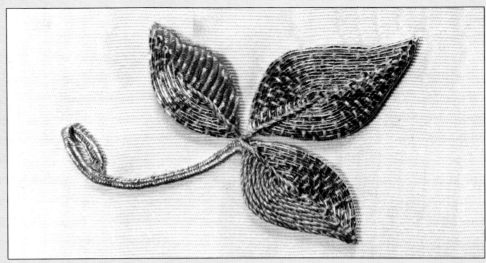

Clockwise from first leaf: Jap and check purl; Jap; Jap and medium gold twist; stalk in gold braid

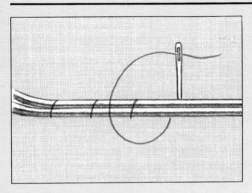

Basic method of couching
1 Secure the fine couching thread with two stitches in the backing fabric and bring it to the right side.
2 Lay the two metal threads on the stitching line, leaving ends of about 3cm at the starting point. Work couching stitches over both threads, placing the stitches about 5mm apart.

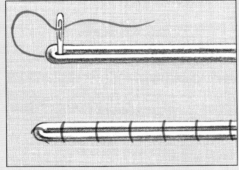

If the thread is sufficiently pliable, bend it double and secure the fold with one stitch. Then couch the double threads in the usual way. Take care to make the stitches the right size: they should be neither so tight as to pinch the threads together nor so loose that they slide about.

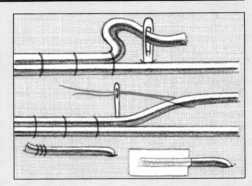

To take the ends through (called plunging), either thread each one into a chenille needle and take it through (using pliers to pull the needle, if necessary) or thread the needle with a loop of ordinary sewing thread and use the loop to pull the end through. On the wrong side, secure the ends with oversewing or sticky tape.

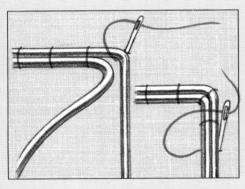

To turn a corner First couch the outer thread at the corner with a diagonal stitch, then couch the inner thread in the same way. Turn the threads in the new direction and continue couching over both threads as before.

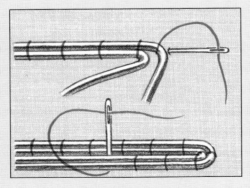

To reverse the direction Couch the threads individually at the turning point, as for a corner. Couch them together close to the turning point to prevent a bulge.

When couching next to previously couched threads, bring the needle up on the outside and take it down between the pairs of threads.

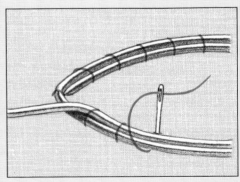

To turn an acute corner when filling a shape
1 Take the outer thread around the corner as shown. Cut the inner thread and take it down just inside the point; restart it and continue couching the paired threads.
2 Work inward from opposite sides of the shape, dovetailing the ends, until the shape is filled.

OR NUÉ

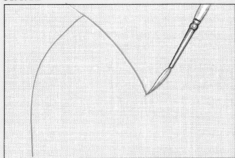

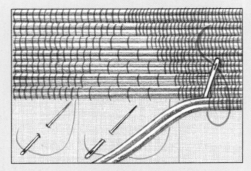

Also known as Italian shading, *or nué* is a method of producing a design by working some of the couching stitches close together, using one or more contrasting colours.

1 Begin by drawing the design on the fabric, using coloured pencils or oil paint and a fine brush.

2 Couch the background (unshaded) areas with matching thread, spacing the stitches as usual. For the shaded areas use silk thread in the chosen colour (or colours), placing the stitches close together. By varying the spaces between the stitches you can create subtle contrasts between the silk and metal threads.

CORDS, BRAID AND PLATE

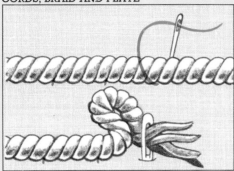

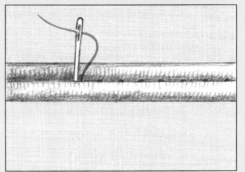

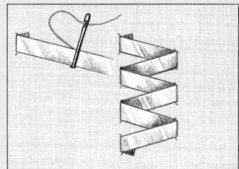

Twisted cord Work couching stitches over the cord at an angle, so that the thread slips down between the twists. Place the stitches several twists apart.

Plunge the cord ends by inserting a large chenille needle into the fabric, then threading the ends into the eye and pulling them through.

Russia braid Apply with small stab stitches, working them down the centre as shown.

Use a stiletto to make a large hole for plunging the ends, and take them through with a loop of thread as shown on page 97.

Plate Couch one end of the plate, then fold the strip back over the stitch at a slight downward angle. Work another stitch over the plate and fold it back as shown. Continue in the same way for the desired length. Fold under the end and secure it with the last couching stitch.

PURLS AND BEADS

Purls can be used in many ways to create interesting patterns and textures. They are normally cut into short pieces, about 1cm long or less, then threaded on to a beading needle and sewn on to the fabric. A rich, ropelike effect can be produced by sewing pieces of purl closely over string, as shown opposite.

Pearl purl is the most versatile type, since it can be applied in longer lines with couching stitches as well as being sewn on with a beading needle.

Beads provide a textural contrast in goldwork, as in other forms of embroidery. They are available in many different colours, shapes and sizes.

When cutting purls, and for holding both purls and beads in readiness, use a box lid lined with felt to stop the purls from springing about.

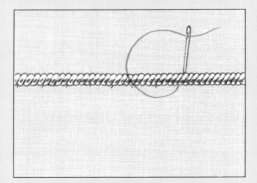

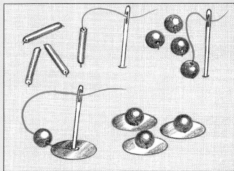

To couch pearl purl Pull the purl gently to separate the coils slightly. (For a 'corkscrew' effect, pull the coils farther apart.) Lay the purl on the stitching line and couch it down with matching thread, pulling the thread so that it slips between the coils and the ends remain on the surface.

To sew purls First cut the purls into short lengths with straight-bladed scissors. Sew them to the fabric with a beading needle and fine thread, picking them up with the point of the needle.

Sew on beads in the same way. Sequins can be sewn on with a bead in the centre, as shown, to avoid having to make a stitch on the surface of the sequin.

A variety of metal thread embroidery techniques is shown in the photograph on the right. Clockwise from top left: *or nué*; pearl purl; couching over cardboard; gold plate; beads and sequins; metal purls; couching over string; gold kid.

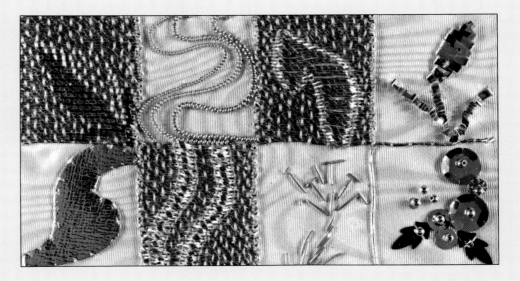

PADDING

The use of padding enhances the effects of metal threads and other materials by creating contrasts of light and shadow. This is especially noticeable when the embroidery moves, as it would do on a religious vestment, for example, since the work catches the light at different angles.

Felt, string and cardboard are the usual materials for padding. Layers of felt are sewn to the fabric as described on page 89. This rounded surface can either be used as a base for appliqué in the form of gold or silver kid or a metallic fabric, or as a base for couched threads or purls.

String is applied to the fabric in lines, and threads are then couched over it at a right angle, covering it completely. The string can be dyed yellow to ensure that it is inconspicuous. Cardboard can also be painted yellow to prevent a white surface from showing through the metal threads.

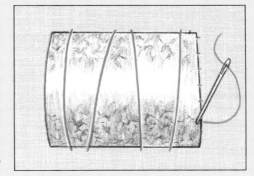

Applying gold or silver kid Tack the piece in place with a few stitches worked over the shape, as shown. Then work stab stitches around the edge, bringing the needle up outside the shape and taking it down into the edge.
Padding with felt Apply several layers of felt as shown on page 89.

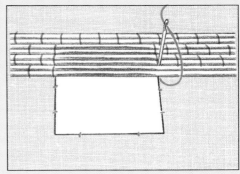

Padding with cardboard Cut pieces of thin card and sew them to the fabric with a few stab stitches.

Fill the area closely with couched threads, working a couching stitch just to either side of the cardboard.

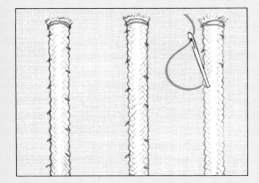

Padding with string
1 Sew the lengths of string to the fabric by working small stitches from alternate sides into the centre. Place stitches about 5mm apart. Secure the ends with two stitches to prevent unravelling.

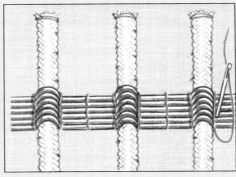

2 Couch the threads over the string at right angles to it, working two couching stitches close to each side of the string to hold the couched threads firmly in place.

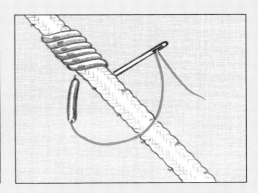

Sewing purls over string Cut each piece of purl long enough to go over the string at a slight angle. Sew them with fine thread and a beading needle, working diagonally over the string and covering it closely.

There are two kinds of cutwork: broderie anglaise, which consists of holes cut in the fabric and edged with oversewing, and true cutwork—also called Richelieu work—which consists of embroidered shapes against a background which is cut away.

Cutwork dates from the nineteenth century. The name Richelieu derives from the resemblance of this type of work to a kind of needle-worked lace fashionable in seventeenth-century France and patronized by Cardinal Richelieu. Both types are most frequently used to decorate clothing, especially lingerie, and household linens, and both are traditionally worked on white fabric with white threads. They can, of course, be worked on a coloured fabric, but they look most effective worked in a matching thread. In Richelieu work, however, a thread one or two shades darker than the fabric is sometimes used to accentuate the lines of the motifs.

Both broderie anglaise and true cutwork must be worked on a frame in order to prevent any distortion of the fabric during the stitching. Neatness is vital in both these kinds of embroidery; the stitches must not call attention to themselves but must provide a smooth outline for the motifs. Since the underside is visible, the threads must be fastened inconspicuously.

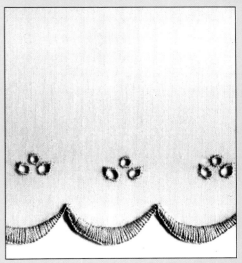

Repeating design for a decorative edge

BRODERIE ANGLAISE

Most broderie anglaise designs consists of round or teardrop-shaped holes, often clustered together in stylized floral motifs. If your design is a repeating pattern, the finished, actual size design need consist only of a single repeat, which you can then move along the fabric when transferring. The direct tracing method (see p.64) is the best choice, since the fine fabric usually allows the design to be seen through it. Shading in the holes on the design helps to make them clear.

The fabric for broderie anglaise should be fairly thin, in keeping with the delicate, lacy effect, and it should be one that does not fray easily. Choose fine threads, such as one or two strands of stranded cotton, or a single strand of quilting thread.

Other surface stitches, such as French knots, satin stitch and thin line stitches may be used with broderie anglaise.

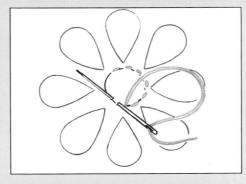

1 Transfer the design.
2 Mount the fabric in the frame.
3 Fasten the thread on the wrong side with two tiny back stitches, and then work running stitches around the marked outline. Do not fasten off.

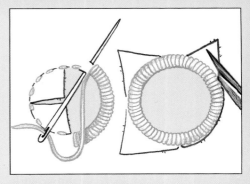

4 Cut across the centre twice with sharp embroidery scissors, or pierce the fabric with a stiletto.
5 Work oversewing stitches evenly over the running stitches, folding each corner of fabric to the wrong side as you work.
6 Fasten off neatly on the wrong side, then trim off the points of the fabric.

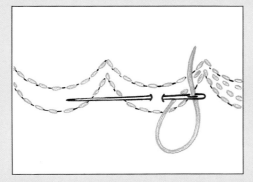

Working a scalloped edging
1 Draw or trace the two lines of the edging on to the fabric. (You can use a coin as a template for the scallops.)
2 Work running stitch, first just inside the outlines, and then to fill in the remaining spaces.

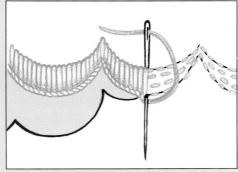

3 Work close buttonhole stitch over the running stitches, keeping them vertical throughout.
4 Carefully cut away the fabric just outside the stitching.

RICHELIEU WORK

Designs for Richelieu work must be carefully planned to achieve a pleasing and workable balance between the solid, stitched areas and the cut-out areas. Shade in the areas that will be cut away, in case the design needs to be modified in some way—by enlarging or reducing some of the shapes, or repositioning them slightly so that they link up at one or more points.

Where a space larger than about one square centimetre will be left, work one or more buttonhole bars across the space, to unify the work visually and to hold the edges of the motifs in place (see below).

Choose an opaque, medium-weight fabric for Richelieu work; plain-woven linen or cotton is a good choice. Use a slightly thicker thread than for broderie anglaise, such as no. 8 pearl cotton or coton à broder.

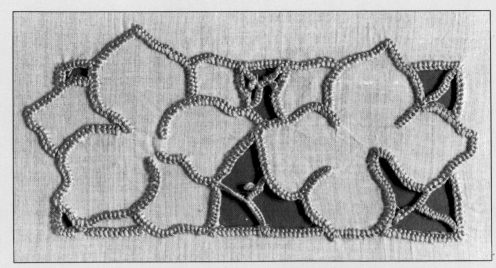

Stylized floral design for cutwork, incorporating branched buttonhole bars and picots

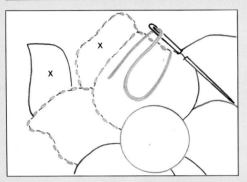

1 Shade the cut-out areas of the final design.
2 Transfer the design to the fabric by pricking or another suitable method (see pp. 64–5). Mark with an X each area that will be cut out.
3 Mount the work in a frame.
4 Work running stitches around the outlines of the areas to be stitched, taking care to work just inside the shapes, not in the marked background areas.

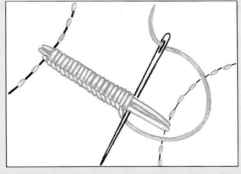

Buttonhole bars When you reach a bar line, take the thread straight across to the opposite edge and make a small stitch. Repeat this twice, so that three strands lie between the shapes.
Work buttonhole stitch over the strands, working back to the first edge.

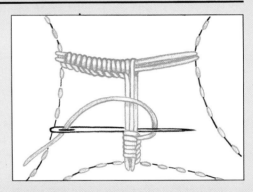

Branched buttonhole bars These are used to join three edges where necessary. Work as for buttonhole bars until you reach the position for a branch. Then lay three strands across to the edge of the motif as shown and work buttonhole stitch back to the first bar. Continue stitching back to the original edge.

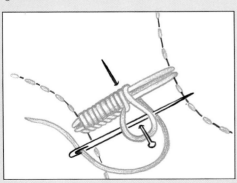

Picots To decorate a bar with a picot, work as above until you reach the centre of the bar. Then insert a pin through the fabric as shown. Loop the thread under the pin, over the strands, then under the loop as shown. Remove the pin and pull the thread tight. Continue the buttonhole stitch.

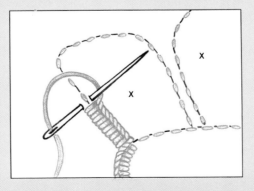

5 Continue working around the design until all outlining and bars are completed.
6 Work buttonhole stitch closely around all the edges, taking care to place the solid edge of the stitching next to the area to be cut away. Where a line crosses a solid area, the stitches can lie either way.

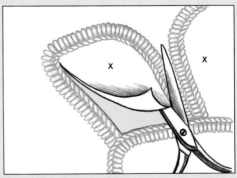

7 When all the stitching is complete, carefully cut out the background areas with sharp embroidery scissors, cutting as close as possible to the stitches. You may find it easier to remove the work from the frame before cutting.

Collectively, cross stitch embroidery, blackwork, pulled and drawn thread work are all 'counted thread' techniques because each stitch is worked over a definite number of fabric threads. The resulting work is regular and somewhat angular.

Cross stitch is both popular and familiar. The stitch is identical to the one used in canvaswork and is used in the traditional embroideries of many countries. In the nineteenth century it was extensively used in the samplers worked by young girls.

Because of its versatility, cross stitch can be used for both lines and fillings, and lends itself also to abstract geometric patterns, especially in border designs. In Assisi work, a limited colour range is used. In this, the backgrounds rather than the motifs are stitched, so that the plain areas form the pattern.

FABRICS AND THREADS
The fabric normally used for cross stitch is evenweave, so-called because it contains the same number of warp (lengthwise) and weft (crosswise) threads over a given measurement. Most evenweave is made of cotton or linen, but it comes in a wide range of textures. The coarsest has 12 or 14 threads per inch, the finest 32 or even 34. Since cross stitch is normally worked over two threads, the fabric's fineness determines the stitch size. However, stitches can be worked over one, three or four threads if preferred.

On some evenweave fabrics, groups of threads form the weave, and the embroidery is worked over one or more thread intersections. Hardanger cloth is woven with double threads while Aida cloth is woven with several groups of threads to form a basketweave pattern.

Evenweave fabric can be bought from specialist shops, but the colour range is limited. Some plain-woven dress and furnishing fabrics can be used, if the number of warp and weft threads per inch is equal. On closely woven fabrics and those with an irregular weave cross stitches can be worked over a canvas grid as shown opposite.

Choose a stitching thread of roughly the same thickness as the fabric threads, so that the embroidery covers the fabric well but not solidly. Cotton threads are most often used for cross stitch, but Persian and crewel wool, linen threads, crochet cottons and silk twists are also suitable.

A tapestry needle is best for cross stitch embroidery, because it does not split the threads. The only exception is in working over canvas, when a crewel or chenille needle may be used.

CHARTS FOR CROSS STITCH
Designs for cross stitch embroidery are normally presented in the form of a box chart. In this type of chart (which is also used for canvaswork designs worked in cross or tent stitch), each square of the chart corresponds to a single stitch. Instructions for charting an original cross stitch design are given on page 29. (The other type of chart—a line chart—is explained and illustrated on the same page.)

Most published cross stitch designs using charts specify the finished size of the work, the weight of the fabric, and the number of threads crossed by each stitch. If any of this information is not included, or if you wish to alter the scale or the size of the finished work, you can easily determine your own specifications as follows.

First count the number of squares on the chart, vertically and horizontally. Next, decide on the finished size of the work, then divide the number of squares by the chosen measurements in inches. (It is best to use inches for these calculations because of the inch-based classification of fabrics.) This will give you the number of stitches per inch. Finally, multiply by two (the usual number of threads worked over) to determine the weight and weave of fabric you should buy.

For example, if the chart contains 100 squares in each direction and you wish the embroidery to measure 10 inches square, there will be 10 stitches per inch. If the stitches are worked over two threads, a 20-thread fabric should be used. Or you could use a 30-thread fabric and work the stitches over three threads—there would still be 10 stitches to the inch.

When working from a chart, first mark the centre of the fabric with two intersecting lines of tacking (see p. 64). Begin working at the centre of the design, as shown below, unless the instructions specify another method of positioning the work.

The use of a frame (see pp. 66–7) is recommended for cross stitch embroidery, since it makes the threads easier to count and helps maintain the work at an even tension.

On this box chart the colours are specified by means of symbols, identified in a key. In other types of chart the squares are filled in with the chosen colours as appropriate (see p. 29).

Here the centre of the motif is marked with two perpendicular lines.

Key
×– red
╱– white
•– blue
○– green

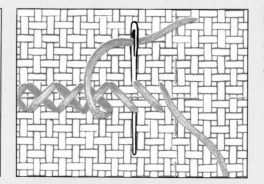

Begin work at the centre of the design (or where instructed), leaving a short length of thread on the right side. After working a few stitches, pull this end to the wrong side, thread it into a needle, and secure it with one or two back stitches in the underside of the stitches worked.

CROSS STITCH

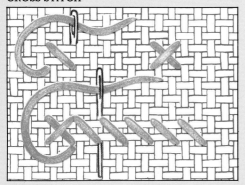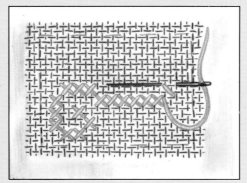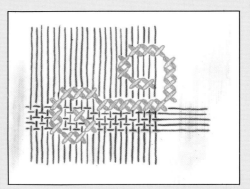

To work a single stitch Work over two intersections, from lower right to upper left, then from lower left to upper right.
To work in rows Work the first 'leg' of every stitch, then work back across them. This ensures that all stitches slant in the same direction.

To work over canvas Choose a gauge of canvas (see p. 124) that will produce a stitch of the desired size. (Do not use interlock.)
1 Tack the canvas to the right side of the fabric, making sure the grain lies straight.
2 Work the cross stitches through canvas and fabric, using a crewel or chenille needle.

3 Remove the tacking. Saturate a towel in hand-hot water and place it over the work for a few minutes to dampen it thoroughly.
4 Pull out the canvas threads one by one. If the embroidered area is large, cut the canvas between motifs to make this task easier.

ASSISI WORK

True to its name, Assisi work originated in the Italian town of Assisi, birthplace of St. Francis. But its antique appearance is deceptive: this type of cross stitch is an early twentieth-century invention.

Assisi work uses both cross stitch and double running, or Holbein, stitch. Double running stitch, used also in blackwork, resembles back stitch but is reversible, that is, the right and wrong sides are identical. In Assisi work it is used to outline the motifs, for borders and for details. Cross stitch is used for the background areas. The motifs themselves contain little, if any, stitching, as the photograph shows.

White or cream evenweave fabric is traditionally used for Assisi work, with bright red or blue for backgrounds and black for the lines. However, any other colour scheme can be chosen.

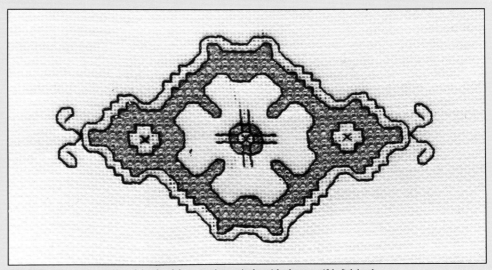

An Assisi design, outlined in double running stitch with the motif left blank

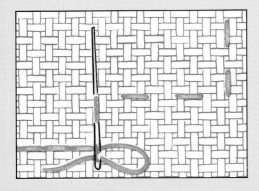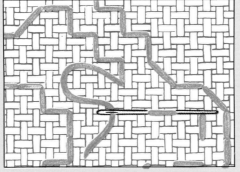

Double running stitch
1 Work a line of running stitches (see p. 69), working each over the same number of fabric threads.
2 Work another line of running stitch, filling the spaces left in the first line and taking care to work into the same holes.

To work an Assisi design
1 Begin by stitching the outlines and any details in double running stitch.

2 Work the cross stitch backgrounds in rows, working in two stages as shown.
3 Add individual cross stitches as required for the design.

Probably of Spanish origin—and certainly evocative of the Moorish civilization that flourished in Spain in the Middle Ages—blackwork first became popular in sixteenth-century England. At that time, its intricate patterns of black thread on white linen, sometimes embellished with gold threads, adorned sleeves, bodices, collars, cuffs, nightcaps and bed linen.

Today blackwork is enjoying a revival. It is used as abstract bands or blocks of pattern on table linens, but more often occurs in stylized pictorial work on panels and wallhangings.

The enormous variety of blackwork designs provides considerable scope for choosing a suitable pattern, either to suggest the texture of an object or simply to provide interesting tonal contrast. The patterns shown below provide some idea of the range. Many can be varied even further by subtracting part of the pattern, by adding new elements or by altering the thickness of the thread used.

Several different stitches are used to form blackwork patterns. They include double running, or Holbein, stitch; back stitch; cross stitch and Algerian eye. Although the patterns themselves are angular, they can be—and often are—used to fill curved shapes, which are then outlined with a line stitch. For such lines, double running or back stitch are the usual choices, but stem, chain or couching may be chosen for a thicker, more flowing line. Other surface stitchery is sometimes added to contrast with or complement the blackwork patterns.

Make a sampler of blackwork patterns, including your own adaptations or original designs, and keep the sampler for reference when designing.

FABRICS AND THREADS

Evenweave linen or cotton (see p. 102) in white or cream is the usual choice for blackwork. It may be coarse or fine, but the fabric's weight will usually govern the density of a given pattern. Fabric with 22 to 26 threads per inch is the most suitable.

Make sure your selected fabric is opaque enough that the threads do not show through from the wrong side. With dense patterns this is rarely a problem, but on an open pattern any 'shadowing' will spoil the effect of clear areas.

Choose a smooth-textured thread to retain the crisp lines of blackwork patterns. Match the thickness of the sewing thread to the fabric threads, but remember that interesting effects can be created by working the same pattern in two or three threads of different thicknesses.

Use a tapestry needle of a suitable size.

BLACKWORK PATTERNS

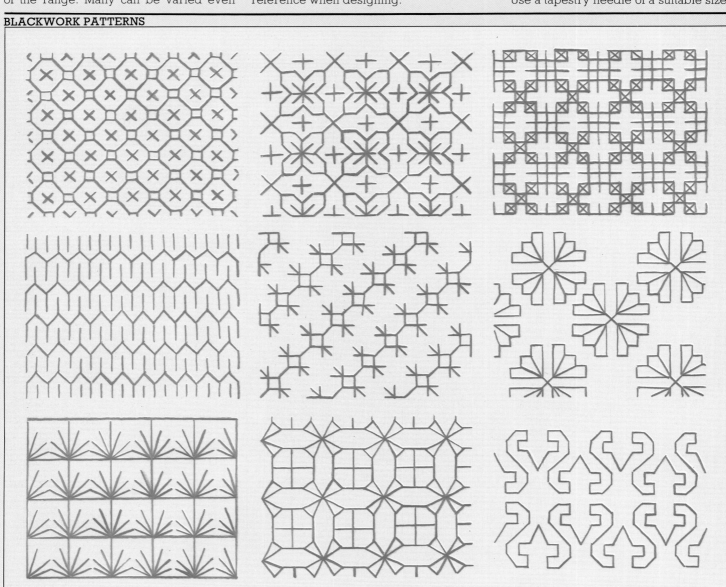

Blackwork patterns can successfully depict a pictorial design motif as shown here. A combination of patterns from the opposite page is used to suggest the texture of the different fruit, and the same pattern is sometimes worked in varying densities by adding or removing elements of it. A thicker thread is occasionally used for details such as the ends of the bananas. All the outlines are worked in double running stitch.

BLACKWORK STITCHES

Two of the stitches often used in blackwork—double running and cross stitch—are shown on pages 102 and 103. Cross stitch is sometimes varied by working a vertical stitch over it, as for Smyrna stitch in canvaswork (see p. 131).

Back stitch is the most commonly used blackwork stitch. Work it as for surface stitchery (see p. 69) but over a specific number of threads—the number varies with, or within a pattern. Algerian eye, which forms an eight-pointed star on the fabric, is another stitch used in some blackwork patterns.

As a rule, stitches should be worked over an even, rather than an odd, number of threads to place one stitch perpendicular to another. The number of threads must be even so that the perpendicular stitch can be centred accurately.

SEQUENCE OF STITCHING

Blackwork patterns are normally presented without specific instructions for working them. It is up to the embroiderer to devise a logical, systematic method of working —one that involves a minimum of backtracking and avoids taking the thread long distances across the back of the work.

Dense patterns are usually worked in rows, with the outlines or framework completed before the smaller elements. Open patterns may entail starting a new thread and fastening off for each motif, in which case start as for cross stitch embroidery (see pp. 102–3). Before beginning to work a particular pattern, study it to identify its component parts, then practise it, revising your method of working if necessary.

Shown right is a pattern composed of back stitch and Algerian eye, explained in five stages to demonstrate how a particular pattern is constructed.

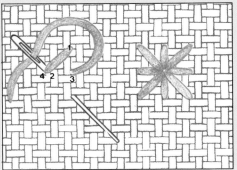

Back stitch To work in a straight line, take the needle back over, then forward under, the same number of threads.

To work around corners, simply follow the line of the pattern, working over and under the correct number of threads as indicated by the pattern.

Algerian eye Bring the needle up at one corner of the eyelet (or where convenient, according to the pattern) and take it down in the centre. Continue in a clockwise direction, working seven more stitches into the same hole. The stitch is usually worked over four fabric threads, as shown.

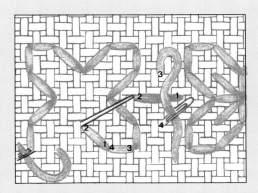

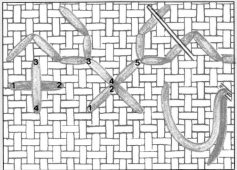

1 Work the main shape in back stitch, taking the needle over two threads (or thread intersections) each time.
2 Work an Algerian eye stitch in the centre of the shape.
3 Work a vertical cross stitch over four threads to the left of the motif.

Repeat steps 1–3 as often as required to complete the row.
4 Work a vertical cross stitch over four threads below the last motif at left.
5 Work four diagonal stitches clockwise over the four threads between the motifs.
Repeat these two rows to form the pattern.

In this openwork embroidery technique some of the weft or warp threads are withdrawn from the fabric. Stitches are worked over the remaining threads in the drawn area to form lacy, decorative bands or borders. There are two basic kinds of drawn thread work, hemstitching and needleweaving. In hemstitching the stitches are worked along the edges of the drawn area, which hold the remaining threads in place and groups them so that they form patterns. Sometimes additional grouping stitches are worked across the middle of the threads. Frequently the hemstitching is also worked through the turned edge of a hem, hence the name.

Needleweaving is a method of strengthening the threads that remain in the drawn area by taking a thread around and through them to group them in a pattern. Besides being a traditional form of embroi-dery, needleweaving also lends itself to free designs, and is used extensively in modern decorative work.

Hemstitching is used mainly for house-hold linens, and in its simplest form is an excellent way of making hems on table-cloths, napkins and place mats. The more elaborate patterns can be used as bands of decoration, either singly or in various combinations. They work especially well on delicate articles of clothing, such as lingerie, blouses and christening gowns, but can also be employed more boldly.

Always remember that withdrawing threads weakens the fabric. A single line of hemstitching is reasonably sturdy, but several bands of lacy hemstitch patterns should not be used on an article that will have much machine washing. Needle-weaving is stronger, but all drawn thread work should be handled with care.

FABRICS AND THREADS

In theory, drawn thread work can be carried out on any fabric from which threads can be withdrawn easily, but in practice certain restrictions usually apply. For table or bed linens, evenweave linen or cotton, available in needlework shops, is the best choice. Its smooth texture does not compete with the subtle patterns of the stitches.

Fabrics with a loose weave are the easiest to work on. The finer the weave, the more difficult the work.

For hemstitching use a thread that matches the fabric in colour and weight. A cotton embroidery thread, such as pearl cotton, coton à broder or stranded is the usual choice. For needleweaving (see p. 109) the choice is wider.

Always use a tapestry needle for drawn thread work to avoid splitting the threads.

BASIC HEMSTITCH

This simple stitch is the foundation of most hemstitching patterns. To learn it, practise working it as shown here, without turning up a hem.

The first step in drawn thread work is to decide how many of the remaining threads are to be grouped by each stitch. A single line of hemstitch used to turn a hem is usually worked with only one withdrawn thread, while for a more open, decorative effect, more are removed. In this example three horizontal threads are withdrawn and three vertical threads grouped with each stitch. This means that the number of vertical threads remaining after the horizontal ones are removed must be a multiple of three.

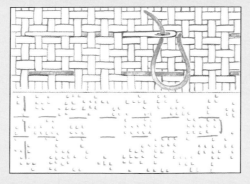

Preparing the fabric
1 Tack along the upper and lower edges of the area to be worked, taking the needle between the horizontal threads as shown.
2 Tack through the vertical centre and across both ends to mark the approximate width.

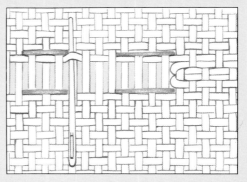

3 Carefully cut the horizontal threads at the centre. Using a tapestry needle, ease them out to the ends, counting the vertical threads to make sure you leave the correct number.
4 Darn the thread ends into the wrong side of the work for about 2cm, then trim them.

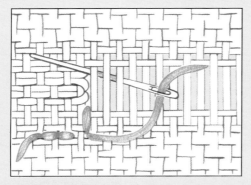

Working the hemstitching
This is done on the wrong side.
1 Leaving an end of about 10cm, work two back stitches to the left of the open area.
2 Work a small stitch over the edge, to the left of the first vertical thread.
3 Slip the needle behind the first three vertical threads, from right to left.

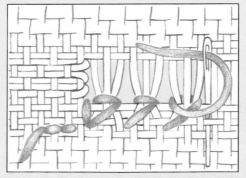

4 Pull the working thread gently to draw the fabric threads together, and work a small verti-cal stitch from back to front to the right of the group.
Repeat steps 3 and 4 to the end.

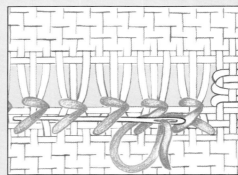

To fasten off, take the needle back through a few stitches on the wrong side. Undo the back stitches made at the beginning and fasten this thread in the same way.

TURNING A HEM; MITRING CORNERS

When a hem is incorporated in the hem-stitching the preparation differs from that for a simple band, as shown opposite. The following instructions are for a hem around all sides of the work. Several threads (nine in this case) are withdrawn. This entails mitring the outer corners and strengthening the inner ones with button-hole stitch. For further reinforcement, additional stitching can be worked at the corners (see p. 108). If only one thread is removed, the ends are threaded into the hem folds as shown below.

Evenweave fabric gives the best results for this kind of work.

Begin by cutting the fabric to the desired size, including an allowance for a double hem. The first turning should be slightly less than the second. For example, for a 1-cm hem, allow 1.8cm extra all around.

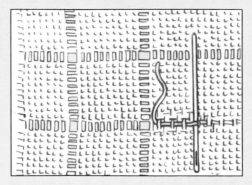

1 Measure to slightly less than the finished depth of the hem along one raw edge and with-draw one thread at this point.
2 Measure to the full depth of the hem and with-draw another thread.

Repeat steps 1 and 2 on the other three sides. These spaces mark the hem fold lines.

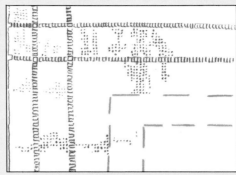

3 Count the number of threads between the two fold lines and add one to the number. Measure off this number of threads from the inner fold line and tack at this point. For example, if there are 10 threads between the fold lines, tack between the 11th and 12th threads. Tack along the inner edge of the border.

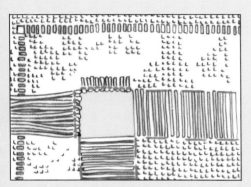

4 Cut the horizontal threads between the two lines of tacking. Withdraw the threads as far as the corner.
5 Fold the threads back as shown. Using matching sewing thread, back stitch them in place close to the corner edge. Trim the ends close to the stitching. Remove tacking.

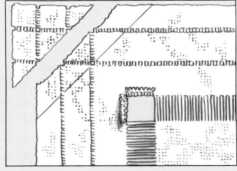

6 Mark a diagonal line where the inner fold lines meet, as shown, then mark another line parallel to the first, through the outer fold lines. (You can use a ruler to ensure straight lines.) Cut along the outer line.

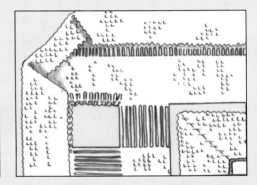

7 Turn in and press the fabric along the remaining fold line. Fold the side edges twice along the two fold lines to form a mitred corner. Tack the hem in place.
8 Join the diagonal edges of the mitre with tiny oversewing stitches.

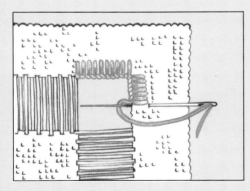

9 Reinforce the corners with buttonhole stitch, using the embroidery thread and working through the folded edge of the hem.

If only one or two threads are withdrawn, this is done after the hem is turned, and the thread ends are simply darned into the hem as shown.

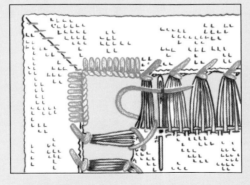

10 Work hemstitching along the outer edge of the drawn threads up to the corners, catching in the hem fold with each stitch.
11 Work hemstitching along the inner edge. At the corners, take the thread around the last and first group of threads on each side before working the vertical stitch.
Hemstitched edges (right), with buttonholing and dove's eye filling in the open corner

DRAWN THREAD WORK

FILLING A CORNER

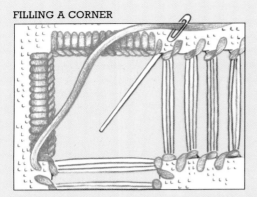

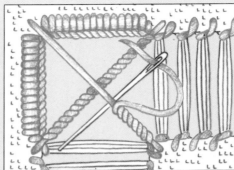

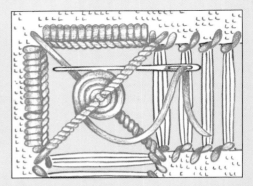

To strengthen an open corner, work button-holing and hemstitching as usual, then work a dove's eye filling.
1 Fasten the thread in the lower left-hand corner (right side facing) and take it across to the upper right-hand corner.

2 Oversew the thread back to the lower left-hand corner.
3 Take the needle under the buttonhole stitches to the upper left-hand corner and diagonally down to the lower right.
4 Oversew the thread as far as the point where the two threads cross.

5 Weave the needle under and over the four threads, as shown, to form a circular motif.
6 When the circle is the desired size, oversew the remaining length of the second thread. Fasten off on the wrong side.

HEMSTITCHING VARIATIONS

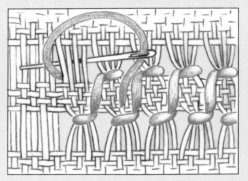

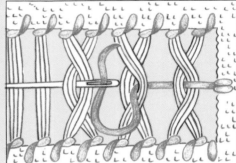

Serpentine or zigzag hemstitch Work hemstitch along each edge of the open area in turn, grouping an even number of threads with each stitch. Work one side, then turn and work the other, grouping half the number of threads with the first stitch, then half from each of the two adjacent groups.

Double hemstitch Withdraw four threads of the fabric, then leave four and withdraw another four. Work over the centre strip of fabric from right to left, as shown, grouping upper and lower threads alternately.

Interlaced hemstitch Withdraw horizontal threads for about 1.5cm and hemstitch both edges. Fasten the thread under the right-hand end. Take the needle under the second group of threads from left to right, then under the first group from right to left, thus twisting them, as shown. Repeat to the end.

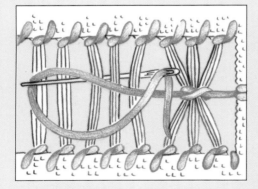

Knotted groups Withdraw threads for about 1.5cm and hemstitch both edges. Fasten the thread under the right-hand end, then loop it as shown and take the needle under the first three groups of threads and over the loop. Pull the thread taut, forming a knot around the first three groups. Repeat to the end.

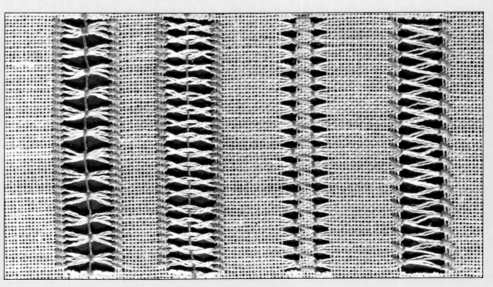

From left to right: knotted, interlaced, double and zigzag hemstitch

NEEDLEWEAVING

The two basic stitches or techniques involved in needleweaving are oversewing and darning. In oversewing, the groups of threads are wrapped to form bars, while darning weaves over and under groups of threads, to form a braid effect. They can be combined in various ways, both with each other and with hemstitching—although this is normally done only where the needleweaving is worked just over the middle of the threads.

Needleweaving can be worked either in regular patterns, or freely. Open areas of needleweaving can be worked in a plain fabric which is then placed over another layer of embroidery to suggest, for example, tree trunks and branches in the foreground of a landscape. For such decorative needleweaving you can use all kinds of fabric and threads.

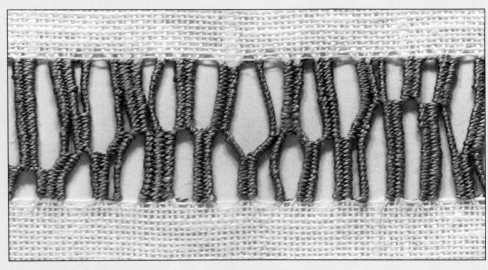

Free needleweaving is often a feature in modern decorative work

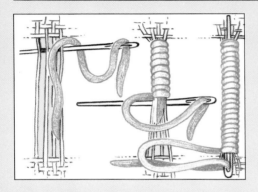

Oversewing Lay the end of the working thread along the threads to be grouped (here four are shown). Take the needle under the threads from right to left, then over and under again, holding the end in place. Continue in this way, pushing the threads smoothly together. To fasten off, take the needle through the work.

Zigzag oversewing Work over a multiple of three vertical threads. Oversew a group of three as shown. At the bottom, work twice over six threads to bring the first and second groups together. Then work upward over the second group, joining it to the next group of three at the top. Repeat to the end.

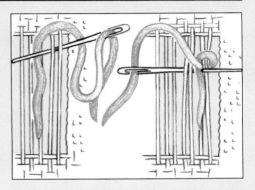

Darning Lay the end of the working thread along the threads to be woven (usually an even number and a minimum of four). Take the needle under the first group of threads (two) from right to left and over the other group and the thread end. Take it under the second group and over the first.

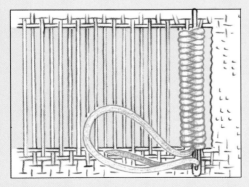

Repeat these two movements, working over and under the threads alternately, and gently pushing the weaving thread into place with the needle until the fabric threads are smoothly covered. Fasten off as for oversewing.

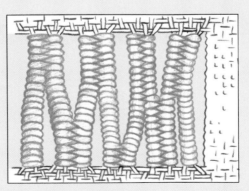

Darning variations are formed by working over adjacent groups in various patterns. The joined groups can be split and oversewn individually. Darning can also be worked over three or more groups. The possible combinations are almost unlimited.

For practising needleweaving, use a fairly coarse fabric and Persian yarn or soft embroidery cotton.

Although darning is slightly more complicated than oversewing, it is easier to learn, since the thread stays in place more readily. Practise darning, then move on to oversewing and combinations of the two.

In pulled work, lacy patterns are formed by pulling the embroidery stitches tightly, thus displacing the fabric threads by drawing some close together and separating others. Unlike drawn thread work, no threads are actually withdrawn, which makes the work stronger by comparison.

Pulled work, also known as pulled thread work and drawn fabric, is like drawn thread work in being a counted thread technique, and is normally worked on evenweave fabric. In both types of embroidery it is the texture and patterns created by the stitches, not the stitches themselves, that are the attraction. They are thus best worked in a thread that matches the fabric. Sometimes you can unravel threads from the edge of the fabric and use them for stitching.

Traditionally, white or cream are used for pulled work. To introduce a contrasting colour, and display the patterns to advantage, use a neutral colour for the work itself, then line it with a fabric of a medium to dark tone. Deep rose might be used under cream, for example, or violet beneath pale grey.

As in the past, pulled work is used today on household linens. In modern embroidery it is also used on cushion covers, lampshades, window blinds, screens and other household accessories. Its potential as a medium for purely decorative work is only beginning to be exploited.

Most examples of pulled work are stitched precisely, over carefully counted threads. However, it is possible to work many of the stitches freely and randomly, creating more modern effects. Pulled work is a counted thread technique that can be enjoyed by those who dislike the laborious business of counting threads.

FABRICS AND THREADS

Any fabric used for pulled work must be of an even weave (see p. 102), and loosely woven. Evenweave fabric in linen or cotton, specially made for counted thread work, can be obtained from embroidery shops. Linen scrim (a coarser, more open form of evenweave) and hessian are suitable for some work. Certain sheer fabrics also lend themselves to pulled work.

Threads used for pulled work must be strong enough to withstand the tension applied to them. As a rule, choose thread of about the same thickness as the fabric threads. Button thread, buttonhole twist, coton à broder, pearl cotton, crochet cottons and threads used for lace making are all suitable.

Use a tapestry needle for the embroidery, to avoid splitting the fabric threads. A large size needle will facilitate the work.

BASIC METHODS

Always use a frame for pulled work; this will help you count the threads and maintain an even tension.

Some pulled work designs are given as line charts (see p. 29), others in diagram form, with the position of each area of stitching indicated in relation to the edge and/or centre. In both cases, mark the centre of the fabric with two perpendicular lines of tacking and work the embroidery outward from the centre. If the design is asymmetrical, scale it up (see p. 21), trace it, and tack the outlines of the stitching through tracing and fabric as shown on page 65. Practise the stitches first on spare fabric.

For the sake of clarity, the stitch diagrams given here show the stitches as they would be if worked untensioned. In most cases, however, the thread is pulled.

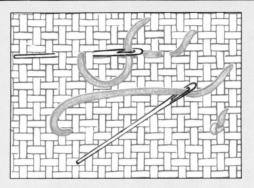

To begin stitching Work a few running stitches toward the starting point along the line to be covered. Then either work one back stitch to secure the thread or anchor it with a knot a short distance away and darn the end in later. When ending a thread, darn it into the wrong side of the work.

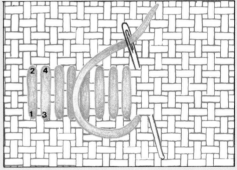

Satin stitch in rows Work vertical stitches over three or more fabric threads, pulling the thread tightly or, for a contrasting texture, leaving the stitches untensioned. Interesting effects can be achieved by random variations in tension within the row.

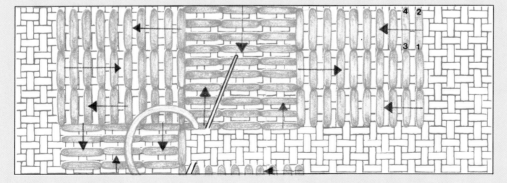

Chessboard filling This consists of rows of satin stitch arranged in blocks and worked in alternating directions. Each block consists of three rows of 10 stitches each, all worked over three fabric threads. Work the blocks in rows as indicated by the arrows.

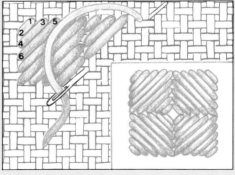

Satin stitch blocks This consists of groups of diagonal stitches worked in a square over any number of threads; here it is five. When the stitches are pulled tightly, a diamond shape results. A group of four, worked in alternate directions, forms a star motif, as shown inset.

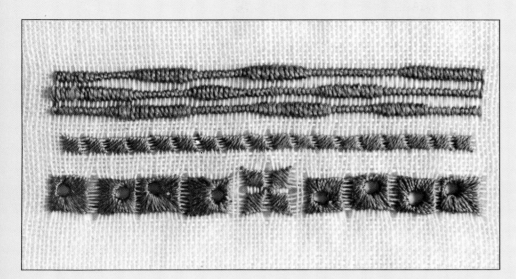

The pulled thread stitches shown in this sampler include (top to bottom): rows of satin stitch with the tension varied randomly to produce irregular lines; satin stitch blocks going in the same direction; four-block motif in satin stitch (centre); freely worked eyelets.

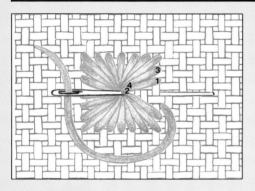

Square eyelets There are several types of eyelet. This type is worked over an even number of threads, with the needle taken down into the centre each time. A medium or tight tension can be used, depending on the desired size of the central hole.

Free eyelets The basic method of working a square eyelet can be varied by placing the hole off-centre, by working over a rectangular area, by varying the tension, and by working only part of the eyelet, so that it seems to emerge from the background. Groups of such irregular eyelets form an interesting 'organic' texture.

Zigzag back stitch This simple stitch makes a subtle pattern for a border. Work back stitch in a zigzag pattern as shown, over the same number of threads each time; here it is three. Pull the stitches tightly.

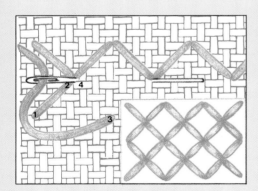

Wave stitch This is essentially zigzag back stitch, worked to fill a space. Work from top to bottom in rows, back and forth, working over two, three or four vertical and horizontal threads. Pull the stitches tightly.

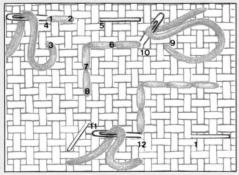

Triangle stitch This subtle diagonal pattern is created by back stitches worked over two sides of a square. Each stitch is worked over two threads and pulled tightly. Work in diagonal rows from upper left to lower right.

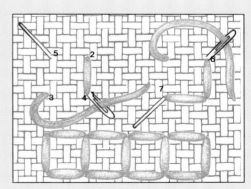

Four-sided stitch This makes an attractive border and can also be worked in rows to fill an area. Each stitch is composed of four back stitches, worked in the order shown, over any number of threads, and pulled tightly.

111

As practical as it is pretty, smocking is a decorative method of gathering fullness in fabric. In the past it was traditionally used at the necklines and cuffs of men's shirts and women's chemises as well as on the bodices of farm workers' smocks. Clothes for babies and young children are often decorated with smocking, and it can also be used to good effect on lingerie and women's casual clothes.

The appealing textures and stitch patterns of smocking lend themselves to use on soft furnishings, such as cushions and curtain headings. Modern embroiderers have also been developing the technique in new ways, for use in panels and soft sculpture.

There are two basic methods of smocking. In the traditional 'English' method, the fabric is first gathered into even folds, called tubes or reeds, and the embroidery stitches are worked over the folds or pleats. In the direct method, used widely in North America, the smocking stitches are worked on ungathered fabric; the stitches themselves gather up the fabric.

Whether you are using the traditional or the direct method of smocking, you will usually need to mark the fabric with a grid of dots. These will serve as a guide when working the gathering, in the traditional method, or the smocking stitches in the direct method. It is now possible to buy a sewing machine attachment that gathers the fabric on a regular grid.

The finished effect is the same in both methods. A piece of smocking normally includes a variety of stitches, the contrasting patterns of which contribute to the charm of the work. The stitches vary in their elasticity: firm stitches such as cable and outline are often used together with the more elastic ones such as honeycomb, to give the work stability. Some other surface embroidery stitches, including chain, feather and herringbone, can also be used for smocking, while French knots, bullion knots, detached chain and other individual stitches can be added once the main stitching is complete.

To emphasize the stitches, work them in one or more colours contrasting with the fabric. To emphasize the texture of the work, use thread to match the fabric.

FABRICS AND THREADS

The easiest fabrics on which to work smocking are soft, smooth, light- to medium-weight, and woven from natural fibres or from a blend of natural and synthetic. Wholly synthetic fabrics tend to be springy and difficult to gather evenly.

Although smocking is usually worked on plain fabric, interesting effects can be achieved with small prints. When gathered up, the print takes on a quite different appearance, so that the gathered area contrasts effectively with the smooth one. Regular patterns such as polka dots, checks and stripes can be exploited in various ways (see p. 47). Small polka dots can serve as a ready-made grid for the gathering. Make sure that the dots follow the grain of the fabric; if not, the gathers will lie incorrectly. Checks and stripes can be gathered in various ways to emphasize different elements of the pattern.

Whatever fabric you select, it is a good idea—especially if you are inexperienced —to buy a small amount first and work a sample or two to see how much fabric will be drawn up by the smocking. As a general rule, you will need three times the finished width of the smocking, but this varies with the fabric, the spacing of the gathers and your own working tension.

Unstranded cotton embroidery threads, such as pearl cotton, soft embroidery cotton and coton à broder are all suitable for smocking. On heavy linen or wool, Persian or tapestry yarn might be used, while silk embroidery or buttonhole thread will give added lustre to the work. For the gathering, use cotton-wrapped polyester or pure polyester thread.

A crewel or chenille needle is used for the smocking stitches.

MARKING THE GRID

Transfers of smocking dots which are ironed on to the fabric are available in haberdashery departments and needlework shops. These are made with a variety of spacings, both vertical and horizontal. The most useful have the dots spaced between 5mm and 1cm apart; the rows may be the same distance apart, farther apart or closer. If you cannot find a suitable transfer for a project, you can make your own as shown below.

Before transferring the dots to the fabric you must decide how many you will need. Making a sample will show the overall width required, but the exact number of pleats or dots may depend on the stitches you are using; some stitches must be worked over a specific multiple of pleats and some must be centred (see pp. 114–15).

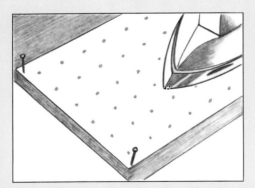

Applying transfer dots Position the transfer inked side down on the wrong side of the fabric (for the traditional method) or the right side (for the direct method). Make sure that the dots follow the grain. Pin the transfer in place at the corners and run a medium-hot iron smoothly over the surface.

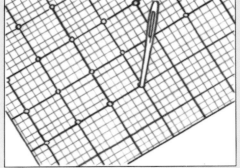

Making your own grid Pierce holes in a piece of graph paper at the chosen intervals, using a large chenille needle. Then position the graph paper smooth side down on the appropriate side of the fabric and mark a dot through each hole with a pencil.

Positioning a grid for a curved area of smocking Slash the transfer (or graph paper grid) between the dots up to the top row. Pin it to the fabric, spreading it evenly to fill the area, and mark the dots as before.

TRADITIONAL SMOCKING

The first stage is to gather up the fabric into even folds, or pleats. The gathering threads, which are later removed, have a dual purpose: besides holding the folds in place they serve as a guide for keeping the rows of smocking straight. They should thus be worked in a contrasting thread. For the same reason, the gathers should not be pulled up so tightly that the thread cannot be seen from the right side.

When transferring dots to the fabric, transfer one more dot than the required number of pleats; the extra dot completes the last pleat when the gathering is worked. It is a good idea also to transfer an extra row of dots above and below the lines for the smocking. These, which are gathered but not smocked, help to keep the folds even and facilitate working the top and bottom rows of smocking.

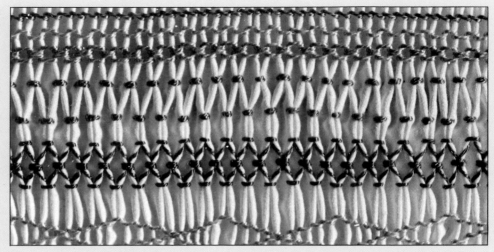

Smocking stitches, from the top: outline, cable, double cable, honeycomb, diamond and trellis (wave stitch worked in opposite directions)

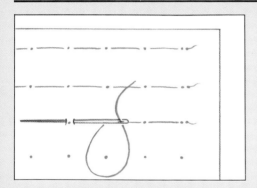

Gathering the fabric
1 Thread the needle with a single strand of sewing thread slightly longer than the width to be gathered. Knot the end, then work even running stitches as shown, picking up a few woven fabric threads at each dot. Do not fasten off.

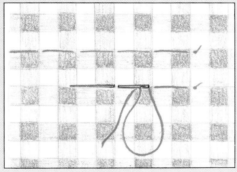

Gathering checked fabric
1 Use one corner of a check as the point to be picked up for each stitch. Take care to pick up this point consistently and accurately on each row.

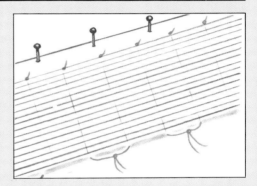

2 When all the gathering stitches have been worked, pin the right-hand edge to a padded surface and pull up the threads two at a time until the folds lie closely and evenly together. Tie the threads together in pairs.

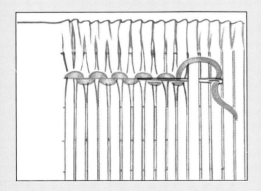

Working the smocking Fasten the thread on the wrong side with two back stitches and work across the pleats in the chosen pattern (cable stitch is shown here), picking up only a few fabric threads with each stitch. Fasten off with back stitches at the end. (All the stitches illustrated on pages 114–15 are worked from left to right.)

DIRECT SMOCKING

In this method the smocking stitches are worked directly on to the fabric without first gathering it. Because the time-consuming gathering process is omitted, this method is potentially quicker than the traditional one, although a certain amount of practice is required in order to work the stitches evenly.

For direct smocking the dots must be applied to the right side of the fabric. Each dot counts as one pleat or fold in the traditional method, so you should transfer the exact number of dots required for the stitches, without adding an extra one.

The stitches are worked in the same way as in the traditional method, except that each stitch is worked through a dot rather than through the top of a pleat.

The method of working direct smocking is illustrated on the right with honeycomb stitch.

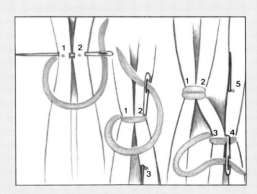

Honeycomb stitch (direct method)
1 Bring the needle up at dot 1, then take it under dot 2 and up again at dot 1. Pull the dots together.
2 Take the needle down at dot 2 and bring it up at dot 3 on the lower line. Join dots 3–4 as in step 1, taking the needle down at 4 and up at 5. Repeat these steps.

SMOCKING STITCHES

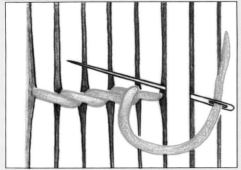

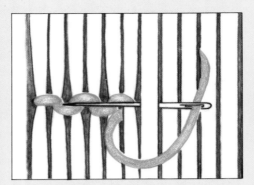

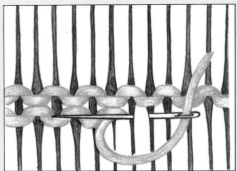

Outline stitch Also called stem stitch, this holds the fabric firmly and can be worked over any number of pleats or dots.
1 Bring the needle up to the left of the first pleat.
2 Take it through the second pleat at a slight upward angle with the thread below the needle. Repeat steps 1 and 2.

Cable stitch This is another firm stitch worked over any number of pleats or dots.
Work as for outline stitch, but keep the thread above the needle for one stitch and below it for the next, continuing to alternate in sequence.

Double cable stitch This is worked over a multiple of four pleats or dots.
Work as for cable stitch, but work two rows to touch each other, reversing the sequence of thread-above and thread-below so as to form the pattern shown.

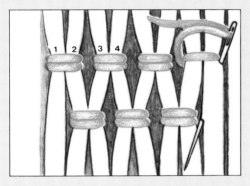

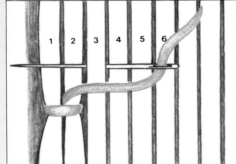

Honeycomb stitch This stitch is worked over two rows of gathering (multiple of two pleats or dots).
Start on the upper row and join pleats 1 and 2 with two back stitches, then take the thread under the work to join 2 and 3 on the lower row. Continue joining pleats alternately on upper and lower rows.

Diamond stitch This stitch forms a pattern over three rows of gathering (multiple of four pleats or dots plus two).
1 Begin on the middle row. Work a back stitch over pleats 1 and 2 with the thread below the needle, and bring the needle out between the pleats.
2 Work a stitch through pleat 3 with the thread below.

3 Work a stitch over pleats 3 and 4 with the thread above, bringing the needle out between the pleats.
4 Work a stitch through pleat 5 with the thread above. Repeat steps 1–4.
To complete the diamond pattern, work another row, positioning the stitches as shown, inset.

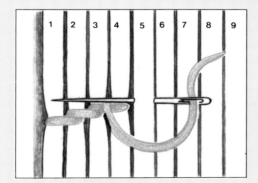

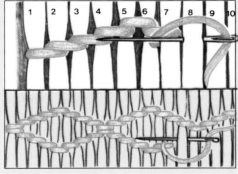

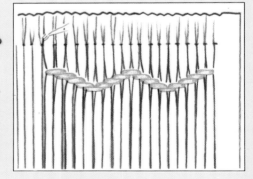

Wave stitch This is worked over two lines of a grid with rows half as far apart as dots (multiple of eight pleats or dots plus two).
1 Starting on the lower line, join pleats 1–2, 2–3, 3–4 and 4–5 with the thread below the needle. Work upward to the upper line as shown, bringing the needle out between pleats.

2 Join pleats 5–6 with the thread above the needle, then work downward, joining 6–7, 7–8 and 8–9 in the same way. Then join 9–10 with the thread below the needle. Continue working up and down across the row.
Trellis stitch is formed by working lines of wave stitch in opposite directions, as shown inset, to form a diamond pattern.

When working large-scale patterns such as wave or trellis stitch, centre the pattern carefully. Mark the point between the two centre pleats with a thread as shown, and begin stitching here. Work to the right-hand side, then turn the work upside down and work to the other side.

EXPERIMENTAL SMOCKING

Like many other forms of embroidery, smocking is now being worked in new and imaginative ways. Some of these new approaches have turned smocking into a new textile art. Panels, wallhangings and soft sculpture exploit the textural possibilities of this work. Such embroidery uses stitches much more freely than is possible on clothing. In some cases the stitches are relegated to the wrong side to allow the folds to 'speak for themselves'. This page gives several ideas to inspire experiments in smocking. For some of these the fabric is prepared as for traditional smocking by working gathers over a grid of dots (see p. 112), but for the random reverse and honeycomb smocking the stitches are worked on the flat fabric, as shown below, to create a texture of interlaced folds on the right side.

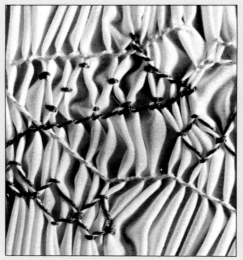
Freely worked smocking stitches

Random reverse smocking

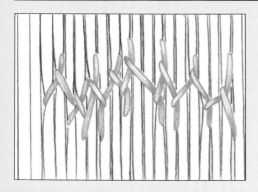

Free surface stitchery can be worked in irregular lines across the work. Gather the fabric on the wrong side as usual, then work the chosen embroidery stitches. The one shown here is Cretan stitch (see p. 74). Do not remove the gathering threads.

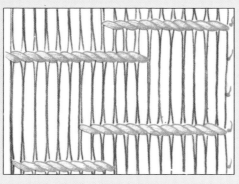

Back smocking For more random stitchery, as shown above, or for motifs, provide a firm base by working lines of outline stitch (see p. 114) just above or below the gathers on the wrong side, using strong sewing thread. The stitching, or back smocking, can be worked all the way across each row or along only part of a row as shown. Remove the gathers when all the stitching is completed.

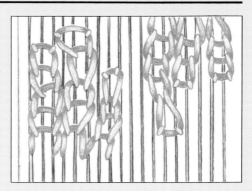

Vertical lines of stitchery can be worked on pleats that have been smocked on the wrong side to hold them in place, as shown left. Open chain stitch is shown here; other possibilities include fern stitch, feather stitch and raised chain band.

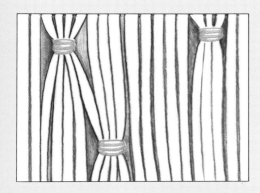

Sculptural effects can be achieved by first smocking deep pleats on the wrong side, as shown above, then joining them on the right side with a few back stitches. Use matching or contrasting embroidery thread.

Random honeycomb can be worked on flat fabric to produce an interesting texture. Choose a firm, lustrous fabric for a rich effect. Mark dots at random on the right side, making sure each one is reasonably adjacent to another. Then join pairs of adjacent dots with two back stitches, taking the thread under the fabric between pairs of dots.

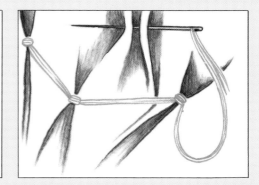

Random reverse smocking is worked in basically the same way as random honeycomb, but on the wrong side of the fabric. Using a double strand of sewing thread, join two adjacent dots with several small back stitches for firmness, then take the thread to another dot without pulling it up, and fasten it. Continue joining dots in a random fashion. The result as seen from the right side is shown in the photograph above.

115

Some of the most imaginitive of all modern embroidery is stitched by machine. And although automatic patterns can be used in interesting ways, as shown in the photograph, more inventive designs are being created with straight stitch and zigzag alone. The most original work is produced by a technique called free machining, in which the machine is adjusted so that the fabric can be moved in any direction.

A great variety of different effects can be created with free machining. Delicate linear designs similar to fine pen drawing, corded effects, and loopy textures are just some of the possibilities. Others include pulled work (see p. 48), cutwork and appliqué. The most recent developments are in the area of machine-made lace (see p. 121).

The speed of machine embroidery has an obvious appeal for those who like quick results, but it can also have a liberating effect on the embroiderer whose hand work tends to be overdeliberate and 'tight'. The machine must, of course, be kept under control, or the result will be a mess, but the act of automatic stitching induces a free, spontaneous approach.

Many decorative effects can be produced with ordinary stitching—that is with the foot on the machine rather than without it, as for free machining. It is a good idea to familiarize yourself with these techniques, especially those that involve adjusting the tension or altering the stitch length, before you try free machining.

In machine embroidery, remember that a mixture of too many techniques may spoil the unity of a design. It is always possible to add texture afterward with hand stitchery, which is slow enough to be applied critically. Mistakes in machine embroidery are notoriously difficult to unpick!

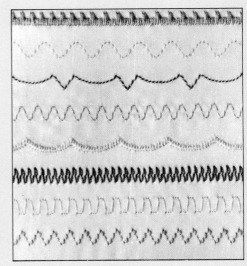

A variety of automatic patterns

SEWING MACHINES

Most modern domestic machines can be used for embroidery. The one essential feature, if you are planning to do free machining, is that it must be possible to lower or cover the feed dog, that is, the jagged teeth that move the fabric along in ordinary stitching. Before you buy a machine, always try it out thoroughly.

Even a machine that does only straight stitch can produce many attractive effects, but the zigzag stitch greatly increases the range of possibilities. A multi-stitch zigzag and a blind-hemming stitch are useful variations. Fancier automatic stitch patterns are an optional extra. If you are buying a new machine, it is not worth spending extra money on these unless you intend to do a lot of this kind of work.

There are some features that are well worth having and, if necessary, paying extra for. One of these is an easily adjusted lower tension. A few machines have a knob-controlled lower tension, which is a great help in working some embroidery techniques; on most, however, the lower tension is controlled by a screw. When trying out a machine, ask the demonstrator to show you how to do this, and make sure that you can do it yourself easily.

A machine with a flat bed—that is, a large surface around the needle—is best for machine embroidery, since it supports the frame evenly. But if you will also be using the machine for dressmaking it is best to buy a free-arm type (ideal for setting in sleeves and other awkward manoeuvres) that will convert to a flat bed with the addition of a metal plate.

A machine on which the teeth can be lowered is generally preferable to one on which they are merely covered, since this allows a framed fabric to lie absolutely flat. It is quite possible to do excellent work on the other kind of machine, but moving the frame with one hand, as is sometimes necessary, requires extra-smooth control.

There are several other features you may find useful: a twin needle, which works parallel lines of stitching; a quilting guide bar (see p. 90); and a speed control, which is often helpful when learning to free machine.

Various different kinds of foot are available for sewing machines. A clear plastic presser foot is suitable for general work and makes the area immediately surrounding the needle easily visible. A cording foot facilitates couching; one type will thread several cords at once. A darning foot is sometimes useful when doing free-machine work.

Always use needles that are in perfect condition—neither blunt nor bent.

CARING FOR THE MACHINE

Many of the problems experienced by beginners in machine embroidery can be traced to lack of practice, plus inadequate understanding of the machine and failure to keep it in good working order.

Make sure you read the instruction booklet thoroughly and familiarize yourself with the various parts and functions of the machine. Many companies offer courses in using their machines, and such courses certainly help you to avoid problems. They may also reveal interesting ways of using the machine that you might never discover on your own.

It is especially important to keep the machine clean and oiled. Bits of fluff under the throat plate, in the bobbin case or between the tension discs can easily cause a malfunction.

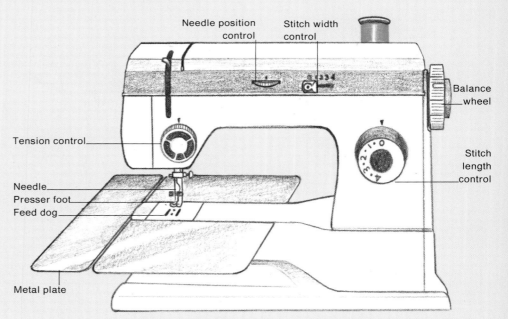

THREADS AND NEEDLES

Many different kinds of thread can be used for machine embroidery, even including knitting yarns. Sewing thread—in cotton, cotton-wrapped polyester or pure polyester—gives good results and comes in a wide colour range. Cotton is graded by number; the relatively fine size no. 50 is generally most suitable for machine embroidery, although for whip stitch (see p. 120) the heavier size no. 40 may be preferred.

Fine silk sewing thread has a rich lustre, but adds considerably to the cost of a project. The same applies to silk buttonhole twist.

Special machine embroidery threads are becoming more widely available. The cotton variety is softer than ordinary sewing cotton and has an attractive sheen. Size no. 30 machine embroidery cotton is roughly equivalent to a size no. 50 sewing cotton; some embroidery shops sell an extra-fine size no. 50.

Rayon and metallic machine embroidery threads are also available. They can be tricky to handle, but with practice can produce excellent effects.

Hand embroidery threads can be used in the machine in many ways. Some of the finer ones can be used in the needle, but medium-thick ones must be used in the bobbin, with the stitching done from the wrong side. Extra-thick, slubbed, and hairy yarns must be machine-couched on to the surface.

A relatively large needle is used for most free-machine embroidery. Sizes no. 90 or 100 are suitable for most purposes; size no. 110 for working on heavy fabrics and using thick thread. For work on delicate fabrics with fine thread, choose a size no. 80.

FABRICS

Virtually any fabric can be used for machine embroidery in which the presser foot is used. However, all thin or slippery fabrics tend to pucker when stitched in a single layer (but see Tip, below).

For free machining the choice is rather more critical. Beginners should select firmly woven fabrics such as calico which are easy to frame up and provide a smooth surface for stitching. Smooth dressmaking fabrics such as poplin, gabardine and cotton-wool blends also work well. With experience you can graduate to sheer, silky and textured fabrics.

Although plain-coloured fabrics are usually best for machine embroidery, you can create interesting effects with printed fabrics. Or you can dye or paint your own backgrounds (see pp. 30–3) to provide a 'structure' for the stitch pattern.

ADJUSTING THE TENSION

For most machine stitching, including embroidery, the tension of the upper and lower threads should be equal, so that the stitches link exactly in the centre of the layer(s) of fabric. Some machine embroidery effects require alterations in tension.

On most machines, the upper tension is easily adjusted by turning a dial. By making this tension tighter or looser than the bobbin tension you can bring the lower or upper thread respectively, to the opposite side.

For some effects, such as feather stitch and cable stitch (see p. 120), the bobbin tension must be loosened. On most machines this entails carefully turning a small screw that controls the tension spring on the bobbin case. For a thick thread it may be possible to remove the tension spring or bypass it altogether.

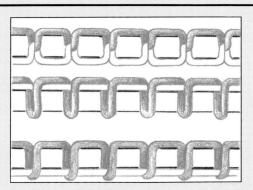

Equal and unequal tensions of upper and lower threads are shown in cross-section.

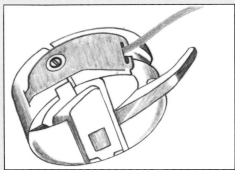

A removable bobbin case controls tension by means of a spring held in place by a tiny screw. A very slight turn of the screw will alter the tension. For thick thread, both spring and screw can usually be removed.

TRANSFERRING THE DESIGN

Various methods can be used to transfer designs for machine embroidery. If the work is to be done with the presser foot, it may be easiest to mark the stitching lines directly on to the fabric. Use tailor's chalk and a ruler for straight lines or paper templates for curved shapes.

If the design is at all complex, dressmaker's carbon, transfer pencil, or the tracing method may be appropriate.

For free machining, it is best to keep any permanent marking to a minimum. The essence of the work is its spontaneous quality, and most of the stitching should be done freehand. It is useful, however, to transfer the main design lines, which will then serve as a guide for the stitching.

Direct tracing with a sharp pencil can be used on sheer or semi-sheer fabrics. Tacking is suitable for thicker fabrics, but use the same thread that will be used for the embroidery so that any bits that cannot be removed will blend into the work.

The pricking and pouncing method can also be used (see p. 65). Small motifs can be transferred on to the framed fabric with the powder only and then stitched immediately.

Another useful method is to stitch the main lines through paper. This is practical where the design outlines do not extend beyond the diameter of the frame. First mark the main outlines on tissue or thin tracing paper. Mount the fabric in the frame as usual (see pp. 66–7). Tack the design to the fabric, then work free running stitch in the appropriate colour(s) along the lines. (Do not use zigzag, or it will be impossible to remove the paper.) When all the main lines have been stitched, carefully tear away the tracing, then work the remaining embroidery.

Machine embroidery, and particularly free machining, consumes a great deal of thread. Whenever possible, buy machine embroidery thread in large reels, for economy.

Back a fine or slippery fabric with a sheer, closely woven fabric such as organza; apply iron-on interfacing to the wrong side; or place a layer of tissue paper beneath the fabric during stitching.

FRAMING THE WORK

The first step in successful machine embroidery, with or without the presser foot, is to make sure the fabric is properly framed. A ring frame is used for all types of machine embroidery. It can be of wood or metal, but must have a screw for adjusting the fit, and should be no more than 1cm thick, so that it will slide under the needle and presser bar. The metal and plastic spring frames (see p. 66) are suitably slimline, but can be used only for lightweight fabrics which can be pulled taut without ejecting the inner ring. A ring with a diameter of 20cm is most useful; larger ones are awkward to use, and small ones give an inadequate working area.

Whether the frame is made of wood or metal, always bind the inner ring with woven tape or bias binding to provide an extra-firm grip.

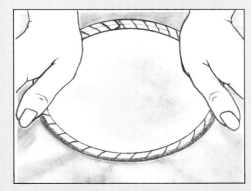

To bind the ring Wrap the end of the tape diagonally around it. Continue wrapping, holding the end in place until it is secure, and overlapping the edges slightly. When you reach the starting point, cut off the excess. Using strong thread, oversew the second end over the first. **To mount the fabric** See p. 66.

The fabric should be as taut as a drum, and the grain should run straight in both directions. Slight adjustments can be made by pulling the edges and tightening the screw with a screwdriver, but if the fabric is not straight it may be better to remove it, tighten the screw, and start again.

EMBROIDERY WITH THE PRESSER FOOT

Designs using either straight or curved lines, or both together, are easily worked with the presser foot on the machine. The most effective work uses several lines together, either in regular patterns or freely flowing designs. Ordinary straight stitch is attractive worked in buttonhole twist or another lustrous thread, using a medium-long (2–3mm) stitch length.

To turn a corner, work up to the turning point, stop the machine with the needle in the fabric, raise the presser foot, turn the fabric, lower the presser foot and continue stitching. Fairly sharp curves can be turned once you have gained some practice in manipulating the fabric smoothly.

Zigzag stitch can be used for many different effects, some of which are shown. Always practise the stitching first on a scrap of the same fabric.

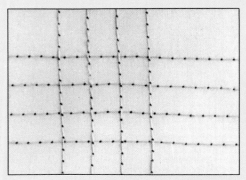

For a 'beaded' line of straight stitch, tighten the upper tension slightly. This brings the bobbin thread to the surface, forming a tiny loop at each stitch.

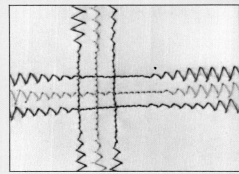

A zigzag stitch can be adjusted in width and length to produce many different effects. Practise adjusting the stitch with your right hand while feeding in fabric with your left. In some machines the needle position can be altered to angle the stitch or produce a straight edge to one side.

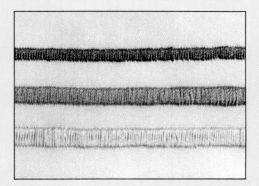

Satin stitch is very close zigzag. On some fabrics a smoother effect can be produced by working the stitch in two stages, with the stitches slightly open. Work the first line slightly narrower than the effect desired, then work a second to the correct width, on top.

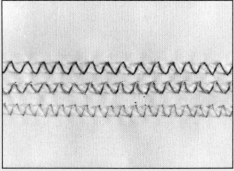

Couching can also be worked with zigzag. Position the foot (raised) over the starting point and slip the thread or cord under the foot as shown. Lower the foot and work zigzag over the cord. Vary the effect by changing the stitch length to reveal more or less of the cord.

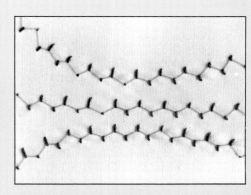

A 'wishbone' effect can be produced by tightening the upper tension. This brings the bobbin thread to the surface. Try using buttonhole twist in the needle and a thin, contrasting thread in the bobbin.

FREE MACHINE EMBROIDERY

The technique of free machining is like drawing with a needle and thread. But unlike normal drawing, it involves moving the drawing surface rather than the implement. The movements will seem awkward at first, but with practice they will become more natural. As you gain confidence an amazing variety of effects will be created —and at high speed.

Spend plenty of time 'doodling' with the machine before you attempt a project. You may well produce some attractive designs in the early stages, but real mastery of the technique requires much practice.

Always make sure that the fabric is correctly framed before you begin. It must be drum-taut, otherwise the machine may miss stitches, the thread may break and the work will be puckered beyond repair when the frame is removed.

'Drawing' using free machine embroidery

USING THE DARNING FOOT

The darning foot can be used for machine embroidery. The technique is essentially the same as for free machining; the teeth are lowered and covered and the stitch length set to zero so that the fabric can be moved in any direction. However, the foot holds down the material at the moment the stitch is being made and so prevents missed stitches.

The darning foot is useful for beginners or the hesitant, but it obscures part of the stitching. Also, because the frame will not slip under the foot, the frame must be removed and reattached every time the work is put on or taken off the machine.

Experienced machine embroiderers sometimes use the darning foot without a frame for large projects. This requires considerable skill since the hands must be used to tension the fabric.

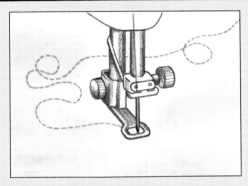

The darning foot has a square or circular opening and can be used for straight stitch or zigzag.

BASIC PROCEDURE
To begin stitching:
1 Set the stitch length and width to 0.
2 Lower or cover the feed dog.
3 Remove the presser foot and the holding screw.
4 Thread the needle and insert the bobbin.
5 Place the framed fabric on the machine, lifting the needle to its highest point.
6 Lower the needle into the fabric to bring up the bobbin thread. Pull the thread through. If the bobbin thread is thick, it may be necessary to pierce a small hole in the fabric with a large chenille needle.
7 Lower the presser bar to engage the tension.
8 Lower the needle and, holding both threads with one hand, work two or three stitches. Cut off the thread ends.
9 Practise moving the frame while stitching, holding it as shown right. Move the frame as smoothly as possible.

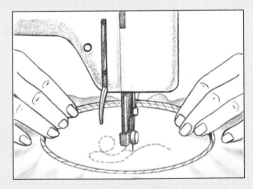

Hold the frame as shown, resting your fingers on the edge. With practice you may prefer to place your fingers on the taut fabric for greater control, but this position is best for beginners. Make sure that your chair is at a comfortable height and your arms relaxed.

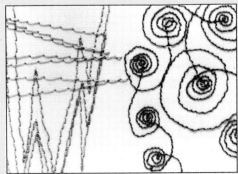

Work in lines, circles and spirals as you progress. To create lines, move the frame back and forth in various directions. Do not stitch quickly in one place or the upper thread may snap. Experiment with all kinds of curves, and try to write your own name or 'draw' motifs. Draw some lines on the fabric and try following them accurately.

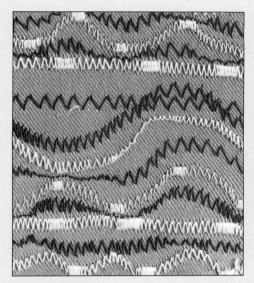

Zigzag lines and curves

Whip stitch

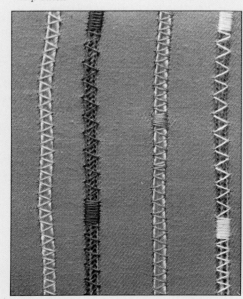

Couching

SPECIAL EFFECTS

A great many different and interesting effects can be created with free machining. The photographs on this page illustrate a small selection. Experiment with your own designs to create patterns with the hallmarks of individuality.

Zigzag lines Set the stitch dial to the desired width and move the frame forward and backward, turning it to form curves. The speed at which the machine is moved determines the stitch length; moving it slowly will produce satin stitch. The stitch width can be adjusted with one hand while moving the frame with the other.

Zigzag used to fill a shape Set the stitch width to maximum (or less, if the shape is small). Move the frame from side to side.

Star and flower motifs are worked with wide satin stitch. Work a few stitches without moving the frame and then, with the needle at the centre point, pivot the work and stitch as before.

Whip stitch is a corded line produced by tightening the upper tension and moving the frame slowly, so that the lower thread wraps around the upper one. Use a fine thread in the bobbin (no. 50 machine cotton, if available) and a relatively heavy cotton in the needle. Run the machine very fast but move the frame slowly. If the upper thread breaks, loosen the tension slightly, and loosen the lower tension correspondingly (see p. 117). Two-colour effects can be achieved by using contrasting colours in needle and bobbin and varying the speed of moving the frame. If the frame is moved quickly, more of the upper thread will show.

Feather stitch This requires a tight upper and loose lower tension. Move the frame quickly in a spiralling motion. The tension of the upper thread pulls long loops to the surface.

Couching can be used to apply a thick thread to the fabric. Use either running stitch or zigzag, holding the thread to be couched with one hand and guiding the frame with the other.

Cable stitch This is produced by using a thick thread in the bobbin and working from the wrong side, so that the decorative thread is on the right side. Frame the fabric in the usual way, but wrong side upward. Wind the bobbin with the chosen thread and use an ordinary sewing or machine embroidery thread in the needle. Loosen the lower tension (see p. 117) so that the bobbin thread can be pulled up easily. The upper tension should be set at 'normal'. Place the fabric on the machine and bring up the bobbin thread. Work the stitching in the chosen design. Tie the thread ends on the wrong side.

Zigzag flower motifs

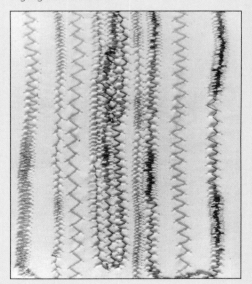

Feather stitch

Cable stitch

LACE

Machine embroidery can be used to make delicate lace by working it on a fabric that is later made to disappear. This can be 'vanishing muslin', which is ironed away, acetate fabric which dissolves in acetone, or a water-soluble material, all available from specialist embroidery shops.

The basic stitching techniques are as for free machine embroidery, except that zigzag can only be used over a line of straight stitch. Remember that all stitching lines must connect, or the lace will collapse once the backing fabric is destroyed. It is advisable to reinforce the principle lines of the design with two or three extra lines of stitching.

Frame the work and use a relatively fine needle to avoid snagging the fabric. A fine thread must be used in the needle, but a thicker one could be used in the bobbin.

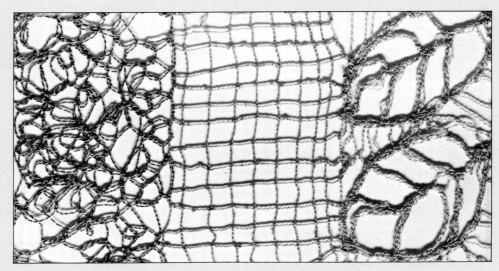

Lacy effects worked in circles and spirals, in straight lines and as a motif

USING DISAPPEARING FABRICS

The disappearing fabrics used for lace machine embroidery are fairly tough but still need careful handling. It is vital that they do not become damp or wet when stored or during use, since this will make them disappear prematurely or destroy their 'vanishing' properties.

Designs can be transferred on to the fabric with a soft pencil. For complex designs it is also sensible to work out a 'flow diagram' for the stitching to avoid overstitching delicate areas and to make sure denser ones are properly worked.

When all stitching is completed, hold the work up to the light to make sure all stitching lines interconnect and that there are no loose ends. Remove the work from the frame. Immerse in solvent or hot or cold water, or iron, as appropriate. Leave flat on a towel to cool or dry, then press.

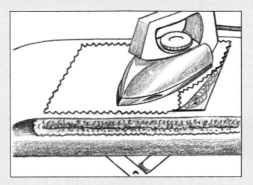

To remove vanishing muslin, place an old towel on the ironing board. Lay on the lace, wrong side up. Cover with a thin, dry cloth. Press with an iron set to the highest possible temperature. Remove the iron from the work as soon as the muslin has vanished or the work may scorch.

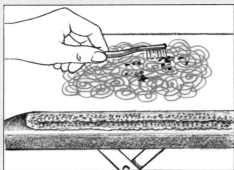

The ironed muslin burns to brown or black then shrivels and becomes brittle as it vanishes. Use an old, clean toothbrush to brush away any fragments adhering to the lace. Always work in a well-ventilated room.

EXTENDING THE RANGE

The advent of vanishing fabrics as backings for machine-worked lace opens up all kinds of possibilities for the inventive embroiderer. As well as ordinary sewing threads, for example, metal and textured threads can be couched into the designs to add impact and interest.

This type of lace work can easily be incorporated into cutwork. Vanishing fabrics soluble in cold water or the iron-away types are best for this kind of work. Lace edgings can be made in a similar way. Another way in which lace designs can be varied is by 'suspending' fabric shapes and motifs into the lace.

It is often advisable to outline shapes and emphasize details in the lace with satin stitch (close zigzag worked over a line of straight stitch); these can be indicated on the fabric.

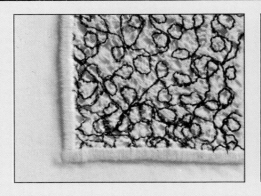

Lace insert incorporated in a cutwork embroidery. To do this, first cut away the desired areas from the fabric, and machine the cut edges with a close zigzag to prevent fraying. Tack on the vanishing fabric, leaving an overlap of a few centimetres. Work the lace, then treat the vanishing fabric to remove it.

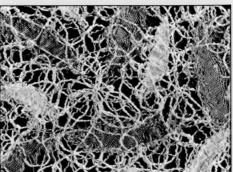

Fabric shape incorporated into machine-worked lace. These should be tacked to the vanishing fabric before the lace is worked. Surface embroidery can be added to the shapes as the lace is being constructed.

Of all the many forms of embroidery, canvaswork, sometimes also called tapestry or needlepoint, is one of the most popular. The most obvious reason is that it is easy to learn. Many people who doubt their ability to master the subtleties of surface embroidery, or lack the patience for cutwork or drawn thread work, for example, find it reassuring to work over a regular, easily visible mesh of canvas threads. Moreover, the work is soothing. But as well as being a relaxing pastime, canvaswork is a versatile type of embroidery. It can be employed to make a variety of useful and decorative objects, from cushions to chair seats. When appropriate thread and stitches are used, such items can be very hardwearing.

Canvaswork is also appreciated for its aesthetic qualities and its potential for creating works of art. In the sixteenth and seventeenth centuries it was often used to imitate tapestries (woven wallhangings) and other woven textiles such as carpets (hence its misnomer, tapestry).

The basic canvaswork stitch is tent stitch. Because this readily lends itself to depicting fine detail, a great many of the canvaswork kits on the market use only this one stitch. Most are realistically pictorial in character. Enthusiastic practitioners of canvaswork are often unaware that any other stitch exists, which is a pity, since one of the main attractions of canvaswork is the marvellous variety of textures that can be achieved.

There are more than 200 canvaswork stitches, some of the most popular of which are shown on the following pages. Satiny effects can be produced with cushion stitch, for example; kelim stitch can give a smooth 'knitted' look, and double straight cross stitch creates a knobbly texture. By using an appropriate stitch it is possible to render the texture of a natural object, such as a pine cone or a weeping willow, much more effectively than through detailed shading with tent stitch alone; indeed, it is possible to create a whole picture or design using only one colour but different stitches.

The grid structure of the canvas and the square-based construction of the stitches will always impose some degree of angularity on the design, but there are ways in which this can be minimized. (See Compensating stitches, p. 131.)

As you will discover when you practise the various canvaswork stitches, most of them are easy to work and cover the canvas relatively quickly. Make a sampler of the stitches that appeal to you, and keep it to use as a reference when designing.

MATERIALS AND EQUIPMENT

Canvas There are two basic types of canvas: single thread, or mono, and double thread, or Penelope. Both come in various widths and are sold by the metre. Of the two, mono canvas is the more useful, since any stitch can be worked over it, and the threads are easier to count than the double strands of Penelope. Mono canvas comes in a wide range of gauges. The gauge of canvas (also called its size or mesh) is the number of threads it contains to 2.5 cm (actually 1 inch since gauge sizes have not yet been metricated). Mono canvas is generally available in gauges ranging from 10 to 24 threads to the inch.

A special kind of mono canvas called interlock is also sold in a few medium gauges. The threads of interlock canvas are actually twisted double threads, which are woven through each other in such a way that they cannot be dislocated. This makes interlock canvas especially suitable for work consisting of straight vertical stitches (such as Florentine work shown on pages 128–9), which have a tendency to slip under the mesh.

Double thread canvas has the advantage that the strands can be separated, if desired, and worked over individually, thus allowing a change of scale for the purpose of showing fine detail. This type of canvas is used for trammed (or tramé) work (see p. 125). To prevent confusion, the gauge of double thread canvas is often given as the number of holes, rather than threads, per inch, and sizes range from 7 to 20 holes per inch.

Rug canvas, suitable for large items such as rugs and wallhangings, is also constructed of double threads. Some is of the Penelope type, while in others the warp threads are twisted around pairs of weft threads to form an especially firm mesh. Rug canvas is available in 3, 5 and 7 gauge.

In the past embroidery canvas was traditionally made of linen, but it is now most often made of cotton, and sometimes of acrylic. Plastic canvas is also available. This is a stiff material which is moulded, rather than woven. It does not fray, and thus eliminates the need for hems. It is useful for rigid objects such as place mats and boxes.

Woven canvas is most commonly available in white or beige, though it sometimes comes in several other colours—shades of tan, yellow and white. The choice is usually a matter of personal preference. Some people find tan or yellow easier on the eyes, but others prefer white because they find the threads easier to count. Ideally, canvaswork stitches should cover the canvas completely, but certain stitches do leave small areas of the canvas visible. In such a case you may prefer to choose a colour that blends unobtrusively with your threads.

When choosing canvas, the main factor to consider is the quality, especially if the item being worked is one that will receive hard wear. Avoid buying canvas that contains knots or other flaws that might cause it to break in use.

Threads Crewel, Persian and tapestry wool are the yarns most often used for canvaswork (see p. 13). Of these, crewel is the most versatile, since it is the finest, and can be divided into strands, so that you can adjust the thickness of the working thread to suit the gauge of the canvas (see p. 124). Tapestry yarn is much less versatile, since it is usually too thick for canvas finer than 12 or 14 gauge, except for vertical stitches. Persian wool comes in a triple strand, and the individual strands, each slightly thicker than a strand of crewel, can be separated, making it almost as versatile as crewel. Both are hardwearing and so are well suited to chair seats, kneelers and other such items.

For large projects worked on rug canvas the obvious choice is rug yarn. This is a thick, single strand yarn made in various fibres, including wool and acrylic.

Cotton threads can also be used for canvaswork. The shiny varieties, such as stranded cotton and pearl cotton, give the work a definite sheen. These threads can either be used for the entire project or combined with wool threads to highlight parts of the design. Silk thread can be used in similar ways.

For purely decorative items you can be more adventurous in your choice of yarns. Some knitting yarns can be used successfully, as can crochet cottons, metal threads and raffia—in fact, anything you like. Pages 50–53 show some possibilities.

Needles and other equipment The needles used for canvaswork are called tapestry needles and have blunt points to prevent them from splitting the threads (see p. 12). They come in sizes ranging from 13 (the largest) to 24 (the smallest). Choose a needle that slips through the mesh easily, but is not so small that the eye frays your chosen thread.

You will also need a pair of dressmaking scissors for cutting canvas and fine embroidery scissors for cutting threads. A pair of tweezers is useful for unpicking bits of thread when removing a mistake. A waterproof marking pen, specially designed for use on canvas, should be used for tracing the design. A set square is ideal for checking that the canvas is square, but any right-angled object, such as a record album, will suffice.

PREPARING THE CANVAS

1 Cut the canvas at least 5 cm larger than the finished work on all sides. If you are working from a full-size design, the size of the finished work will, of course, be the same as the area of the drawing or tracing. If you are working from a chart, the finished work will probably be larger (or, in some cases, smaller) than the chart, and its size must be calculated. The box on page 128 will help you to make this calculation. Also, the method of preparing the canvas for charted designs is slightly different from that shown here (see p. 128).

When cutting canvas, always cut the vertical edges parallel to the selvedge (the firmly woven edges of the canvas), since this makes the work stronger.

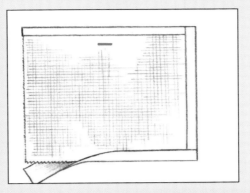 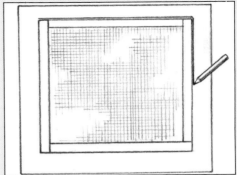

1 Mark the top of the canvas with pen or a thread so that you can be sure to place the design correctly.
2 Bind the cut edges with masking tape to prevent fraying. (Omit this step if you are mounting the work on a slate frame.)

3 Check that the corners of the canvas are square, and if not, pull the canvas gently into shape. Place the canvas on a piece of blotting paper or other tough paper and draw around the edges with a pencil. Save this template for use when blocking the finished work (see p. 136).

TRANSFERRING THE DESIGN

Pictorial and free abstract designs are best transferred to the canvas by tracing. The main lines, including the outlines of the design, are first darkened, which makes them visible through the mesh. The design is placed underneath the canvas and its outline then traced on to the canvas using a waterproof pen. When working the embroidery, you use the outline as a general guide and refer to the detailed plan for the colours and stitch patterns.

If the design is elaborate, with many colours, you may prefer to paint the colours on to the canvas. In this case, follow steps 1 and 2 (right), then paint in the colours using oil paint thinned to the right consistency with turpentine.

Some designs, especially the more geometric ones, are worked from charts (see p. 29 and pp. 128–9).

 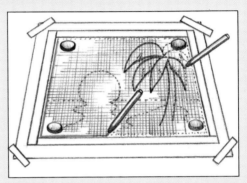

1 Darken the main lines of the design, including the edges, with a black felt-tipped pen. You can omit details and incorporate them later as you proceed with the work.
2 Tape the design on to a flat surface. (If the design is on tracing paper, place some opaque white paper under it.)

3 Tape or weight the canvas on top of the design, aligning the canvas threads with the edges of the design. Trace the outside edges on to the canvas, running the marking pen smoothly along the channel between two threads.
4 Now trace the main lines of the design itself. Trace any curved lines as curves; do not try to square them up to fit the canvas grid.

USING A FRAME

As a general rule it is best to work canvas embroidery on a frame. This can be either a slate frame or a stretcher frame (see pp. 66–7). A ring frame is not suitable, since it will not accommodate the stiff canvas.

The use of a frame will prevent the canvas threads from becoming distorted. New, unstitched canvas is stiff, because of the stiffener or size applied to it during manufacture, but when you start to handle and stitch it, it softens and the threads may slip out of alignment. This is particularly true if a strongly diagonal stitch, such as continental tent or slanted Gobelin, is used, or if you work with a firm tension. As a result, the finished piece will be warped, and blocking it to its original shape will be difficult, if not impossible.

However, there are some cases where a frame may not be necessary. For instance if the piece is small; if the stitches used entail working in different directions, so that a pull in one direction is balanced by a pull in the opposite one; or if you normally work with a relaxed and even tension. (Even in the last case, however, certain stitches will always require a frame.)

To mount canvas on to a stretcher frame, use the method shown on page 67, after first preparing the canvas and transferring the design as shown here. If you are using a slate frame, follow the method shown on page 67, but instead of hemming the side edges and inserting string, bind the edges with wide woven tape. Do this by folding the tape over the raw edge of the canvas and machine stitching or back stitching through all the layers.

MATCHING THREAD TO CANVAS

Before you buy all the thread for a project, make sure that it is suitable for the gauge of your canvas and for the stitches you are using, so that the thread will cover the canvas completely. (If you have decided to use a particular type of thread, you may prefer to match the canvas to the thread rather than vice versa.) The examples here are worked in basketweave tent stitch, each in a thread well suited to working this stitch on the particular canvas. Alternatives are given where appropriate. Bear in mind that a thicker thread—or more strands—may be needed for some stitches, especially vertical ones, and also that different brands of the same type of thread vary slightly in thickness. Work a sample of each stitch you plan to use before making a final decision on thread and canvas.

22 single: stranded cotton, 4 strands (shown); French crewel, 2 strands; coton à broder, 1 strand

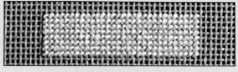

18 single: no. 5 pearl cotton, 1 strand (shown); coton à broder, 2 strands; stranded cotton, 6 strands; English crewel, 2 strands; Persian, 1 strand

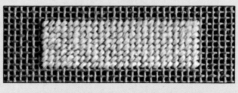

16 single: English crewel, 2 strands (shown); French crewel, 3 strands; stranded cotton, 6–7 strands

14 single: tapestry, 1 strand (shown); English crewel, 3 strands; French crewel, 3–4 strands; Persian, 2 strands

12 single: English crewel, 3 strands (shown); French crewel, 5 strands

10 double: Persian, 3 strands (shown); English crewel, 4 strands

ESTIMATING THREAD AMOUNTS

It is best to buy all the thread for a project at one time, to avoid variation in dye lots (although this will not matter much if areas of a particular colour are separated by other colours). Because some stitches need more thread than others to cover a given area, it is difficult to estimate precisely how much you will need. However, as a rough guide, 4 grams of crewel wool, used in three strands and worked in basketweave tent stitch on 14-gauge canvas, will cover 34 sq cm. Less will be required for most other stitches, but it is best to estimate generously; extra thread will always come in useful for a later project.

WORKING CANVASWORK STITCHES

If the canvaswork is being done on a frame, you must work with a stabbing movement, preferably using both hands, as shown on page 68. If you are working without a frame, you can use either the same stabbing method (with one hand) or a sewing movement, in which the needle is used as shown in the stitch illustrations.

Always take the needle up into an empty hole if possible. When the needle and thread are taken down into a partially filled hole, they smooth the fibres down; if brought up into it, the opposite happens. In some cases this is unavoidable, but the fewer threads in one hole, the less likelihood of their being split by the new stitch.

There are no general rules about the order in which to work the canvaswork rows, but there are several alternative approaches, depending on the design. If you start at the top and work down you will not be touching the stitched areas as you work, so they will receive less handling. On the other hand, if the design has a border it is a good idea to work the whole border first, as this will help to keep the work square. And if there are several colours, it makes sense to work one whole colour area at a time, preferably leaving the paler colours until the end.

Take care not to use so long a thread that it becomes frayed; as a general rule a length of crewel or Persian wool should measure no more than 50 cm. Move the needle along the thread occasionally to avoid weakening the yarn at the point where it is held in the eye. (For hints on threading the needle, see page 68. Left-handed readers should refer to the note on that page about direction of working.)

Note Throughout this section numbers are used, where necessary, to indicate the order of inserting the needle.

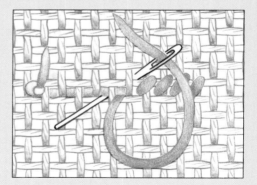

To begin work Knot the thread and take the needle through to the wrong side, a short distance ahead of the starting point. Work over the thread, then cut off the knot.

To end work (or to begin a new thread alongside some stitching) weave the thread through the stitches on the wrong side, as shown on page 68.

TENT STITCH

The basic stitch used in canvaswork is tent stitch. Some people call it petit point and refer to cross stitch or half cross stitch as gros point, but these two terms are properly applied to the size of the stitch (*petit* meaning small, and *gros* large), which is determined, of course, by the canvas gauge. In general petit point describes work containing more than 16 stitches per inch.

The names continental and basketweave refer to the two different ways of working tent stitch. The appearance of the stitch is the same on the right side, but continental tent is worked vertically or horizontally, whereas basketweave tent is worked diagonally. Basketweave tent is preferable, because it does not distort the canvas. But both stitches cover both sides of the canvas completely.

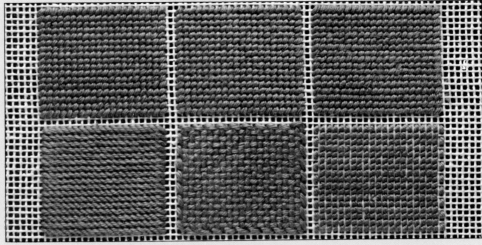

Continental tent, basketweave tent, half cross stitch seen from the front (top) and the back (below)

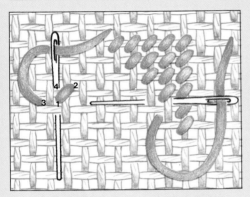

Continental tent stitch This stitch should be used sparingly, particularly if the work is not on a frame, since it tends to distort the canvas. Work in rows, either horizontally or vertically. On the second and following rows work as shown, so that the needle comes up through an empty hole. At the end of a row, either fasten off (see p. 68) or take the thread through to the wrong side of the work ready for the next row.

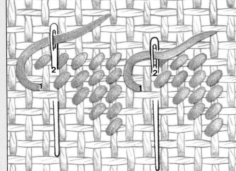

Satin stitch This variation of continental tent is worked over two or more threads. It can be combined with ordinary tent to give an interesting shantung-like texture to a background. Or it can be worked in various patterns and slanted in different directions.

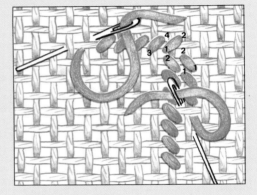

Basketweave tent stitch This stitch gets its name from the woven effect produced on the wrong side. It should be used in preference to continental tent wherever possible, since it does not distort the canvas. Begin at the upper right-hand corner (turn the work, if necessary), and work as shown, in diagonal lines alternately up and down.

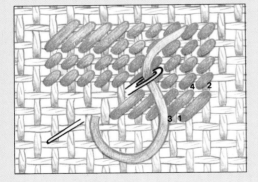

To turn a 90° corner Begin the next row one stitch up or down from where you would normally begin, at the edge of the worked area.

For a 45° angle, work the next row as if to continue the 90° angle, then on the following row work the last stitch just beside the first stitch of the previous one.

HALF CROSS STITCH OVER TRAMMING

Like tent stitch, half cross stitch covers one intersection on the right side to produce a small diagonal stitch, but on the wrong side the thread crosses only a single canvas thread. This makes half cross considerably weaker than tent stitch (although more economical) and thus unsuitable for any item that will receive hard wear. Also, the stitches have a tendency to slip under the mesh, and thus should only be used on interlock or double thread canvas.

Half cross is often used over tramming (or tramé). This is a method of laying horizontal threads along paired threads of Penelope canvas and then working over them. The resulting effect has a slightly ridged appearance. (Tramming may be done on single canvas, see p. 126.)

To tram the canvas Bring the yarn up between a pair of threads and take it down where the colour changes.

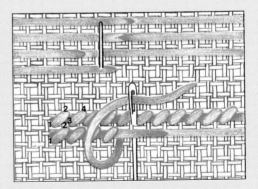

If the trammed line needs to be longer than 5 cm, secure the thread by taking it down and bringing it up behind the previous vertical thread as shown.

Using matching thread, work half cross stitch as shown over the tramming, bringing the needle up below the horizontal threads, taking it down diagonally over one intersection and up directly below.

125

VERTICAL STITCHES

The stitches illustrated on these two pages, though vertical in their structure, form horizontal patterns. The stitches are created by taking the thread vertically over the horizontal threads of the canvas (in two cases they are slanted and taken over one vertical thread also). They are all worked in rows. Despite the basic similarity in their formation, vertical stitches can be used to produce a range of different effects.

The Gobelin stitches are named after the famous Gobelins tapestry works in Paris, whose products they resemble. These stitches are well suited to backgrounds that require a stitch more textured than tent stitch, but do not demand a strong pattern. All of the Gobelin stitches lend themselves well to shaded effects, as does random straight stitch. Start with one colour at the top of the work and change gradually to lighter or darker shades in the following rows. One of the best stitches for shading is random straight stitch. This stitch is smooth and flat, making it ideal for backgrounds, yet it has an interesting texture because of the varied lengths of the individual stitches.

Regular patterns of vertical stitches can be created with brick stitch or Parisian stitch, while Hungarian and Hungarian diamond stitches both form diamond patterns.

A special category of vertical stitches, called Florentine work, or Bargello, is described and illustrated on pages 128–9.

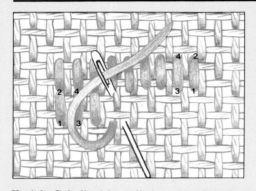

Upright Gobelin (also called straight Gobelin) This stitch has a strongly horizontal character and, if worked over only two threads, a ridged texture. Work in rows over two or more horizontal threads. The vertical canvas threads will show slightly between the rows, so use a fairly thick thread to cover them as far as possible.

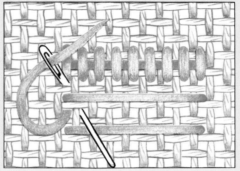

Upright Gobelin over tramming This method accentuates the ridged effect and prevents the canvas from showing through; it also produces a firmer fabric. Work the tramming (see p. 125) between alternate pairs of threads on single or double canvas, then work the upright Gobelin stitches over them.

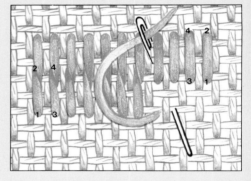

Encroaching Gobelin This form of Gobelin makes a smooth texture of interlocking stitches that covers the canvas completely.

Work in rows over three horizontal threads. On the second and following rows, the stitches are taken up into the previous row to the left of each stitch.

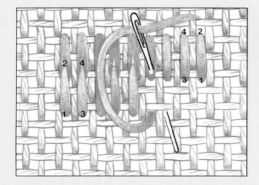

Split Gobelin This is essentially the same as encroaching Gobelin, except that the needle is taken down into the centre of the upper stitch, rather than to one side of it. Take care to insert the needle into the correct hole of the mesh each time. Split Gobelin is especially good for subtle shading effects.

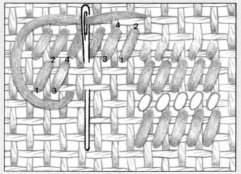

Encroaching slanted Gobelin This also gives a diagonal effect, and the stitches can slant to the right, as shown, or to the left. It must be worked on a frame. Work the stitch over three or more horizontal threads and one vertical thread. Here it is shown worked over five horizontal threads.

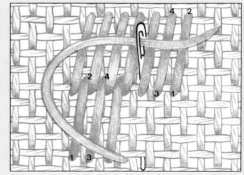

Slanted Gobelin This stitch gives a close fabric with a diagonal effect, and must be worked on a frame, otherwise it will distort the canvas. Work in rows over two or more horizontal threads and one vertical thread.
Variation Work a line of tent stitch between two rows, using contrasting thread.

Clockwise from top left: upright Gobelin, Hungarian, brick (over 2 and 4 threads), split Gobelin, random straight, encroaching slanted Gobelin, Parisian, Hungarian diamond, slanted Gobelin with tent, encroaching upright Gobelin

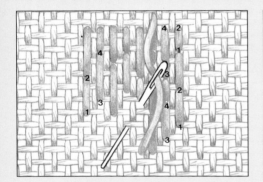

Random straight stitch Work in rows, varying the length of the stitches as desired, to create texture. Avoid ending two consecutive stitches between the same two horizontal threads. For extra-subtle shading, use two colours, working over a three-row grid: one colour for the upper row, and the other for the lower, with a mixture of the two colours in the needle for the intermediate row.

Brick stitch Work over two horizontal threads in a zigzag pattern as shown, working back and forth across the canvas. For a more strongly vertical effect, work the stitches over four threads instead of two. When all the rows have been worked, fill in the gaps at the top and bottom with short vertical stitches.

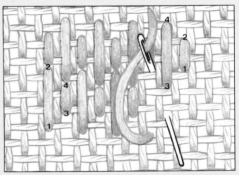

Parisian stitch Work in rows, making the stitches go over two and four threads alternately. For a two-colour effect, work all the long stitches in one colour, and the short stitches in another colour. Fill in the gaps at top and bottom with appropriate colours to maintain the pattern.

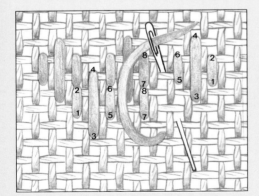

Hungarian stitch Work this stitch in groups of three, one long and two short, across the canvas, leaving one hole between each group. On the second and following rows, work back across the canvas, filling in the gaps as shown. For a two-colour effect, work alternate rows in different colours.

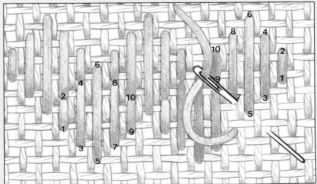

Hungarian diamond stitch This is a larger-scale version of Hungarian stitch, and also lends itself to two-colour patterns. It is worked in groups of five, with the longest, central stitch crossing six threads. These longer stitches make the work slightly less durable than Hungarian stitch.

FLORENTINE WORK

The type of canvaswork known as Florentine or Bargello, consists of upright stitches arranged in steps to form zigzag or curved repeat patterns. This work was brought to a high degree of refinement in sixteenth-century Florence—hence the name. Its alternative designation is derived from the Bargello Palace in Florence, which contained some particularly fine examples.

Today Florentine work retains an enormous popularity. The stitch is simple and covers the canvas quickly, and the number of effects that can be created is virtually infinite. Also, it is easy to design your own embroideries in Florentine work once you understand the few simple principles of forming the pattern lines.

There are two main categories of Florentine pattern, row designs and motif designs. In a row design all the rows are identical and repeat a regular colour sequence. The pattern might consist of zigzags, curves or a combination of the two. All the stitches are the same length —except in the case of Hungarian point designs (see opposite).

In a motif design the basic unit is a medallion shape. This might be a lozenge, an oval, a honeycomb cell or even a stylized flower. Often the upper and lower outlines of the shape form a mirror image.

Either of these two types of design can be adapted to form four-way Florentine patterns (see p. 29). In these patterns a square is divided into four triangles and the repeat worked to fill each triangle so that it radiates out from the centre.

The finished effect of a piece of Florentine work is determined not only by the arrangement of the stitches but also by the choice of colours. Vividly contrasting colours can be used for dramatic impact, or several shades of one colour for a restful effect. One of the most striking types of Florentine pattern, called flame stitch, uses both shading and sharp contrasts to enhance its dramatic lines.

Florentine work is suitable for many different items, including cushions, spectacle cases, chair seats and evening bags. If the item will receive hard wear, it is best to avoid using stitches more than four canvas threads deep, otherwise there is a risk of snagging. A hardwearing yarn, such as crewel or Persian, is a better choice than tapestry wool. For purely decorative objects, the choice of thread is wider.

WORKING FROM A CHART

Designs made up of repeating patterns, such as Florentine work, are not traced on to the canvas, as described on page 123, but worked from a chart. Published designs for canvaswork are generally presented in chart form, since this method saves space (the chart is usually considerably smaller than the finished work) and enables the embroiderer to copy the original exactly.

Where a design consists of a repeating pattern, only the basic repeat will usually be given on the chart. It can easily be duplicated the required number of times both across the canvas and up and down it. Designs consisting of a single symmetrical motif may have only one half (or one quarter) charted; the design is completed by working a mirror image of the chart.

The two basic types of chart, line charts and box charts, are discussed on page 28. Line charts are used for Florentine work; box charts for designs worked in tent stitch.

PREPARING THE CANVAS

Before you cut the canvas, check the size of the finished work—this is usually given in the instructions. But you may wish to use a canvas with a different gauge to the one recommended, in which case you must count the number of lines across and down the chart and divide the result by the gauge of your canvas. For example, if there are 96 lines both across and down on the chart, and you are using 16-gauge canvas, the finished area will be 15 cm square, 96 ÷ 16, being 6 in (canvas gauge has not yet been metricated).

Use a single thread canvas for Florentine work.

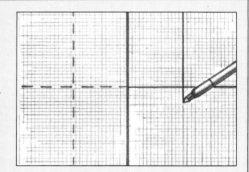

1 Cut the canvas to the required size (finished size plus at least 5 cm all around). Mark the top and bind the edges with masking tape as described on page 123. Mount the canvas on the frame, if you are using one.
2 If the centre of the chart is not already marked, find it by drawing two straight lines through the middle. Mark the exact centre of the canvas with tacking or a waterproof marking pen.

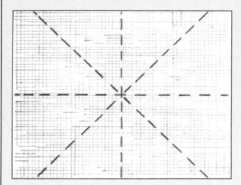

For a four-way Florentine design Mark the canvas on the diagonal, between opposite corners, with tacking, keeping the stitches fairly small to avoid straying off the true diagonal. Remove the tacking as you work.

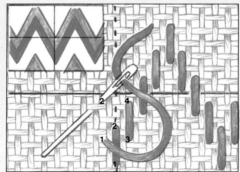

3 Begin stitching at the centre. For a row design you can choose any row, working to the right or left of the centre, then to the other side. Refer to the chart frequently to ensure accuracy.

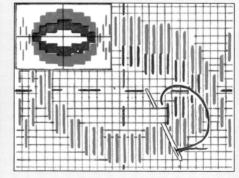

For a Florentine motif design Work the upper and lower framework, starting at the centre and working outward, then fill in the spaces, referring to the chart frequently. For a four-way design, choose a dominant line near the centre and work it first, then fill in the centre and surrounding area.

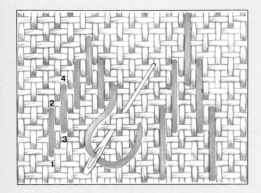

Basic Florentine stitch Zigzags are formed by taking stitches up over three or more threads with 'steps' between stitches. The step is the number of threads left between the base of adjacent stitches. Expressed numerically, the first number denotes stitch length, the second step. The example on the left is 4.2, on the right 6.4.

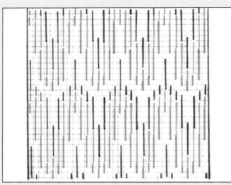

Hungarian point A distinctive spiky pattern is produced by using two lengths of stitch in a regular sequence, as shown. The short stitches normally cover two threads, the long ones four or six. In every vertical line two long and two short stitches alternate for the entire length.

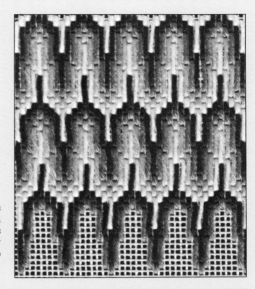

TYPICAL FLORENTINE PATTERNS

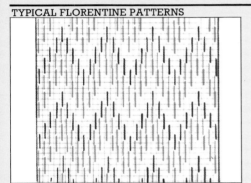

Flame stitch In its simplest form this pattern consists of even zigzag lines worked in a shaded colour sequence such as the one shown here. These stitches follow a 3.2 formation.

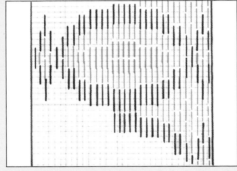

Oval medallions Like other curved designs, these are formed with blocks of stitches. The 'frame' of this oval is made up of stitches four canvas threads deep. Inside and outside the frame, the stitch length varies.

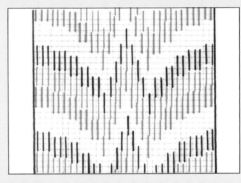

Zigzags and curves The combination of these makes some of the most dramatic Florentine designs. Here again, shading is used to heighten the effect. The stitches are all four threads deep.

CROSSED STITCHES

There are many different crossed stitches in the canvaswork repertoire. Most of them give the work a knobbly texture and so contrast effectively with flatter or smoother stitches, such as tent (see p. 125) or cushion (see p. 132). Some of them also combine well with each other: for example, large cross stitches worked over four threads can be interspersed with upright cross, as shown in the photograph. The stitches can be worked in two different colours for a lattice effect.

Two colours can also be combined in the same stitch, thus transforming its appearance. If worked in one colour, rice stitch, for example, produces a rough-textured fabric with no strong pattern, but if the corner stitches are worked in a contrasting thread, a lattice pattern emerges. Similarly, Smyrna stitch in one colour

forms a square, bumpy texture; but if a different colour is used for the vertical cross on top, an upright grid pattern is produced.

Some crossed stitches have a horizontal or vertical character (depending on the direction of working); long-armed cross and herringbone fall into this category. Both produce a plaited effect. Two colours can also be used effectively in herringbone stitch to bring out its zigzag structure.

Another way of adapting some of these stitches is to use only one colour but to work part of the stitch in a matt-finish thread and part in shiny thread. This technique is illustrated in the sample of double straight cross stitch and rice stitch in the photograph. When working a design, you could highlight a small part of an area in this way, leaving most of the

stitches in the matt thread.

You can also vary the scale of some of these stitches. Rhodes stitch, for example, could be worked over six threads in part of the design and over three elsewhere. This is a good way to achieve unity and variety at the same time.

Practise these stitches using different threads and combinations of threads and working them, where possible, in different sizes, to see some of the endless variety of effects you can create.

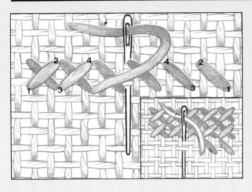

Cross stitch Work in rows, horizontally or vertically, taking two diagonal stitches over two or more canvas threads in each direction. For an even tension, and to ensure that all the top stitches slant the same way, you can work a whole row in two stages. Cross stitch can also be worked over one mesh on double canvas, as in the inset.

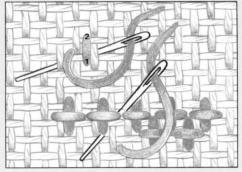

Upright cross stitch This small stitch creates a firm, pebble-textured fabric on its own, or it can be used in conjunction with other cross stitches.

Work in rows as shown, completing each cross before starting the next.

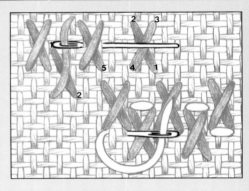

Alternating oblong cross stitch These stitches are formed like ordinary cross stitches, but are twice as tall as they are wide. They do not cover the canvas well if worked in rows, but if staggered, as shown, they make an excellent background. Back stitch may be used in conjunction with these stitches to help cover the canvas threads.

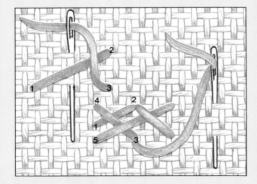

Long-armed cross stitch Also called long-legged cross, this stitch produces a plaited effect.

Work in rows, from left to right or right to left, over three horizontal and six vertical threads. For a neat edge, begin and end the rows by shortening the 'arm' as shown.

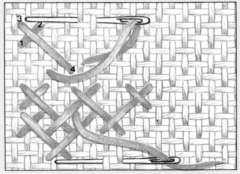

Herringbone stitch This is formed like the same stitch in surface stitchery (see p. 73), but rows are worked close together for an interlaced look.

Work in rows, always in the same direction, taking the short stitch (1–2) over two horizontal threads and the long stitch (3–4) over four. Be careful not to split the stitches in the row above. Fill in any gaps at the top with cross stitches.

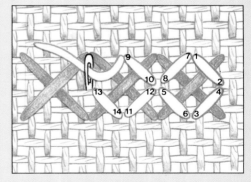

Rice stitch Also called crossed corners or William and Mary stitch, this is worked in two stages.

First work ordinary cross stitches, but over four horizontal and four vertical threads. Then work four stitches, in the order shown, over the legs of each cross.

A finer, or contrasting, thread is often used for the small stitches.

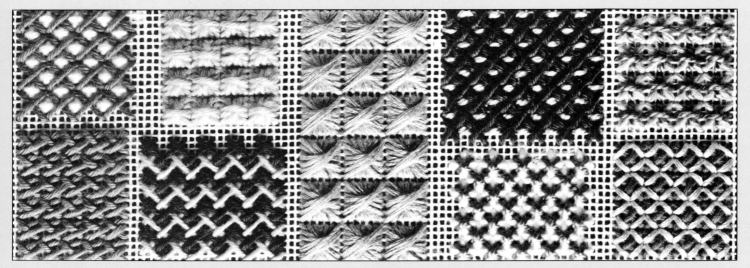

Clockwise from top left: cross and upright cross, double leviathan, Rhodes, alternating oblong, Smyrna, rice, double straight, herringbone, long-armed cross

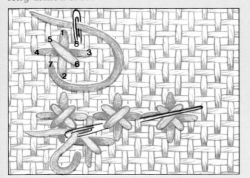

Double straight cross stitch This is a highly textured, firm stitch with a diagonal character. Work an upright cross stitch over four threads (1–2, 3–4). Then work an ordinary cross stitch on top (5–6, 7–8).

Work in rows, fitting each row into the spaces left in the previous row.

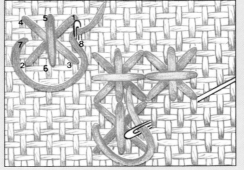

Smyrna stitch Also known as leviathan or double cross, this stitch has a square, bumpy texture but does not cover the canvas thoroughly. It is effective worked in two colours, which makes an attractive grid pattern.

Work a cross stitch over four threads (1–2, 3–4), then work an upright cross on top (5–6, 7–8). If desired, the top stitch of the cross can be vertical instead of horizontal.

Double leviathan stitch Similar to Smyrna stitch, this covers the canvas better. Use a relatively thin thread to prevent the centre from becoming too bulky.

First work a cross stitch over four threads (1–2, 3–4). Then work two intersecting stitches over each arm of the cross (5–6, 7–8, 9–10, 11–12). Finally, work an upright cross on top (13–14, 15–16).

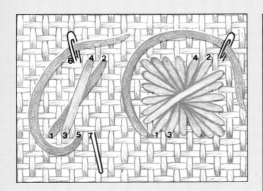

Rhodes stitch This simple stitch, named after the English embroiderer who invented it, forms small pyramids on the canvas.

Work over a square of three or more threads (six are used here), working anti-clockwise, and moving one vertical thread to the right at the bottom and one thread to the left at the top, for each stitch. Continue in this way until the square is filled; end with a long diagonal stitch.

COMPENSATING STITCHES

The grid structure of canvas and the angularity of canvaswork stitches can pose a problem when the embroiderer attempts to fill a curved shape. The solution is to fill in awkward corners with 'compensating' stitches. These are part of, or scaled-down versions of, the stitch being used within a certain area. There are no 'official' compensating stitches that correspond to the full-size ones; the embroiderer must use her own judgement.

Where possible, work half (or a third, or a quarter, etc.) of the stitch being used. You can sometimes miniaturize the stitch, or use a smaller stitch that resembles it in some way. For example, upright cross stitch might be used to fill in gaps along the edges of Smyrna stitch.

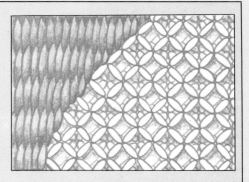

The illustration shows work done in rice stitch and encroaching slanted Gobelin (see p. 126), with tent stitch and various other compensating stitches used to fill in the curves. Tent stitches can always be used to cover any few remaining bare canvas threads.

131

SQUARE STITCHES

Many, if not most, canvaswork stitches are square, because of the structure of the canvas, but certain stitches have squareness as their dominating characteristic, and the patterns they form make them especially suitable for depicting stonework or tiling.

Scottish stitch, for example, is ideally suited to windows, particularly if the surrounding tent stitches are worked in a darker thread, while weaving stitch realistically suggests basketweave. Cushion stitch (also called flat stitch or satin stitch squares) is perhaps the most versatile of these. It has a pleasing texture and makes an interesting yet unobtrusive background. Brighton stitch, a variation of cushion stitch, softens the gridlike pattern by cutting off the corners and placing an upright cross at the intersections.

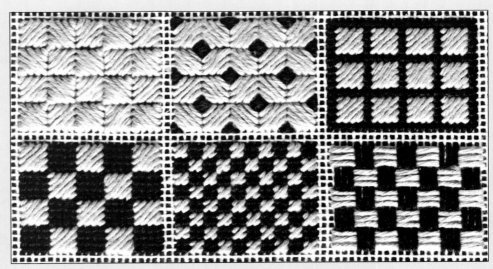

Clockwise from top left: cushion, Brighton, Scottish, weaving, small chequer, large chequer

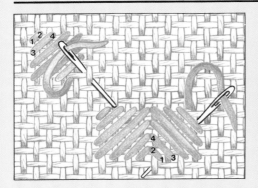

Cushion stitch Make blocks by working stitches diagonally as shown, over one, two, three and four, then three, two and one intersection(s). Change the direction of working in alternate squares or, to vary the stitch, work all the squares in the same direction.

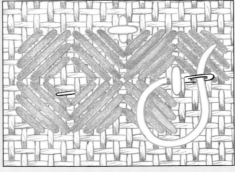

Brighton stitch Work as for cushion stitch, but omit the first and last stitches over one intersection.

Fill in the resulting spaces with upright cross stitches (see p. 130) in a shiny thread or contrasting colour.

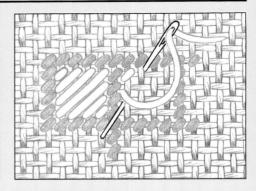

Scottish stitch This can be worked over different numbers of threads. Here the centre squares are worked over four vertical and horizontal threads.

First work a grid of continental tent stitches (see p. 125), spacing the lines four threads apart. Then fill in the spaces with diagonal stitches as shown.

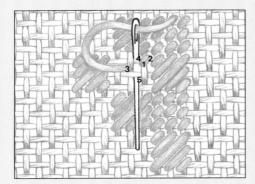

Large chequer stitch In this stitch, squares of satin stitch alternate with those of tent stitch.

Work the satin stitch squares in diagonal rows from upper left to lower right, working the central thread over three canvas threads, as shown, or over four. Then fill in the remaining squares with basketweave tent stitch (see p. 125).

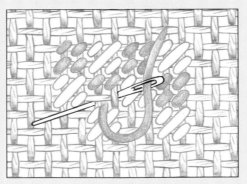

Small chequer stitch In this scaled-down version of chequer, the squares emerge only if worked in two colours.

Work as for large chequer stitch, completing the satin stitch squares first, then filling in with the tent stitches.

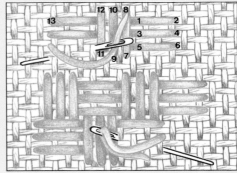

Weaving stitch Work groups of three straight stitches over four threads, alternating the direction as shown, and working back and forth in rows across the canvas.

To emphasize the woven effect, use two colours: one for the horizontal and one for the vertical stitches.

DIAGONAL STITCHES

The stitches shown on this page all give a strongly diagonal character to the work. The effect can be subdued, as in small diagonal mosaic, or bold and striking, as in Moorish, Byzantine and jacquard. The steps in Byzantine and jacquard can be emphasized by using contrasting colours for different rows, or they can be softened by the use of graduated shades of the same colour. For jagged stripes, try working Milanese stitch in two colours. These large-scale stitches need to be worked over a correspondingly large area for their patterns to emerge.

The diagonal mosaic stitches work well in smaller areas, but can also be used in larger ones. Attractive narrow diagonal stripes can be produced by working small diagonal mosaic in two or more contrasting colours, as shown in the photograph.

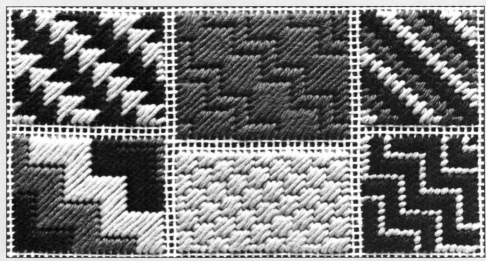

Clockwise from top left: Milanese, jacquard, small mosaic, Moorish, large mosaic, Byzantine

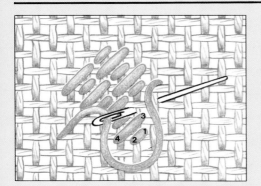

Small diagonal mosaic stitch Work up and down diagonally across the canvas, working stitches over one and two intersections alternately.

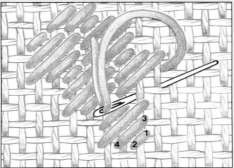

Large diagonal mosaic stitch This is basically the same as the small version, but worked over a maximum of three intersections (going over one, two, three and then two and one). Worked in a single colour it has a 'honeycomb' appearance.

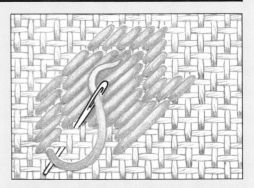

Moorish stitch This stitch consists of diagonal rows of stitches, worked from top left to bottom right and covering two, three, four, five and six intersections, alternating with 'steps' of satin stitch (see p. 125) worked over two threads.

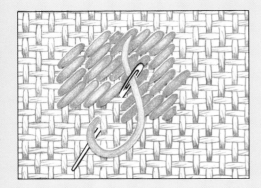

Byzantine stitch This consists of regular steps of satin stitch (see p. 125), arranged to form a zigzag pattern. Here each horizontal and each vertical step is four stitches wide (counting the corner stitch twice), but the basic pattern can be varied by increasing the number and depth of the stitches.

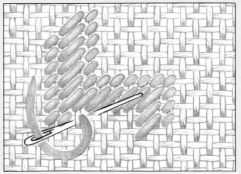

Jacquard stitch This is similar to Byzantine, but the satin stitches are separated by rows of continental tent stitch (see p. 125). To maintain the correct method of working the tent stitch, you will need to bring the needle up on alternate sides of the step as shown.

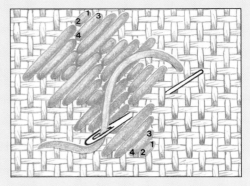

Milanese stitch Diagonal rows of interlocking triangles form this stitch, which creates an intriguing brocaded effect.

Work up and down the canvas alternately, working over one, two, three and four intersections, and fitting each row into the edges of the preceding one.

VERTICAL PATTERN STITCHES

With one exception, all the stitches on this page form strongly vertical patterns. They contrast with those given on pages 126–7 which, although vertical in their structure, actually form horizontal patterns. The exception is leaf stitch which, as its name indicates, forms pretty leaf-shaped motifs, perfect for depicting foliage. What it has in common with the others is that it is formed mainly by working diagonal stitches in vertical rows.

Kelim stitch, also called knitted stocking stitch, has the finest 'grain' of all these stitches, and makes a smooth, firm fabric. Stem stitch is a wider version of kelim with (usually) a line of back stitch worked between alternate rows. Fishbone and fern stitches form plaited effects on the canvas.

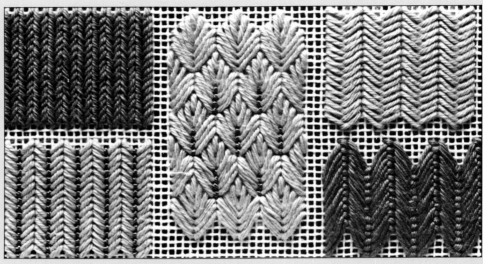

Clockwise from top left: kelim, leaf, fern, fishbone, stem

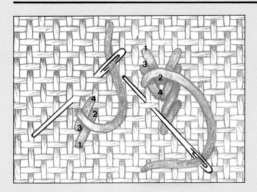

Kelim stitch This stitch is worked over one vertical and two horizontal threads. Begin at the lower right-hand corner and work up and down, changing the slant of the stitches in alternating rows as shown.

The stitch may be worked horizontally if preferred.

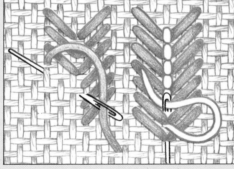

Stem stitch This stitch consists of slanting stitches worked in vertical rows.

Begin at the lower right-hand corner and work up and down over two vertical and horizontal threads, as shown. Then work back stitch between alternate rows where the stitches point downward, using a contrasting thread if wished.

Fern stitch Like stem stitch, this stitch gives a pleasing ridged effect. Begin at the top and work each row downward as shown, working each complete stitch over three vertical and two horizontal threads.

A flatter, wider effect can be obtained by working over five vertical threads.

Fishbone stitch This attractive pattern consists of long diagonal stitches worked over three canvas intersections crossed by short stitches.

Start at the upper left-hand corner and work alternately down, then up, slanting the second row of stitches in the opposite direction. Take care to work the short stitches over just one intersection; finding the correct hole can be tricky.

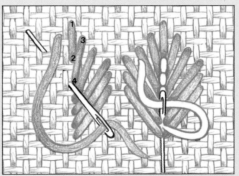

Leaf stitch Begin with the centre stitch (1–2), placing it between the third and fourth vertical threads from the edge of the area to be filled. Then work each side. On subsequent rows, take care to place the stitches accurately.

Leaf stitches can be used in blocks or as individual motifs, and lines of back stitch may be added to suggest stems.

TIED STITCHES

The three stitches shown below are each formed by 'tying' or 'holding' a longer strand or loop in place with a short stitch.

Knotted Gobelin is the simplest of the three, consisting of rows of long diagonal encroaching stitches held in place with half cross stitches. It can be worked in two or more colours, as shown.

Rococo stitch consists of groups of four vertical stitches, each secured in the centre with a short horizontal stitch, forming an oval shape.

Velvet stitch is one of several canvaswork stitches that duplicate the pile of a woven carpet. When working velvet stitch, keep the loops even and hold them in place by working them over a knitting needle; hold the needle just below the stitching, as shown below. The loops may be trimmed evenly or left uncut.

Clockwise from top left: square eyelets, diamond eyelets, velvet (uncut), Rococo, knotted Gobelin, velvet (cut), ray, star-shaped eyelets with back stitch

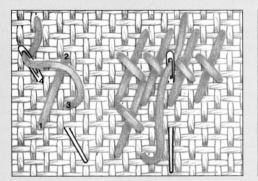

Knotted Gobelin Work in rows from left to right, starting at the top.

Take each stitch up over six horizontal and two vertical threads, then work a half cross stitch over the centre of it as shown.

On subsequent rows, begin four threads down and work into the spaces left above.

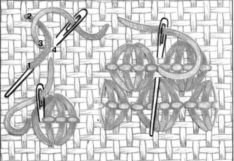

Rococo stitch Work four vertical stitches from bottom to top over four threads. After pulling each one through (gently), work a back stitch over the centre of it. On subsequent rows, skip one thread; this gives the stitch a better shape. If the canvas shows, cover it with back stitches.

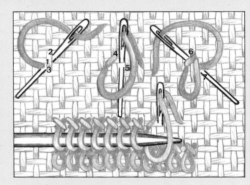

Velvet stitch Work a stitch over one intersection (1–2) and bring the needle up again (3) in the first hole. Leaving a loop, take the needle down again (at 4) in the same hole as 2. Bring it up to the right of the loop, one thread down, at 5 and work a diagonal stitch (5–6). Bring the needle up into position for the next stitch at 7 (being the same hole as 5).

Work the next row above, missing one thread.

EYELET STITCHES

The stitches in this group are formed by working a number of individual stitches into the same hole, to produce a radiating effect. One of them, ray stitch, is really one quarter of a square eyelet.

The larger the eyelet, the more difficult it is to place the stitches smoothly so that they do not overlap at the hole. It is often helpful to enlarge the hole first by inserting a point such as a fine knitting needle into it. Always work all the stitches down into the hole, bringing the thread up at the edge. In order to fit all the stitches into the hole, it might be necessary to use a finer thread than normal for canvaswork, which may leave the canvas visible at the edges. In this case, back stitch may be worked between the eyelets if appropriate to the design. A certain amount of experimenting is often necessary to get the right effect.

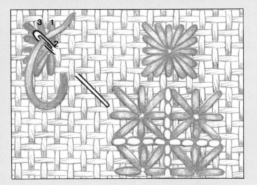

Square eyelet Start at the top edge and work either clockwise or anti-clockwise around a square of four threads, working into each hole as shown.

When moving to the next row, take the thread under the stitches on the wrong side to avoid crossing the hole.

For a star shape Work into every alternate hole. Add back stitch at the edges if desired.

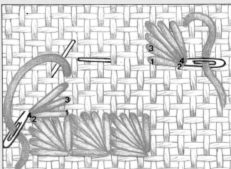

Ray stitch This is also called fan stitch.

Start with the bottom row and work upward, beginning with a horizontal stitch (1–2).

Work over a square of three threads, taking the needle down into every hole on two adjacent sides. The direction of the stitches can be reversed on alternate rows for a different texture.

If you have spent considerable time and care in working a piece of embroidery, it would be shortsighted to give insufficient attention to the finishing stages. Many fine pieces of stitching are spoiled by inept or careless finishing and making up. Inadequate blocking, wobbly seams and lumpy corners can become obvious, to the detriment of the embroidery itself.

A simple solution to these problems is to take the embroidery to a shop that offers a making up service, although this can be expensive. In the case of a complex project, such as a pair of slippers or a handbag that will be mounted on a frame, it may be well worthwhile paying for a professional finish, but simple articles such as cushions, wallhangings and panels are relatively easy to make up yourself.

It is wise to plan the making up before you begin work on a project, since your design decisions may be influenced by the availability of certain fabrics, trimmings and other items. If you are making a cushion, for example, you should find out whether the required size of cushion pad is available. Buy the pad at the outset so that you will have it when you need it.

Before mounting embroidery for a panel (see p. 138) discuss the framing with a professional framer. (Do not attempt the framing itself unless you are experienced in this craft.) Decide whether you want the work surrounded by a mount. If no suitable colour of cardboard mount is available, you may prefer to double-mount the panel on a fabric-covered board, as shown on page 138.

Making up embroidered clothing requires some knowledge and expertise in dressmaking, explanation of which lies beyond the scope of this book. The crucial thing to remember is that the embroidery should usually be worked before the garment section is cut out accurately, unless you are following a pattern that specifies otherwise. To position embroidery, lightly mark the outline and seamline of the piece on the fabric with tailor's chalk. If the work is quilting, you will need to add about 5cm all around to allow for the fabric taken up by the quilting itself. The closer and more numerous the lines of quilting stitches, the greater the take-up will be.

If the embroidery has been worked on a frame, leave it on the frame until you are ready to make it up. It will thus remain in good condition and require little, if any, pressing or blocking. (If it has become soiled, either wash it gently in cool soapy water or have it dry cleaned.)

BLOCKING SURFACE STITCHERY

The process of blocking, or stretching, is the technique of smoothing a completed piece of stitchery, removing creases and restoring the fabric's shape. If the work has been done on a slate or stretcher frame it may need only a light pressing, but if it has been worked on a ring frame or looks at all puckered it should be wet blocked.

Materials You will need a piece of plywood or hardboard at least 5cm larger than the embroidery, a sheet of blotting paper slightly larger than the fabric, adhesive tape, drawing pins or carpet tacks (for plywood or hardboard respectively), a set square, hammer and pliers.

1 Tape the blotting paper to the board.
2 Immerse the embroidery in cold water, then gently squeeze out (do not wring).

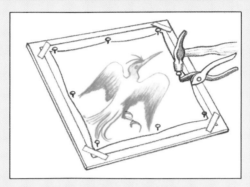

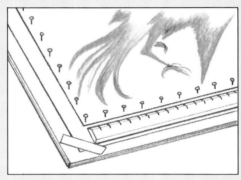

3 Place the embroidery right side up on the board on top of the blotting paper. Pin or tack each corner to the board, checking each one with the set square to make sure it is square.
4 Tack or pin the fabric at the centre of each side, placing the first two pins or tacks opposite each other. Use pliers, if necessary, to pull the fabric taut.

5 Continue pinning or tacking, always placing each tack opposite the last, and checking with a ruler to make sure the edges are straight. The pins or tacks should be about 1.2cm apart.
6 Allow the work to dry thoroughly before removing it from the board.

BLOCKING CANVASWORK

Canvaswork should always be blocked. If the work has been done in the hand it will almost certainly be distorted, and even work done on a frame will benefit from the freshening effect of the blocking process.
Materials These are basically the same as for blocking surface stitchery, plus a spray bottle and a wet cloth or sponge. First mark an outline of the entire canvas on blotting paper. Measure two adjacent sides of the work and use a ruler and set square to draw the square or rectangle.

1 Tape the blotting paper to the board.
2 Check the canvas to make sure no stitches are missing by holding it up to the light. Trim the thread ends closely on the wrong side.
3 If there is a selvedge, slash it at intervals of about 4cm in to prevent puckering.
   If you have bound the edges of the canvas with masking tape, do not remove it.

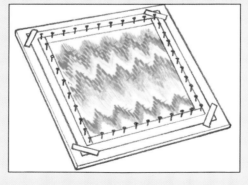

4 Place the work right side down on the board if the stitching is fairly flat and right side up if highly textured. Moisten it slightly.
5 Pin or tack it in place within the drawn outline, corners first, pulling it to fit. Tack through the tape, placing the tacks about 1.2cm apart.
6 Wet the work thoroughly and leave it to dry.

PRESSING

Certain kinds of embroidery, such as cutwork, drawn thread, pulled work, appliqué and smocking are never blocked. However, depending on whether or not the work has been done on a frame, such embroidery may need pressing.

A light touch is essential for pressing embroidery. It should always be pressed from the wrong side and placed over a clean, folded, thick towel to cushion the stitches. Use either a steam iron or a dry iron over a damp cloth, set to a temperature suitable for the fabric. Apply the iron gently for a moment, then lift it off and apply it to the adjacent area; do **not** move it back and forth as in ironing. In some cases it is sufficient to hold the iron just above the fabric and let the steam do all the work.

Metal thread embroidery requires no pressing, since it is always worked held perfectly taut on a frame.

WALLHANGINGS

A wallhanging is easy to make up. Only basic sewing skills are required, but it is important to make sure that the embroidery fabric and the lining lie smoothly together. For the lining, choose a firmly woven fabric such as a furnishing cotton or dupion, lighter than the embroidery.

Materials Besides the lining fabric, you will need sewing thread to match the embroidery fabric. For hanging the work you can either use two lengths of dowelling, one 3cm longer than the upper edge, and some cord, **or** a strip of Velcro to fit across the finished wallhanging, a batten the same length and a length of curtain weights for the lower edge. The size of dowelling or batten will depend on the weight and nature of the finished embroidery, but 1cm is suitable for most purposes.

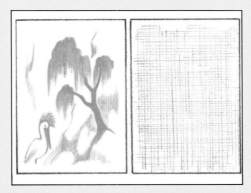

For a small or medium-sized wallhanging
1 Trim the embroidery to measure 1.2cm more all around than the finished size.
2 Cut the lining to the same size as the embroidery.

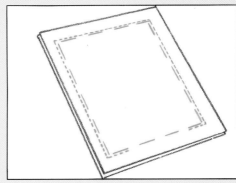

3 Place the embroidery and lining with right sides together. Pin and then tack around all four edges.
4 Machine stitch or back stitch by hand 1.2cm from the edge. Leave about 10cm open on the lower edge for turning.

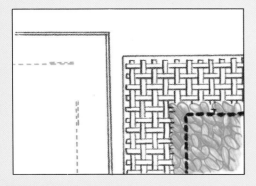

If 1cm dowelling is to be inserted, leave a gap of 2cm in the stitching at each corner, as shown.
For canvaswork embroidery, stitch just inside the edges of the embroidered area to prevent any canvas threads from showing. A line of tent stitch can be added first, if necessary, to avoid spoiling the design.

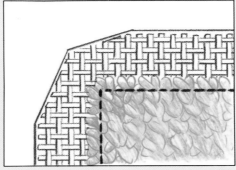

5 Trim the seam allowance to 5mm, or 1cm for canvaswork, tapering the corners as shown. Turn to right side; poke out the corners. Insert curtain weights, if using.
6 Press the edges flat; work on the lining side and push the stitching out to the edge.
7 Close the edges of the gap with slip stitch.

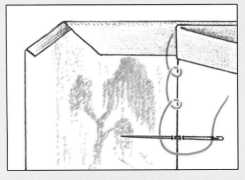

For a large wallhanging
1 Prepare the two fabrics as in steps 1 and 2 above.
2 Press under 1.2cm on all edges of both fabrics, mitring the corners as shown.
3 Place the fabrics wrong sides together. Fold back the lining along the centre. Work lock stitch loosely through both fabrics.

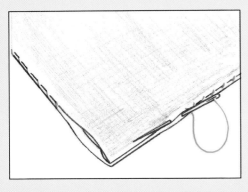

4 Tack and slip stitch the fabrics together around the top and side edges, leaving gaps for the dowelling, if used.
5 Hang up the work and leave it for a few days to 'settle' (it may stretch a little) before finishing the bottom edge.

For hanging with dowelling Slip the dowelling through the gaps; tie the cord to the upper length.
For hanging with Velcro Separate the Velcro strips and glue the stiffer one to the batten; fix the batten to the wall. Slip stitch the softer Velcro strip to the hanging.

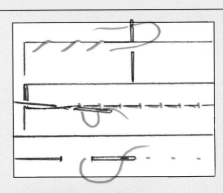

SOME USEFUL STITCHES
Oversewing (top) is used to neaten raw edges.
Slip stitch (centre) is used for hemming and for joining two folded edges.
Prick stitch (above) is a variation of back stitch used for inconspicuous top stitching.

PANELS

An embroidered panel can be framed with or without a mount, or can be sewn to a fabric-covered board, see below. Ideally, it should not be covered with glass, which detracts from its tactile quality, but if it is likely to become damaged by dirt, as in a city home, it should be glazed.

Before framing, the embroidery is mounted on a board, as shown here. For a smooth effect, cover the board first with flannelette or thin wadding. (This is not necessary for canvaswork.)

Materials You will need a piece of stiff cardboard or thin hardboard the size of the finished work, plus a small allowance to fit under the frame rebate if you do not want to lose any of the design. To cover the board first you will also need a piece of flannelette 3cm larger all around than the board, as well as fabric glue and strong thread.

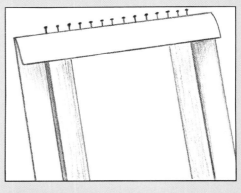

To cover the board
1 Apply thin strips of glue close to the edges on the wrong side of the board.
2 Place the board, glue side up, on the flannelette and fold the fabric edges over it, mitring the corners, as shown. Allow the glue to dry thoroughly.

To lace the embroidery
1 Centre the board on the wrong side of the work. Fold the upper edge over the board and fasten with pins inserted through the edge into the fabric or cardboard. (If using hardboard, tacks may be needed.) Turn and fasten the lower edge in the same way, making sure that the embroidery lies straight.

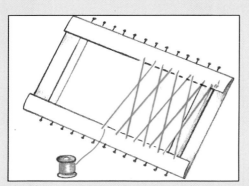

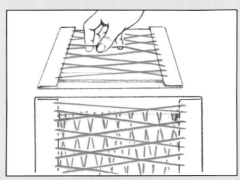

2 Leaving the thread on the reel, and starting in the centre, work herringbone stitch between the two edges out to one side. Fasten off securely.
3 Measure off and cut through enough thread to reach the opposite side and stitch as before, but do not fasten off.

4 Remove the pins or tacks. Starting at the fastened end, pull each thread firmly to tension the fabric evenly. Fasten off the remaining end.
5 Fold over the side edges, pin them in place, and lace them together in the same way.

To double mount a panel
1 Cover a board with fabric, as for the panel itself, and to the same size.
2 Slip stitch the turned corners.
3 Sew the panel to the mount fabric using a curved upholstery needle.
Fabric-covered or cardboard window mounts are also ideal for panel display.

NEATENING CANVAS EDGES

If the edges of a piece of canvaswork are not to be seamed or laced over a board, they must be turned under and neatened in some way. In many cases the edges are simply turned under and pressed, then a lining stitched or glued to the wrong side.

Leather, or the various imitation leathers and suedes, make excellent linings for some articles, such as coasters, belts and bags, since the edges of these materials do not need finishing, thus preventing excess bulk. The lining is simply cut to the finished size and either applied to the wrong side of the embroidery with fabric glue or sewn in place with small oversewing stitches.

Woven fabrics are sewn to the canvas in the same way, with the edges turned under. First trim the canvas edges to 2cm and press them firmly to the wrong side, using a steam iron or a dry iron over a damp cloth.

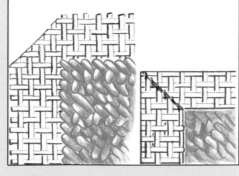

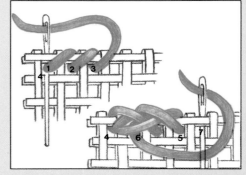

To mitre a corner
1 Trim across the corner, leaving two canvas meshes between the cut edge and the work.
2 Fold the cut edge over the corner and press.
3 Turn the edges over the work and sew the diagonal folds together using button thread.

Modified long-armed cross stitch can be worked over the folded canvas edges to prevent any canvas threads from showing.
Begin the stitch with three oversewing stitches, working over two horizontal threads. Then take the needle back through the starting point and work in the order shown.

PIPING AND BINDING

A piped edge gives a professional look to cushions and some garments. For such an edge you will need bias binding and piping cord. You can either buy bias binding or make your own from strips of fabric which are then joined. The fabric for bias strips should be light- to medium-weight and fray-resistant. The amount to buy depends on the number of joins that are acceptable. As a rough guide, 90cm of fabric 90cm wide will yield nine strips 3cm wide, the longest measuring about 1.2m, the shortest about 70cm.

Piping cord is available in several thicknesses. Most is preshrunk, but for safety buy 10cm extra for each metre you need. Immerse the cord in boiling water for five minutes, then leave to dry flat.

For measuring and marking you will need a metal ruler and tailor's chalk.

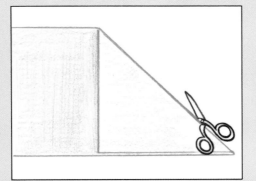

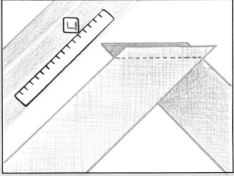

To make bias strips
1 Straighten the fabric edges, if necessary, by cutting or pulling along a thread.
2 Fold the fabric diagonally, so that two adjacent edges are aligned. Press the fold lightly. Cut along the crease. This cut edge lies on the true bias of the fabric.

3 Measure and mark the bias strips using the cut edge as a guide. The width of each strip should be the circumference of the piping cord plus twice the seam allowance (normally 1.2cm).
4 Cut the strips and join them along the straight grain as shown.

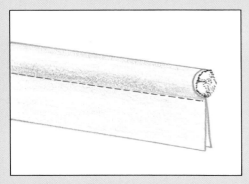

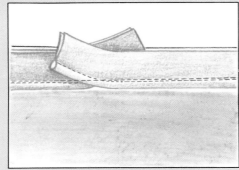

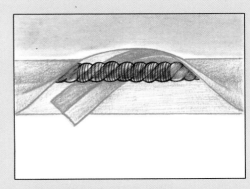

To make and attach piping
1 Fold the bias strip over the piping cord, with right side out and raw edges together. Tack (optional) and then machine close to the cord, but without 'crowding' it. Use a zipper foot and a long stitch, and stretch the fabric gently as you go. Alternatively, sew by hand, using a small running stitch or back stitch.

2 Pin and tack the piping to the right side of the edge to be piped, with the raw edges of the piping aligned to the raw edges of the article. Stitch the piping in place close to the first line of stitching, inside the seam allowance. Clip any curves.

To join ends of thick piping Cut the cord so that the ends overlap by 2cm. Cut two strands from one cord, one from the other, and wind remaining strands together. Bind with thread.

Thin piping can be joined in a similar way, but often it is acceptable to simply abut cut ends of piping. Tack them in place if necessary.

BINDING AN EDGE

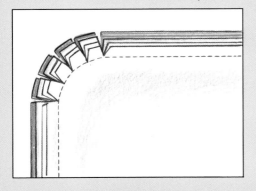

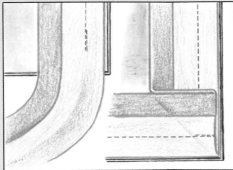

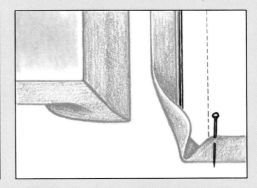

3 Place piped fabric and unpiped fabric pieces right sides together. Tack and then machine very close to the cord, using the zipper foot. Alternatively, back stitch by hand.
4 Trim the seam allowance of each of the four layers to different widths (called grading). Make any extra clips in curves as needed.

1 Cut and join bias strips. Fold and press in the edges to meet at the centre.
2 Open out the fabric along one creased edge and stitch the binding to the main fabric, along the crease, with right sides together. At corners, end the stitching at the turning point. Fold the strip as shown and continue stitching, beginning at the raw edge.

3 Turn the binding to the right side and press. A pleated mitre is formed at the corner.
4 Fold the binding to the wrong side, and slip stitch the pressed-under edge over the existing stitching. Fold the corner to form a mitre, as shown, and secure it with tiny oversewing stitches.

CUSHION COVERS

The simplest kind of cushion cover is made by stitching the front and back, right sides together, with a gap left on one side. The cover is then turned right side out, the cushion pad inserted and the edges of the opening slip stitched in place.

This method is perfectly satisfactory, but if the cover will have to be removed for washing or cleaning you will need to insert a fastening of some kind. A zip fastener is most commonly used, and this is concealed best if the seams of the cushion are piped.

Always buy a cushion pad slightly larger than the finished size of the cover. This will make the cushion plump and reduce wrinkling at the corners.

It is easiest to insert a zip before the front and back of the cover are joined. If the embroidery has a top and bottom, insert the zip in the lower edge, or in the side seam if you prefer. The zip should be 8–10cm shorter than the finished length of the seam itself, thus making it easier to join the seam at the corners.

1 Attach the piping to the front of the cushion cover as shown in step 2, page 139.

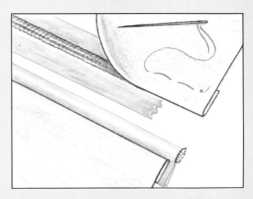

2 Turn back the seam allowance on the edge where the zip is and press to bring the piping to the edge. Press under a corresponding seam allowance on the back cushion piece.
3 Pin and tack the folded edge of the back piece over the closed zip, overlapping it by the same amount at each end; cover the teeth completely.

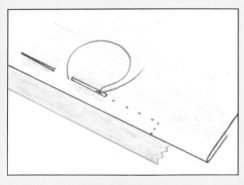

4 Stitch by hand, using prick stitch (see p. 137), or by machine, using the zipper foot. Stitch 3mm from the edge and across both ends.
5 Pin the piped edge over the zip so that the piping overlaps the folded (back) edge. Tack in place.

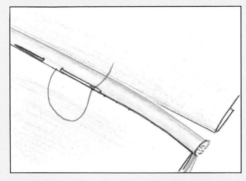

6 Work prick stitch invisibly between the front cover fabric and the piping.
7 Open the zip, then tack and stitch the front and back sections together close to the piping, as shown in step 3, page 139. Use hand stitching if necessary to work close to the ends of the zip.

MITRING CORNERS ON A HEM

There are several ways of mitring corners on hems. One method is shown in the Drawn thread work section on page 107. In that method, threads are withdrawn to mark the hem fold lines to ensure that the number of threads between fold lines is uniform, but a simpler method, for general use on closely woven fabrics, is to simply press the folds.

On sheer fabric, however, it is better to use the method shown here, which produces a mitre that is less noticeable from the right side. When cutting the fabric add twice the depth of the finished hem to all sides.

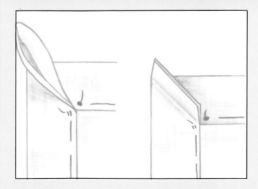

1 Fold half the hem allowance to the wrong side, overlapping the folds at the corners. Press, then fold again, leaving the corners free as shown. Tack the hem in place.
2 Press each corner first to one side, then to the other, creasing the fabric diagonally.
3 Cut off the corners 5–7mm from the crease.

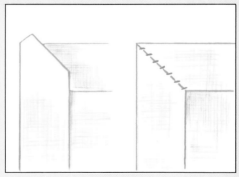

4 Slip one cut edge under the other and press the edges flat.
5 Turn under the seam allowance on the top cut edge and slip stitch it in place. Take care to work through the hem only, not through the outer layer of fabric.
6 Complete the hem.

TRIMMINGS

Embroidered soft furnishings and articles of clothing are often embellished with trimmings. A decorative braid or cord might be sewn around the edges of a cushion or a fringe could be added to the lower edge of a shoulder bag. A single tassel could provide the finishing touch on a bell-pull; while several tassels could be attached to a wallhanging.

Haberdashery and furnishing-fabric departments of stores usually offer a range of trimmings in various colours, but you may not find exactly the colour or type you need, and it is often more effective to make the trimmings from the yarn or thread used for the embroidery.

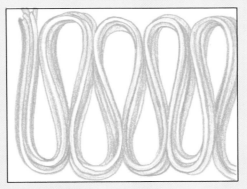

Stitched fringe
1 Take several lengths of yarn and fold them serpentine fashion, as shown, making the loops twice the finished depth of the fringe, plus 2cm.
2 Machine stitch twice through the centre of the loops, placing the lines of stitching 2cm apart.

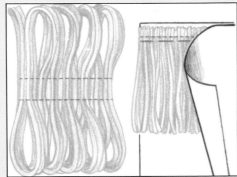

3 Cut between the lines of stitching.
4 To insert the fringe in a seam, place it as shown, with the stitching along the seamline. Tack it in place.
5 Tack the other fabric piece on top and stitch through all layers.
6 Trim the ends of the fringe.

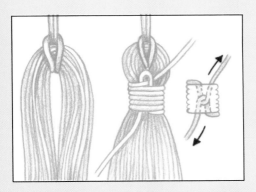

To make a tassel
1 Wind the thread around a piece of cardboard the depth of the finished tassel.
2 Cut through the ends. Loop a strand of yarn around the folded strands.
3 Bind another strand tightly around the tassel. Slip the end through the loop; pull both ends firmly. Trim ends and push inside.

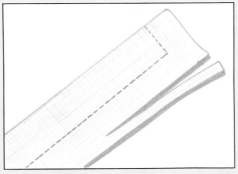

Rouleau can be used for shoulder straps or ties, either in single lengths or plaited.
1 Cut strips of fabric on the straight grain, four times the finished width of the rouleau.
2 Fold each strip in half lengthwise, with right sides together, and stitch down the centre and across one end. Trim the seam a little.

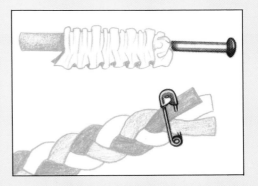

3 Turn the rouleau right side out by attaching a length of thread to one end and pulling it through the tube, using a bodkin or blunt-ended needle.
4 For a plaited rouleau, pin three strips together at one end and plait them, then either knot the ends or sew them together, as appropriate to the project.

Twisted cord
1 Estimate the number of strands needed by twisting a few together, then cut them to three times the finished length.
2 Knot the strands together at each end. Slip one end around a doorknob and insert a pencil in the other end. Turn the pencil clockwise until the strands are tightly twisted.

3 Fold the strands in half and hold the knotted ends together. The strands will twist around each other again of their own accord. Shake the cord to smooth out the twists.
4 Make another knot at each end. Trim the strands evenly.

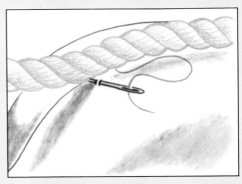

To sew the cord to a seam Use a single thread and sew through cord and fabric diagonally, working from alternate sides and catching in only a few fabric threads. Leave a small gap in the seam for the ends, then cross them and slip stitch the fabric edges in place.

THE EMBROIDERY DESIGN COLLECTION

The Embroidery Design Collection comprises more than 30 patterns, each with complete working instructions and photographs of the finished embroidery. Each pattern is a designer original, and the designs have been carefully selected to cover a wide range of techniques, both simple and complex. They include many different items, from clothes and household linen to pictures and wall-hangings, and cater for different tastes as well as varying levels of embroidery proficiency.

Many patterns also suggest 'options' – ideas for altering, adapting or changing the design to suit individual needs, notions or colour schemes. Reference to both the Design Your Own and Embroidery Basics sections of the book will be helpful when following the patterns in the Embroidery Design Collection.

CONTENTS

CHOOSING THE DESIGN

Interest in combining different techniques, in this case tie-dyeing and pulled thread work, was the idea behind this design. The embroiderer has chosen a simple design of diamond shapes against a subtle blue-grey background. Additional colour and texture are afforded by the corded embroidery worked in pearl cotton.

MATERIALS

28cm white muslin, 116cm wide
Pearl cotton no. 2 in white, yellow and pink
Sewing thread and button thread in any colour
Sewing needle and fine tapestry needle
1 tin cold-water dye in blue or blue-grey
Tailor's chalk

Finished size: the finished scarf measures approximately 114cm by 26cm

METHOD OF WORKING

First hem the fabric by rolling it between the fingers to form an even hem, then stitch with small running stitches worked in sewing thread; press.

Tie-dyeing
Following the Pattern Design illustration, mark out the diamonds using tailor's chalk. Then follow the diagram for the steps in tie-dyeing (and see book, pp. 32–3).

First make running stitches around the edge of each diamond. Use button thread, fastening it securely at the start and leaving a long end for wrapping around the shape when drawn up (A). When all the stitching is complete, gather up the threads for each diamond, wrap the long end several times around the gathers and fasten off by rethreading the needle and taking it through the bundle (B).

For the border, make running stitches all around about 2cm from the hemmed edges, then gather up tightly and fasten off.

Make up the dye according to the manufacturer's instructions and immerse the scarf in the dyebath for the length of time recommended.

Leave to dry with the gathering threads still in place. When dry remove all the threads and press (C).

Embroidery

Select the squares to be embroidered, indicated in blue on the Pattern Design diagram below. Either follow the diamond designs illustrated, or design your own. Using the tapestry needle, work rows of straight vertical stitches over three warp (horizontal) threads, pulling the stitches fairly tightly as you go to draw the fabric threads together. This is a pulled work technique called coil filling stitch.

OPTIONS
The scarf could be varied by using diamond shapes in different sizes—for example, a large one in the centre surrounded by smaller ones. A variety of other embroidery stitches could also be used. The colour scheme could be made brighter by using hot-water dyes, which give much deeper shades.

Designed by Donna Rumble

DIAMOND DESIGNS

TIE-DYEING

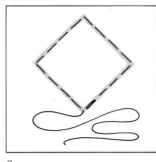
a

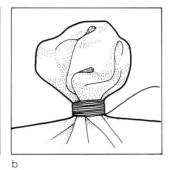
b

c

PATTERN DESIGN

middle point

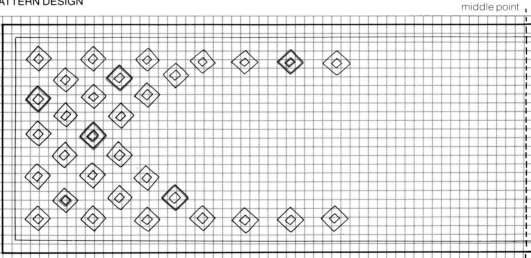

middle point

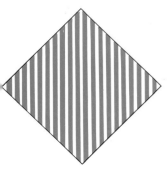

each square = 1cm/³⁄₈in

CHOOSING THE DESIGN

The bluebell and convolvulus were used as the basis for these cards partly because of their design possibilities and partly because of their symbolic significance. In the 'language of flowers' the bluebell is said to mean constancy, while the convolvulus symbolizes bonds. The embroiderer has treated the twining stem of the convolvulus in a stylized way so that it forms a heart shape, while the spray of bluebells tied with a simple bow is depicted quite naturalistically.

MATERIALS

40cm pure silk such as Nanshan, 50cm wide

1 skein each stranded embroidery cottons —for the bluebells: dark blue, light blue, dark green, light green, white and natural. For the convolvulus: pale yellow, darker yellow, 2 silvery greens, cream and blue-grey

Small piece backing fabric such as linen (for convolvulus)

30cm cream satin ribbon, about 3mm wide

Mounting cards with windows; small amount thin cardboard

Crewel needles, sizes no. 8 and 9

Tracing paper, pencil, pounce powder

Finished size: both embroideries measure 8cm by 9cm

METHOD OF WORKING

Bluebell design

Cut a piece of silk 20cm long and wide enough to fit in a small ring frame. Trace the design and transfer it to the silk by the pouncing method (see book, p. 65). Mount the silk in the ring frame. Work the embroidery following the colours shown in the photograph.

Using two strands of dark green thread, work the large leaves in satin stitch and the main stems in stem stitch. Work the petals in satin stitch with one strand of blue, using the paler shade for the left side of each one and the darker shade for the right side, to create a light and shadow effect. Before stitching the last top petal, outline the area with a few split stitches or stem stitches and work the satin stitch on top (see book, p. 78). This gives a slightly raised look, and 'lifts' each petal up from the one underneath.

Use one strand of natural for the stamens and one strand of green for the small pieces of stem, varying the shade as desired. The small leaves and wisps can be worked in either satin or stem stitch. Finally, work the forget-me-nots in white satin stitch, with either blue or natural for the centres. Position the ribbon across the stems as shown, secure it with a few stem stitches and then tie a bow, anchoring it unobtrusively with a few stab stitches if necessary.

Convolvulus design

Transfer the design as for the bluebell and mount the silk on top of the backing fabric.

Embroider the leaves first with satin stitch, using two strands of the lighter green thread for one side and the darker for the other. Couch the stems (see book, p. 71), using three strands for the laid threads and two for the couching, varying the shades of green. Satin stitch the flower bases in green, 'lifting' the raised edge as described for the bluebell. Work each flower in satin stitch using pale yellow thread, adding a few stitches of cream to lighten the centres. Use one strand of the darker yellow for the centre spots. Work the butterfly in blue-grey, adding small yellow spots with one strand of thread.

MAKING UP

Trim each embroidery to 1cm smaller all around than the outer edge of the mounting card. Cut a piece of thin cardboard to the same size and attach the edges of the embroidery to it with fabric glue, then attach the mounted embroidery to the back of the front piece of the mounting card so that it shows through the window. If you are unable to obtain a suitable windowed card you can make your own from the mounting boards sold in art shops; cut out the window with a sharp knife.

Designed by Caroline Davis

THE BLUEBELL

THE CONVOLVULUS

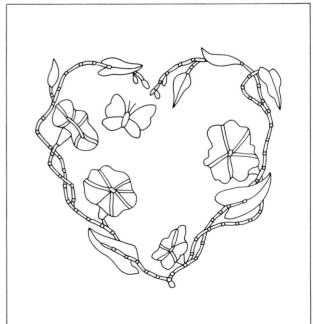

CHOOSING THE DESIGN

The idea for this design came from a photograph. A series of tracings was made, gradually simplifying the intricate details into broader, flatter areas until the right image was achieved. In this case the designer wanted to give a general impression of the goose, emphasizing the wing feathers. The colours of the threads were selected in much the same way as an artist selects paint colours, choosing shades to create an impression, with the freedom to rearrange them as necessary while working.

First the outside edge and then each main area was outlined in running stitch, this being the basic stitch used for the whole picture. Each area was then developed in turn, blending the colours and tones by eye. The gradations of colour, in the sky for example, were achieved by using a single thread instead of a double one where one tone or colour becomes darker or lighter.

MATERIALS

Linen canvas (available from artists' suppliers) at least 27cm by 22cm, or large enough to stretch on a slate frame
Note Linen canvas provides a solid background, but any similar close-mesh natural-fibre fabric can be used.
Threads
Stranded cotton in a selection of colours. Since this kind of embroidered painting is largely a matter of personal choice, it is not possible to specify precise colours. However, as a general guide, you will need the following:
8 skeins in shades of grey-blue and blue (for the sky and pond, arranged in different ways)
7 skeins in shades of grey, brown, beige and white (for the goose)
2 skeins pink-beige (for the beak)
2 skeins green (for the pond bank)
1 skein each light beige and donkey brown (for the border)
Scraps of red-brown and black (for the eye)

Crewel needles, 1 medium and 1 fine
Hardboard or mounting board, 15cm by 11cm
Gummed paper strip or string (See Finishing Off below)

Finished size: the complete picture, with mount, measures 20.5cm by 16.5cm. The area of embroidery is 15cm by 11cm.

METHOD OF WORKING

Trace the design from the diagram below and transfer it to the canvas (see book, p.64). The diagram is actual size and shows the direction of the stitches. Stretch the canvas on the frame, if you are using one.

Outline the outside edge in running stitch (see book, p.69), then outline each main area in the appropriate colour, before filling in the areas of the design with the stitches indicated.

Referring to the diagram and the colour photograph as necessary, continue the work in running stitch on each area in turn, except for the wing feathers, using one or two strands of thread as required. The medium needle, with two strands of thread, will cover the large areas best, while the fine needle, with one strand of thread, can be used for any small details, such as the eye and the beak.

Work the wing feathers in fly stitch (see book, p.77), varying the size and direction of the stitches to create texture and detail.

Finally, work the border in satin stitch (see book, p.78).

FINISHING OFF

Using a damp cloth or a steam iron, press the embroidery on the wrong side. If the canvas is distorted, gently pull and stretch it back into shape.
Mounting
Stretch the canvas over the piece of board or hardboard. If you are using mounting board, secure the canvas at the back with gummed strip; if hardboard, lace the canvas at the back as shown on page 138 in the book.

Hardboard is the best choice if you are not intending to frame the picture. If you are, then mounting board is quite adequate, since it will be held by both glass and backing.

Designed by Ljiljana Rylands

KEY

satin stitch

running stitch

fly stitch

CHOOSING THE DESIGN

This abstract geometric design exploits the vibrant effects that can be created by the juxtaposition of blending and contrasting colours. Additional interest and texture have been created by the use of the free and inventive stitchery in colours chosen to contrast with the painted squares and stripes.

MATERIALS

5.5m white heavy cotton fabric, 90cm wide
Screen frame with three panels, each with an inside measurement of 56cm by 148cm

Threads

Stranded embroidery cotton: 6 skeins turquoise in a light and darker shade; 6 skeins pink in a light and darker shade; 4 skeins pale green; 1 skein pale lilac; 1 skein mid-blue; 4 skeins pink shaded to white; 3 skeins white; 2 skeins red

Fabric paints or printing inks in 10 colours: 4 shades of blue; 2 shades of lilac; 2 shades of green; pink and red (see Note below)
2 large rolls adhesive tape, 2cm wide
1 large roll masking tape, 2.5cm wide
1 large and 1 small paintbrush
Long ruler; set square; pencil
Staple gun and staples
Jam jars for mixing paint
Note Most fabric paints are available in only a limited colour range, so you will have to mix them to obtain the shades used here. To mix the 10 colours you will need red, pink, green, blue, black and white.

Finished size: each panel measures 148cm by 56cm, without the frame

METHOD OF WORKING

Preparing the fabric

Cut out three rectangles of fabric, each 60cm by 158cm. Iron one piece thoroughly and lay it on a wipe-clean surface (or lay two layers of clean paper underneath before painting). Using masking tape, fix the fabric firmly to the work surface, making sure that the grain is quite straight.

To mark each rectangle, first rule a line 56cm long along the bottom, leaving an equal margin below and at each side. Using the set square, draw a vertical line at right angles from one corner and extend it to 148cm. Mark the other sides in the same way. Measure and draw a margin all around the rectangle the exact depth of the recess in the screen frame. Using ruler and set square, and measuring carefully, mark in the squares and stripes from the diagram.

Painting the fabric

Mix the colours so that you have 10 blending but distinct shades. Paint the fabric according to the photograph or your own design. Paint one colour at a time, masking all the areas for each colour. Paint as evenly as possible, forcing the colour through the fabric without leaving any excess lying on top or beneath to form blotches. Leave each area to dry thoroughly before starting on the next. To fix the colours, iron on the back with a hot iron.

Making the screen

Trim the excess fabric outside the design, leaving the small margin, then turn this under so that the fold is on the edge of the design, and press. Staple the fabric to the top recess of the frame, working from left to right and placing the staples about 1cm apart, then turn the frame the other way up and staple the other short end, pulling the fabric slightly to stretch it. Staple the sides.

The stitching

The embroidery for the squares, indicated by blue lines in the diagram opposite, consists of long stitches running diagonally across each square or block of squares. The larger areas also have stitches worked vertically and horizontally to outline each square or block. The colours contrast with the painted colours, and are changed for every pair of squares. Use six strands of thread throughout, starting at the inner corner of each square. Knot the thread to secure it at the start, and fasten off by sticking the thread to the side of the frame on the wrong side with masking tape. Sew all the diagonals first, then the outlining stitches, following the diagrams.

The stitching inside the stripes and in the free areas is a series of long and short stitches arranged in a zigzag pattern and running the length of each stripe. Using the diagrams as a guide, vary the size and direction of the stitches, allowing some stitches to extend over the edges.

When complete, trim all the threads on the inside of the screen. Cover the staples in the screen recesses with strips of wood.

Designed by Christine Calow

MAKING UP

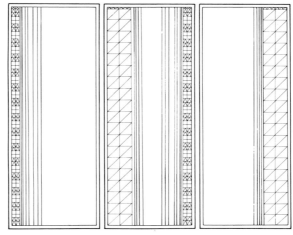

SMALL PATTERN SQUARES

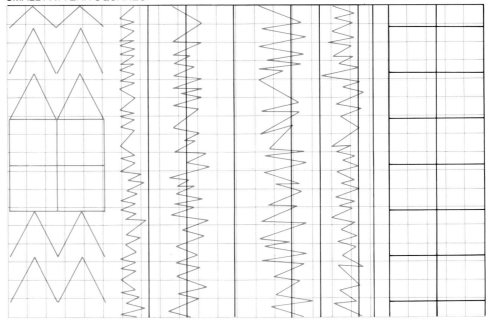

LARGE PATTERN SQUARES

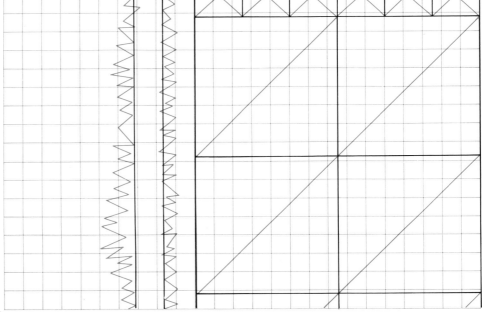

one square = 1cm/³⁄₈in

CHOOSING THE DESIGN

The simple dog-rose motifs, in bright sunny colours, are worked in buttonhole and fly stitch, rather than a more solid filling stitch, to give a feeling of airiness to this design. The French knots in the centres add texture.

MATERIALS

1.2m white poly/cotton fabric, 114cm wide
Stranded embroidery threads: 2 skeins each deep yellow, pale yellow, cream and leaf green
1 reel white sewing thread
Crewel needle, size no. 9/10
Tracing and dressmaker's carbon paper

Finished size: the diameter of the tablecloth is 110cm

METHOD OF WORKING

Preparing the cloth

Cut off the selvedges. Make an exact square by folding the fabric diagonally and trimming off the excess. Press the fold, then fold in half twice more as shown, so that there are eight thicknesses of fabric; press well. Measure from point A to point B as shown in the Pattern Design diagram below and mark off this measurement along the bottom (long) edge. This is point C. Mark several points between B and C exactly the same distance from point A, then join them to form a curve. Cut along the curve through all thicknesses to make a perfect circle. The folds will serve as a guide for placing the motifs.

To prevent fraying, work the hem before starting the embroidery. Turn under 2cm then 3cm to make a double hem and tack well. The cloth illustrated was hemstitched by hand, but a quicker alternative would be to use machine straight stitch. For a more elaborate hem an embroidery stitch could be chosen, such as herringbone, fly stitch or chain stitch, in either white or a contrast colour.

The embroidery

Trace the outlines of the motif and transfer it to the fabric using dressmaker's carbon paper (see book, p. 64), placing each one centrally over one of the creases and 11.5cm from the hem.

Two strands of thread are used throughout for the embroidery. Start with the whole flower, working the inner petals in buttonhole stitch in deep yellow. The spacing of the stitches is an important part of the effect: they should not be so close together that the fabric does not show, and they must radiate out from the centre so that there is more space between stitches at the outer edge than in the middle. You will find it easiest to start at the centre of each petal and work first to one side and then out to the other side.

Work the second row of petals into the first row, using the paler yellow thread. To keep the same density of stitches it will be necessary to increase their number. Work the outer row in cream, again increasing the number of stitches to maintain the density. Finally, work deep yellow French knots in the centre. Work the second flower in the same way, filling in the small areas in straight stitch as indicated on the pattern design.

Work the leaves in fly stitch (see book, p. 76), starting at the tip and using the vein of the leaf as the centre of the stitch. Space the stitches a little farther apart on the leaves and fill in with straight stitches.

FINISHING OFF

Wash the cloth if it has become at all soiled. Iron it on the wrong side while damp on a pad of felt or a clean blanket. This will stretch the embroidery while retaining its texture.

Designed by Margaret Horton

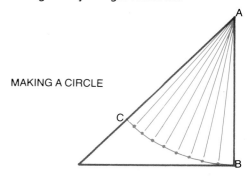

MAKING A CIRCLE

MAKING UP

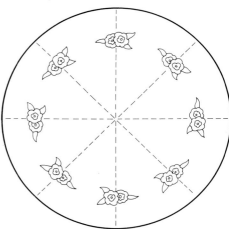

PATTERN DESIGN

fold

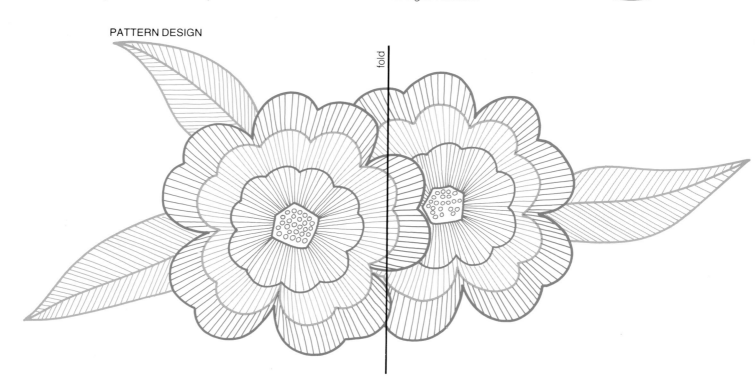

CHOOSING THE DESIGN

For this rag book the designer has chosen as her theme the sequence of night and day, starting with the north star, the herald of night, and ending with the rising sun. The bright colours make the images easily recognizable to a small child, as well as rendering the creatures of night—the bat and the owl—less frightening.

MATERIALS

Fabric
80cm fine white cotton fabric, 90cm wide
70cm fine black cotton fabric, 90cm wide
Small piece terylene wadding
Threads
1 reel black machine thread
Stranded embroidery cotton: 1 skein black, 1 skein yellow
Coton à broder: 1 skein each in black, yellow, blue, red or pink, white
1 reel gold lurex thread

Needles and pins
Fabric paints in black, blue, yellow, red
Artist's paintbrushes, small and large
Dressmaker's carbon paper, pencil

Finished size: each page measures 18cm by 23cm, the cover 38cm by 23cm

METHOD OF WORKING

Painting the fabric
Enlarge the designs and transfer them to the white fabric, using carbon paper. Transfer the stitching lines around the sun on page 4 also, since you will need them as a guide for the embroidery. The design for the star on the front cover can be taken from page 1. Cut out the pages and front cover, allowing a margin of 1cm all around.

Practise fabric painting on a spare piece of white fabric. When you feel confident, place the terylene wadding under the fabric and paint in the outlines of each shape, using the black paint and a small brush. Leave to dry, then press with a hot iron under a damp cloth to fix the paint.

Referring to the photograph, paint in each area in the relevant colour, leaving the owl and all the background areas until last. For these areas a colour wash technique is used. Dampen the fabric slightly with a brush so that the colours run into one another when applied; paint the paler colours first. Try out the technique on some spare fabric – if too much water is used the colours will spread out too far. When painting the background, take care not to cover the black lines: paint just outside the outline and allow the paint to run up to it. When dry, fix as before.
The embroidery
Page 1. Work the eye of the moon in satin stitch using two strands of black thread.
Page 2. Work seeding stitch (see book, p. 76) for the bat's wings and tail, using gold lurex thread and white coton à broder. Work the eyes in satin stitch.

Page 3. Work the owl's eyes as before, then work zigzag stitch around them with one strand of yellow thread. Work the body in plush, or knot stitch, shown below, using blue, yellow and pink coton à broder.
Page 4. Work the sun's eyes in French knots, using black coton à broder. Place the knots as close together as possible.

MAKING UP AND FINISHING

Cut the black fabric to the same size as the painted pages and front cover. Seam around each edge with right sides together, leaving an opening at the bottom edge to turn. Turn to the right side and press, poking the corners out well, then slip stitch to close the opening.

Pin and tack along the edges and then diagonally across as for quilting (see book, p. 91). Press lightly along the edges on the wrong side, using a cloth under the iron.

Using two strands of black embroidery thread and running stitch, embroider on top of all the black outlines through both thicknesses of fabric. Work the sun's rays in yellow coton à broder and running stitch.

To assemble the book, slip stitch each page in turn to the centre of the cover, stitching 8mm from the edges on both back and front to secure the pages thoroughly.

Designed by Claire Johnson

KNOT STITCH

PATTERN DESIGNS

PAGE 1

PAGE 2

PAGE 3

PAGE 4

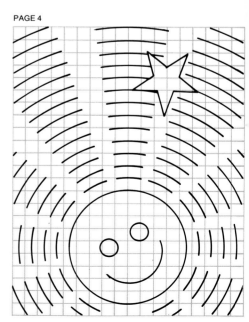

one square = 1cm/⅜in

CHOOSING THE DESIGN

Each of these three bow ties makes use of a different embroidery technique, but in all of them the embroidery is quite sub-dued, so that the effect is more that of a printed and textured fabric. The white tie is couched in a diamond pattern, while the larger diamond pattern on the grey tie is machine stitched with a twin needle and then embellished with French knots. The black-and-white tie is simply satin stitched within the pattern of the printed checks.

MATERIALS

The white tie
50cm white linen-textured polyester, 90cm wide
Pearl cotton size no.5 in red and grey
The grey tie
50cm grey linen-textured polyester, 90cm wide
Sewing thread in pale grey and black
The black-and-white tie
50cm black-and-white checked brushed cotton, 90cm wide
Pearl cotton size no.8 in red, dark grey, black and white
Crewel needle; sharps needle
Tailor's chalk, tracing paper

Finished size: each tie is 87cm long and measures 5.5cm at the widest point

METHOD OF WORKING

For all three ties, make a paper pattern by enlarging the one given. Note that the pieces must be cut on the bias.
The white tie
The couching is best worked on a ring frame, but this is not essential. If using a frame, mark but do not cut the two top pieces on the fabric, leaving sufficient for the back pieces. Mark the 1cm seam al-lowance and stretch the fabric in the frame.

The laid threads form a diamond grid pattern, and are placed about 8mm apart. You may find it helpful to mark the position of the stitches along the seam allowance before starting. Using the red thread and the crewel needle, lay all the threads in one direction first, starting and finishing each 3mm outside the seam line. The last long stitch should be placed about 20cm from the centre seam. Work the laid threads in the opposite direction then, using the grey thread, make small stitches over each intersection.

Remove the work from the frame and cut out the four pieces.
The grey tie
Cut out all four pieces. The grid pattern is machined on the top two pieces with a twin needle, with the rows of stitching approximately 1cm apart. Mark along the edges as before, then stitch first in one direction and then in the other using the pale grey thread. When both sides are complete, make a small French knot at each intersection using the black thread.

The black-and-white tie
Cut out the four pieces. Work blocks of satin stitch on the top two as shown, using red, grey, black and white pearl cotton.

MAKING UP

Join the centre seams of backs and fronts. Trim the seam to within 5mm of the stitch-ing and press open. With right sides together, stitch the backs to the fronts, leaving an opening for turning as shown. Trim the seam, clip the corners and turn to the right side, poking out the edges well. Press, then slip stitch the edges of the opening together.

Designed by Ariella Green

CUTTING PATTERN

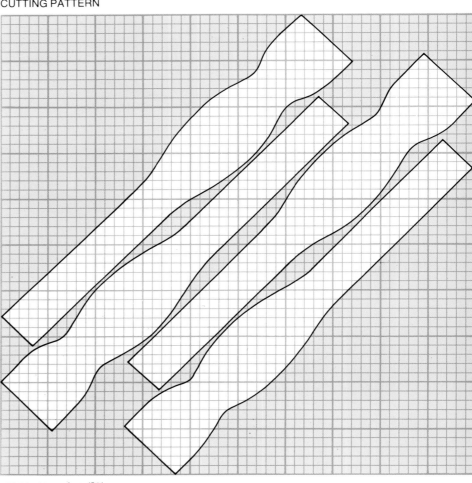

one square = 1cm/⅜in

MAKING UP

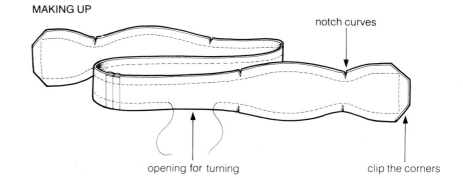

notch curves

opening for turning

clip the corners

CHOOSING THE DESIGN

Nothing gives a more individual look to clothes than hand-made buttons, especially if they are made by the dressmaker to complement a particular garment. All these buttons can be made quite easily from inexpensive materials.

MATERIALS

Dorset buttons
Curtain rings, 2.5cm and 2cm in diameter
Threads, such as pearl cotton, coton à broder, soft embroidery or crochet cotton
Tapestry needle

Toggles
Any embroidery thread sold by the hank

Covered buttons
Self-covering buttons
Evenweave linen or fine, soft canvas

Tapestry needle
Coton à broder or stranded cotton

WORKING THE DORSET BUTTONS

Thread the tapestry needle with a long length of thread (about two and a half arm's length.) Tie the free end to the curtain ring and buttonhole closely around the edge. Catch the short end under the first few stitches to secure it, and cut it off closely. When the ring is covered, slip the needle through the first stitch worked to join the stitches together.

Turn the stitches firmly on the ring so that all the loops are on the inside. Hold the thread to the front of the ring and pass it up over the top of the ring and down the back to the starting position. This forms the first spoke of a wheel. Continue to make spokes in this way, moving around the ring as evenly as possible.

Join the spokes in the centre by working a cross stitch over the middle; centralize the stitch by pulling gently but firmly.

Next the spokes are filled in. Back stitch from one spoke to another, beginning in the centre and working under spokes 1 and 2, then back under 2 and 3. Continue until the ring is filled with stitches, varying the colours if desired by joining a new thread into the back of the button.

WORKING THE THREAD TOGGLES

Fold a hank of thread until you have the required thickness, then wrap another thread, in a contrast colour if desired, evenly around it. When the hank is well covered, fasten off by pulling the thread back through the hank to the centre top and working a small buttonholed loop.

The toggles can be varied by working a row of buttonhole stitch at each end of the wrapped section, or by working detached buttonhole stitch to form a mesh over the wrapping; both are shown in the photograph. Attractive toggles can also be made using random-dyed thread (see book, p.52).

WORKING THE COVERED BUTTONS

Mount the fabric in a ring frame (see book, p.66) and, using the measuring guide on the button card, draw a circle on the fabric. Mark the approximate centre, then work the design of your choice from those given below (see book, Blackwork pp.104-5 and Canvaswork pp. 126-7). The canvaswork stitch shown here is diagonal satin stitch; Scottish or mosaic stitch would create a similar pattern. Before removing the embroidery from the frame, run a gathering thread around each circle, 2.5cm from the edge. Cut out and cover the buttons, according to the manufacturer's instructions.

OPTIONS
Buttons of the types shown can be made in almost any threads, colours or combinations of colours, so it is possible to match or blend with any garment.

Designed by Gail Marsh and Jacqueline Blackburn of *Bottom Drawer*

DORSET BUTTONS

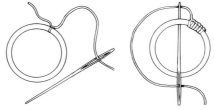

THREAD TOGGLES

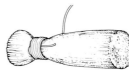

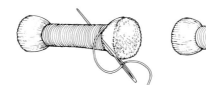

BLACKWORK BUTTON

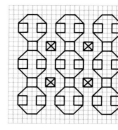

CANVAS BUTTON

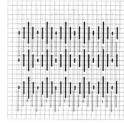

CHOOSING THE DESIGN

The hat was inspired by Peruvian designs, which make use of bold, stylized shapes and juxtapose bright colours. The motifs on this hat are less ethnic representations.

Felt, which is available in bright, clear colours, is ideal for this kind of bold, simple design. It also has the great advantage of not fraying, so the appliqué shapes can be smaller and more elaborate than is possible with woven fabrics.

MATERIALS

Fabric
25cm square pale blue felt
23cm squares of felt in red, pink, yellow and grey
Small piece red felt
Threads
1m yellow satin ribbon, 1.5cm wide
1.4m green satin ribbon, 5mm wide
1m green satin bias binding
1 reel cotton sewing thread in red, yellow, green, black and pale blue
1 reel silver lurex thread
1 skein yellow embroidery thread for tassel

Bonding web for appliqué shapes
20 grey mother-of-pearl 4-hole buttons

Finished size: to fit child aged about 2–4

METHOD OF WORKING

Draw up the pattern pieces to size from the cutting pattern overleaf and make a template for each of the appliqué shapes from thin cardboard (cereal packets are ideal).

Iron bonding web to the backs of the four 23cm felt squares, but do not remove the paper backing. Cut out pattern pieces A, B and C from the pale blue felt and D from the small piece of red felt.

Place the templates on the backing of the felt squares, and draw around them. Cut out the shapes from the appropriate colours.

Using herringbone stitch, either by hand or machine, attach a length of green satin ribbon 4.5cm from the bottom of piece A.

Remove the backing paper from the backs of the hearts and three of the bears, leaving it on the fourth bear, since this will be attached after the seam is made. Iron shapes in place as indicated in the Making Up diagram, then stitch the hearts in place using back stitch and a double thickness of red sewing thread. Attach the bears using stab stitch and yellow thread, picking out the details—nose, mouth and eyes—with black satin stitch.

Remove the backing paper from all but one of the pink clouds and from all the suns. Iron them on above the green ribbon, placing the suns between alternate clouds so that the clouds overlap them by about 1cm. Stitch the clouds using blanket stitch and red thread, and the sun using

stab stitch and yellow thread, working long, straight stitches for the sun's rays.

Lay three of the grey clouds in place, remove the backing paper and iron on to piece B. Stitch, using back stitch and a single thickness of lurex thread, then use running stitch in a double thickness of lurex thread for the rain.

Stitch piece A to piece B, using close machine zigzag stitch to join them edge to edge. Tack, and then sew, the red ribbon over the seam so that the lower edge of the ribbon just covers it. Sew on the buttons, using green thread for contrast. Join piece C to piece B in the same way, and stitch green satin ribbon over the seam, using a suitable machine embroidery stitch if your machine has one, or by hand if not.

MAKING UP

Sew centre back seam using a small ladder stitch. Press open. Try the hat on the child if possible, and make any small adjustments at this stage. Appliqué the remaining bear and cloud over the seam and stitch as before.

Fold the yellow ribbon in half over the two lower edges of each earpiece and back. Place the red ribbon so that its edges butt up to the yellow one; tack in place and then stitch, using green thread and a machine satin stitch about 5mm long. Tack green bias binding to the bottom of the hat, tack earpieces in place and secure both earpieces and bias binding with machine satin stitch in yellow.

Sew about 40cm of green ribbon to the bottom corners of each flap and knot at the ends to prevent fraying. Make the tassel (see book, p. 141) from yellow embroidery thread, fit it into the cone at the top of the hat and stitch in place. Finally, steam the work in front of a kettle spout to 'pick up' the fabric and stitching.

OPTIONS
Felt appliqué can be combined with machine stitching for a great variety of different items from outer garments to wallhangings. Felt cannot be washed, however, so it is not suitable for anything that needs frequent laundering. Sequins or beads could be used instead of buttons, and the stitching can be varied to create different effects, colour combinations and textures.

Designed by Victoria Brown

CUTTING PATTERN

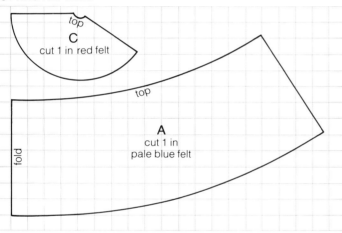

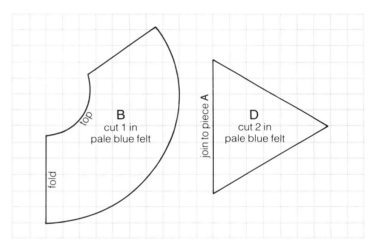

C cut 1 in red felt

A cut 1 in pale blue felt

B cut 1 in pale blue felt

D cut 2 in pale blue felt

join to piece A

one square = 1.25cm / ½ in

APPLIQUÉ SHAPES

SUN
cut 6 in yellow felt

TEDDY BEAR
cut 4 in yellow felt

HEARTS
cut 4 in red felt

RAIN CLOUDS
cut 4 in grey felt

CLOUDS
cut 4 in pink felt

MAKING UP

piece C

piece B

piece A

piece D

CHOOSING THE DESIGN

The starting point for this design was a drawing of a garden made by the embroiderer one hot summer. Because the embroidery is intended to convey the effect of regular garden borders, the design concentrates on the shapes of the yuccas and red-hot pokers against the wall, not on the small details. The motifs are repeated in rows; the sun is also repeated at regular intervals. The warm colours were chosen to accentuate the summery atmosphere.

MATERIALS

Fabric
1m cotton fabric, 90cm wide, for backing and lining
90cm blanket or felt, 90cm wide
1m grey cotton fabric, 115cm wide
50cm green cotton fabric, 90cm wide
50cm yellow cotton fabric, 90cm wide
50cm each of printed cotton fabrics, 90cm wide: yellow-and-white stripe, green stripe, and pattern suitable for a wall

A reel of machine embroidery thread in each of about six colours, to match and blend with appliqué fabrics, plus dark red and dark brown for flowers
1m bonding web, 90cm wide
50cm heavy iron-on interfacing, 90cm wide
Machine needle, size no.90

Finished size: the wallhanging measures 86cm by 63.5cm

METHOD OF WORKING

The wallhanging is worked in sections, two for the central panel and seven for the borders, as shown, so that each section can be comfortably accommodated under the sewing-machine foot. The appliqué is done first, the pieces being assembled and applied to the background by the bonding web method (see book, p.83). The work is then tacked in one piece to the blanket or felt, and the surface machine stitching carried out before all the pieces are joined. You should allow a 2.5cm seam allowance around all sides of the panels for joining up.

Cut the appliqué pieces for panels A and B, outlined in black on the charts overleaf; apply the bonding web to the fabrics before cutting, but leave the backing on. Cut patterns for the sun motifs by enlarging those given in panels A and B overleaf and cut out 21 small suns and one large one. Cut out a piece of the green-striped fabric 90cm by 20cm and set aside to make binding and loops later.

Cut out 38cm-wide strips as follows: two in the pattern chosen for the wall, 3.75cm and 2.5cm deep; two of yellow-and-white stripe, 11.5cm and 20cm deep; one of grey, 11.5cm deep; two of green stripe 3.75cm deep; and one of yellow cotton 5cm deep.

Cut out two pieces of grey backing fabric: 38cm by 45cm for section A and 38cm by 40.5cm for section B. Assemble the cut pieces on the grey fabric as shown on the panel charts overleaf, remove the backing from the bonding web and iron on, leaving a 1.2cm seam allowance all around. Make sure that those pieces which have to be overlapped by others are ironed on first.

Cut out two pieces of blanket or felt to the same size as the appliqué work and tack both layers together firmly (see book, p.91). The machine embroidery, outlined in blue on the panel charts overleaf, is essentially free, and it will be helpful to look at the photograph to get an idea of the stitches and colours used. Try out the stitches on spare pieces of fabric before starting each one; the fabric allowance is sufficient to make test pieces of each.

The stitches used are mainly satin and zigzag, with the widths varied to create different effects. There is a double row of straight stitching inside the satin-stitched border of the large sun; below this are wavy lines of satin stitch in white and grey. The yuccas are in dark brown, red and

reen satin stitch, and the red-hot pokers ave satin stitch for the leaves, while the owers are worked in random zigzag with e foot removed from the machine (this nust be done very carefully). On panel B here are rows of grey satin stitch below e first line of suns, and close satin stitch elow and beside the yuccas in dark red-rown.

When the central panels are complete, ut the fabric for the borders as shown; use rey fabric as backing for the outer bor-ers and green for the inner ones. Cut 17 uns in yellow-and-white striped fabric for ach long outer border and 10 for each hort one. Work the appliqué and em-roidery as for the central panels.

FINISHING OFF

o join the central panels cut a strip of terfacing about 5cm deep and the width f the panels. Place the panels edge to dge and iron the interfacing on to the ack. Cover the join with a wide row of ecorative satin stitching. Join the border

pieces to each other and to the central panel in the same way, satin stitching over each join.

To make the edging strips, cut two strips of green-striped fabric 5cm by 66cm and two 5cm by 89cm. Join one short strip to the top by placing right sides together and working a 1.2cm seam. Turn to right side, turn the raw edge under and hand hem at the back. Repeat for the bottom binding strip and then for each side.

To make the loops for hanging, cut three strips of the same fabric, each 5cm by 13cm. Fold in half lengthwise, turn in 1.2cm on the long edges and machine close to the edge. Fold each in half and attach at equal intervals to the wrong side of the hanging so that about 4cm projects above the edge to take the hanging rod.

Finally, cut a piece of lining fabric to the same size as the wallhanging, press under the 1.2cm seam allowances on both, and hand stitch wallhanging to lining around all four sides.

Designed by Chris Crilly

MAKING UP

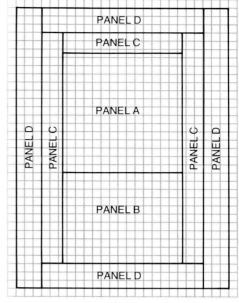

one square = 2.5cm/1in

PANEL A

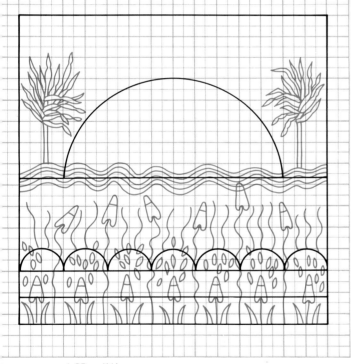

one square = 1.25cm/½in

PANEL B

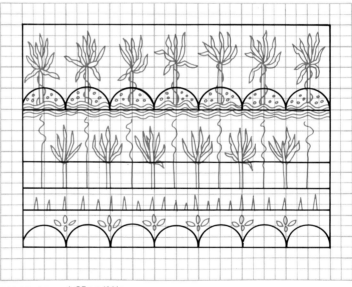

one square = 1.25cm/½in

PANEL C

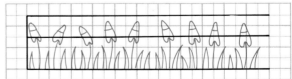

PANEL D

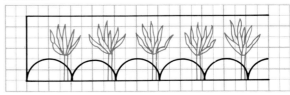

one square = 1.25cm/½in

CHOOSING THE DESIGN

The design, although giving the appearance of quilted patchwork, is actually painted straight on to the satin fabric by dabbing on special fabric dye. A measured drawing was made first, with the squares and zigzags placed in a pleasing arrangement. The design was then transferred and the different areas coloured before machine quilting was worked around each one. This technique produces a luxurious appearance and enhances the patchwork effect.

Note The back of the cushion, tied with bows, is shown in the photograph.

MATERIALS

Fabric

1.1m white silk crepe satin, 115cm wide
1.1m 225g polyester wadding, 90cm wide
1.1m plain cotton fabric, 90cm wide

2 reels white cotton or polyester sewing thread
Fabric paints: 2 pots gold, 1 blue, 1 green
Cushion pad, 70cm by 45cm
Old sheet or similar for laying under fabric while painting

Tailor's chalk, pins, ruler, set square, paintbrush

Finished size: the cushion measures 70cm by 45cm

METHOD OF WORKING

Marking and painting the fabric

Cut or rip the silk into two pieces, 50cm for the front and 55cm for the back. Spread out the old sheet on the floor or on a large table and pin the silk pieces to it. If you are working on the floor, pin right into the carpet. If you are using a table, use drawing pins to tense the back fabric. Pin in the order shown in the diagram, so that the silk is held taut, with the grain straight.

Draw in the pattern lines as shown in the diagram, using tailor's chalk, ruler and a set square. Each colour square is 15cm by 15cm. Note that the pattern for the back has an extra allowance in the middle for the fabric to be cut and seamed. Paint each area in the colour shown, using a dabbing action. You may find it helpful to hold a piece of card over the edge of the area next to the one you are painting. Leave to dry, or dry with a fan-heater or hairdryer, while the fabric is still pinned in place.

Remove the pins and iron the silk under a clean cotton cloth with a hot iron for one to two minutes to set the paint.

Quilting

Cut the wadding into three pieces across its length, a 50cm piece for the front and two for the back, measuring 37cm and 22cm. Cut off the two pieces of yellow silk from the end of each rectangle, leaving the seam allowance at the edge of the pattern and set aside. Cut across the back piece 2.5cm from the end of the zigzag pattern.

Work the front first. (A different procedure is followed for the back.) Cut the cotton backing fabric to the same size as the silk, and make a three-layer sandwich with the wadding in the middle and the silk on top, right side up. Pin through all layers, then tack to hold them firmly in place (see book, p.92). Set the sewing machine pressure foot to low and start quilting, using a medium stitch length. Work from the centre out, in the order shown in the diagram, starting with the yellow zigzag. Machine in the same direction each time to prevent the shapes from twisting. Stitch around the edges of the design last, using a machine zigzag stitch 2.5cm from the edges of the pattern. Trim away any excess fabric.

For the back, tack the silk to the wadding only, since the ties are sewn on before the backing is added. Cut the backing fabric to the same size as the two back pieces.

To make the ties, cut 10 strips of yellow silk each 6cm wide, fold in half lengthways, right sides together, and stitch down both long sides. Turn to right side, using a knitting needle or bodkin to help you push the end through. Press, then stitch five ties to each cushion back piece with raw edges matching and right sides together. Make sure they are evenly spaced and that each tie lines up with its opposite number across the opening. Place the cotton backing on top and, with wrong sides together, join to silk and wadding with a 2.5cm seam. Turn to right side, stitch again and press. Pin and tack to the other two layers as before, then work the quilting in the same way, referring to the diagram for the order of stitching.

MAKING UP

Lay the front and back cushion panels on top of each other with right sides together, pin and then tack the outside seams, matching the pattern squares and quilting lines. Seam, then trim the corners and turn through to the right side. Insert pad and tie bows.

Designed by Elizabeth Lippiatt

FRONT

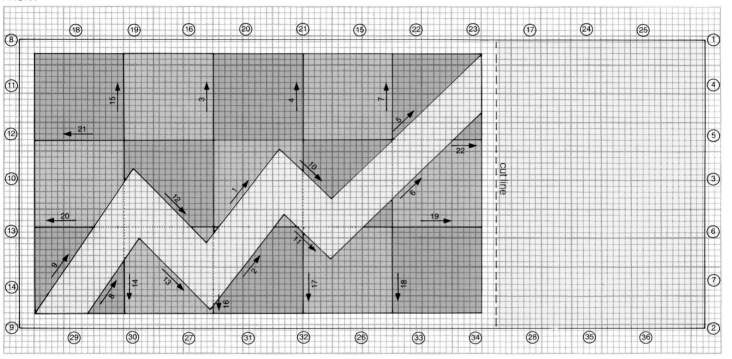

BACK

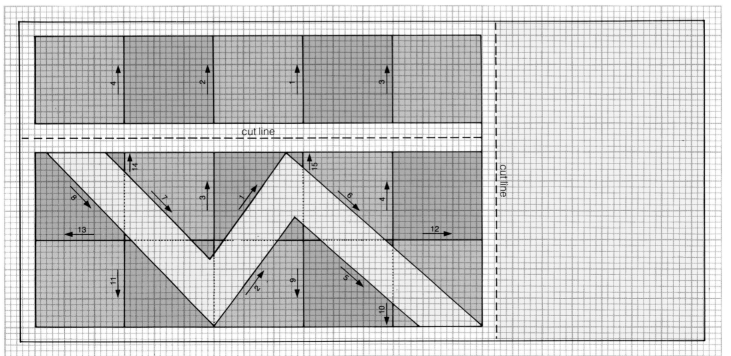

five squares = 5cm/2in

CHOOSING THE DESIGN

This form of quilting combined with appliqué is thought to have developed as a response to the more traditional methods taught to Hawaiians by the missionaries. The motifs represent the shadows cast by the island flowers of Hawaii and bear the names of the plants that inspired them, while the quilted lines echo the waves of the sea. The designs, usually executed in bright primary colours, are cut in one piece by the method children often use for making snowflake patterns in paper—by folding a square of fabric into eight, cutting shapes into it and then opening it out. Intricate designs can be made in this way, which can either have a starting point in nature, like these, or else be quite random and abstract.

Three of the four cushions—breadfruit, carnation and clownflower—are traditional Hawaiian designs, and the fourth was developed in a similar way; it is based roughly on a sunflower shape. Try experimenting with different paper patterns, opening out the paper to assess each one until you arrive at a pleasing design.

MATERIALS

(For each cushion)
Fabric
1m cotton fabric, 90cm wide in background colour
50cm cotton fabric, 90cm wide in contrasting colour for appliqué
50cm 100g polyester wadding, 90cm wide
Threads
1 reel quilting thread or cotton sewing thread in a colour to match appliqué fabric
1 reel sewing thread in background colour

Quilting needle, size no. 10 or finest available
40cm zip fastener
Cushion pad, 46cm by 46cm or nearest available size
Beeswax block
Sheet of fairly stiff paper, 43cm by 43cm

Finished size: Each cushion measures 46cm by 46cm

METHOD OF WORKING

The template
Make the template by folding the square of paper into half, then half again, then diagonally to form a triangle one-eighth the size of the original square. Enlarge your chosen design from the charted diagram below, draw it on to the triangle and cut out. Open out the paper to make sure the design is as intended, then cut out one triangle. This forms the template. Mark the centre point of the design, by referring to the colour photograph. Mark the longest side on the template also; this must be placed on the bias of the fabric with the other two sides on the straight grain.

The appliqué
Cut out a square measuring 43cm by 43cm from the appliqué fabric. Fold the fabric square in the same way as the paper, pressing each fold in turn and taking great care to be accurate. Cut out two squares each measuring 43cm by 43cm from the background fabric. Fold and press one square of background fabric in the same way, then open it out.

Carefully pin the paper template to the folded triangle of appliqué fabric through all eight thicknesses, making sure to match the centre points, the bias and the straight grain of fabric. Mark all around the edges of the template with a pencil (not a biro or felt-tipped pen), remove the template and repin the folded layers of the fabric together.

Cut through all thicknesses, using very sharp scissors. Open out and pin on to the background fabric, carefully matching the fold lines. Pin along the fold lines, then tack the appliqué approximately 5mm from the edges.

Appliqué the design by hand, using tiny hemming stitches (see book, p. 85) and a matching thread. Turn about 3mm under as you go. On curves and points, oversew at the outside edges to prevent possible fraying. To make the points look as neat as possible, turn them under at the top first then down each side.

The quilting
Cut a slightly larger square of wadding 45.5cm by 45.5cm, and lay it on top of the backing fabric. Lay the completed design on top of the wadding. Starting from the middle, secure all three layers together with tacking stitches in lines spaced about 7.5cm apart.

Wax all quilting thread before use by running it over the beeswax to strengthen it and prevent tangling. Place work in circular quilting frame and quilt all around the edges of the appliqué (see book, p.91) with small, even stitches. Fill in the background with evenly spaced contoured lines about 1cm apart. The motifs themselves can also be quilted, but this is not strictly necessary. (You may find it helpful to mark the lines first with a water-soluble pen; the marks can be washed out when the work is complete.)

The quilting can be done by machine if quick results are desired.

MAKING UP

Cut out the cushion back to measure 43cm by 45.5cm. Cut this piece of fabric in half down the long side and insert the zip between the cut edges, turning under 1.2cm on each side to give a square the same size as the front.

Cut two strips of background fabric to measure 43cm by 5cm, and another two to measure 45.5cm by 5cm. With right sides together, tack and then machine sew the shorter strips of fabric to the sides of the cushion front, stitching 1.2cm from the edge. Turn to right side and press seam open. Join the longer strips of fabric to the top and bottom, as shown in the Making Up diagram below, stitching across the side strips. Turn to the right side, over the raw edges. Tack, then machine, the cushion back to the strips, leaving one edge open. Turn right side out and hand hem the opening, turning 1.2cm under.

Designed by Angela Madden

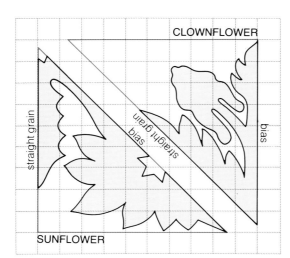

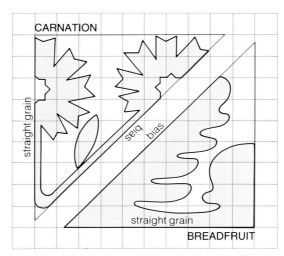

one square= 2.5cm / 1in

CHOOSING THE DESIGN

For small items such as these baby bootees, a simple motif is the best choice. The embroiderer has chosen the rabbit motifs both for their associations with childhood and because they can be treated in a simple, stylized way. The central rabbit is cut out from felt and appliquéed, while the others are outline-embroidered with running stitch.

MATERIALS

Fabric
20cm white brushed cotton, 90cm wide
20cm white cotton, 90cm wide
18cm 50g terylene wadding, 30cm wide
18cm heavy sew-in Vilene interfacing, 14cm wide
Scrap of white felt

White sewing thread
White stranded embroidery cotton
2 small press fasteners; 2 small buttons
Tailor's chalk; tracing paper
Small piece thin cardboard for template

Finished size: the bootees measure 11cm long and 5.5cm wide at the widest point

METHOD OF WORKING

Make a paper pattern by enlarging the one given in the diagram. Cut out two of each piece from white cotton and brushed cotton. Cut out two pieces A and B from wadding and two of D from Vilene.

To make the soles, trim off the 5mm seam allowance from the Vilene and mark a trellis pattern as shown, using the tailor's chalk. Place the pieces on the cotton, matching the edges of the Vilene to the seam allowance of the cotton. Tack in position and machine on the marked lines.

Tack the wadding to the wrong sides of pattern pieces A and B, and seam the sides of B, matching notches. Trim the wadding close to the seams.

Make a template for the rabbit motif by tracing the design given, then cut out two rabbits from felt and pin them in place on the centre front of each bootee. Apply by stitching all around the edges with back stitch, using three strands of embroidery thread. Work a cluster of French knots for the tail. Mark the outlines of the other rabbits by drawing around the template, positioning them as shown on the pattern. Work the outlines in back stitch, with French knots for the tails as before.

Attach the tops of the bootees to the soles, matching points a and b. Turn to right side. For the straps, stitch the cotton and brushed cotton pieces together, leaving an opening at the centre back for turning, as shown. Trim the seams and turn to the right side. Matching points c at centre back, and with right sides together, overstitch the straps to the backs of the bootees.

Lining
Stitch together the brushed cotton pieces for the backs, front and soles, allowing 9mm seams. Trim seams, then trim 4mm from the top edges. Turn over a further 5mm at the top edges and press well. Tack the linings into the bootees, pushing them down well into the corners.

Turn over and tack the 5mm seam allowance at the top of the outer bootees, then slip stitch the lining to it.

Sew press fasteners on to the straps and bootees; sew on the buttons as decoration.

Designed by Margaret Horton

CUTTING PATTERNS

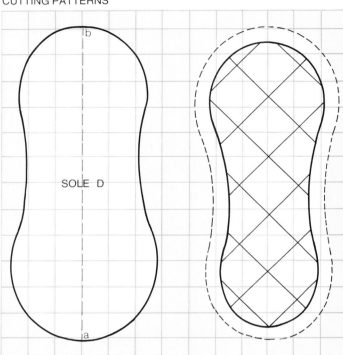

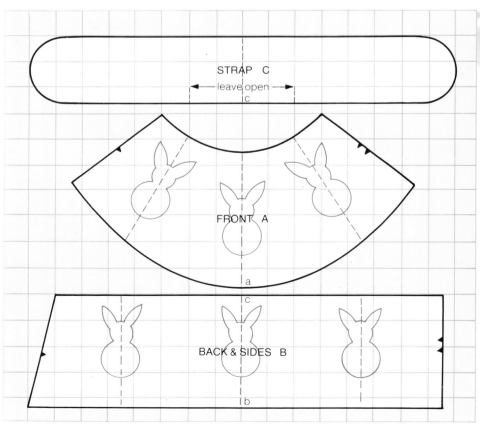

one square = 1cm/³⁄₈in

CHOOSING THE DESIGN

The design for this photograph album cover is derived from print samples which were created in Victorian times to edge advertising and visiting cards. Metal thread techniques are combined with the use of ribbon in this basically floral design. It would be most appropriate for a special album, containing photographs of a wedding, christening or other ceremonial occasion.

MATERIALS

Fabric
40cm handwoven Indian silk at least 80cm wide, in cream
40cm calico, 90cm wide for backing
Small piece yellow felt
Piece gold kid, 10cm by 7cm

Threads
1 reel cream silk thread
6m Japanese gold substitute size 3k
1m imitation Grecian cord
70cm pearl purl, size 3
80cm bright check purl, size 5
40cm smooth purl, size 5
40cm rough purl, size 1
1m cream ribbon, 7mm wide
50cm cream ribbon, 2mm wide

Crewel needle, size no.9
Chenille needles, sizes no.18 and 20
Piece of lightweight card

Finished size: to fit standard size photograph album, 27cm by 30cm

METHOD OF WORKING

Cut the silk and calico to measure 80cm by 40cm, and tack them together. Transfer the design from the Pattern Design chart below on to the silk fabric using the tracing and tacking method.

Couch down the imitation Grecian cord (see book, p. 97) on design line 2. Pull out the size 3 pearl purl to approximately double its length and stitch into position inside the Grecian cord (1).

Cut out three circles from card approximately 1.3cm in diameter (an old greeting card is suitable). Stitch each one down at four points, by bringing the needle up in the background fabric and then through the card. The card can be prepared by piercing with holes before placing in position.

Couch down ten rows of Japanese gold substitute (3) using the bricking method (see book, p. 98). At the top edge stagger the turned ends of the rows. At the bottom edge the ends should be taken down separately and staggered. Take all the ends down when the rest of the work is complete as it is easier to control the purl when it lies on the top rather than underneath. This also applies to the imitation Grecian cord.

Baste the zigzagged ribbon into position before finally stitching it along each side with small stitches in a matching sewing thread.

Flowers and leaves
Cut out felt padding for the flowers and leaves (see book, p. 98). Three graduated layers of padding are used for the flowers and two for the leaves. Stitch in position.

Cut the rough, check and smooth purls on a velvet board, into pieces about twice

PATTERN DESIGN

one square = 1.25cm/½in

MAKING UP

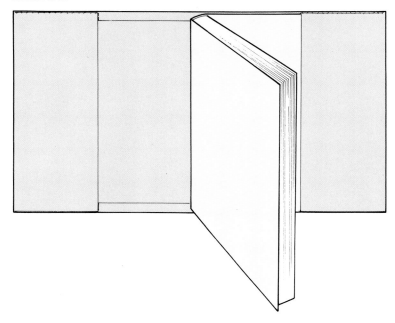

as long as their width. Purl is most effective if the larger sizes are cut squarish and the fine ones long; this works better than using them in a random way.

The top flower has five check purls in the centre of the petal; these are stitched on first and the five smooth ones are stitched around, filling the petal, thereby covering the felt. The lower flower is composed of rough purl in the centre and check purl around to complete the petal.

Trace the leaf shape on to a piece of card. Draw around this shape on the wrong side of the kid and cut around it. This will make the kid fractionally bigger so that it covers the felt adequately.

Couch down the imitation Grecian cord stem (4). Then stitch pearl purl to join up leaves to the stem, stitching a small amount as veining on the leaves. It is easier to stitch on kid if the needle position is found by putting indentations in the kid from the wrong side, checking that the needle position is correct before perforating the kid. (A hole where the kid has been pierced inadvertently will show.)

Using the fine ribbon, make French knots for the centre of each flower, using a size no.20 chenille needle.

Take down all ends using a size no.18 chenille needle. Take the imitation Grecian cord down in three parts, the underneath section of cord first.

MAKING UP

Turn under 5cm at the top and bottom of the cover. Check that this fits your photograph album, then tack. Fold in 12.5cm at either end and check against your album; press. It is always difficult to calculate the thickness of fabric when making up, so checks should be made at each stage.

Fold under 2cm of the 12.5cm to neaten the raw edges and tack. Slip stitch together at the top and bottom and both sides, as shown in the Making Up diagram below. You may have to carry out the final stitching when the album cover is on the album. Remove the tacking.

OPTIONS

Cream and gold are used here, but silver yarn could be used with white and silver-grey ribbons. A greater tonal value could be achieved by using golden-brown ribbons, or the gold metal thread retained and a new colour scheme devised by changing the background material, the stitching thread (as used for the bricking) and the ribbon, and by using a coloured leather instead of gold kid.

A photograph could be placed on the front cover as well as the initials of the owner or recipient, or such memorabilia as dried flowers from a wedding bouquet.

Designed by Janice Williams

CHOOSING THE DESIGN

A sketch of freesia flowers inspired this design for cutwork. The curve of the spray fitted well into the top of the camisole, requiring only a little adjustment to create a pleasing and balanced design. It is essential to ensure that flowers and leaves touch, otherwise the embroidery will fall apart when the open parts of the design are cut away.

Texture on the flowers and leaves is created by twisted chain stitch, bullion knots and trailing, a kind of stem stitch. The outline is worked in buttonhole stitch.

MATERIALS

1.5m pink satin, 90cm wide
Threads
1 reel pink sewing thread
1 reel pink silk twist
2 skeins pink stranded cotton

Crewel needle, size no. 10

Finished size: to fit bust 90cm (size 12)

METHOD OF WORKING

Use two strands of cotton throughout, except for the bullion knots which are worked in silk twist.

You must work all the embroidery before cutting out the garment, so be careful to place the embroidery design on the fabric in a position which allows plenty of room for the rest of the garment to be cut. Trace the design on to the cloth with a sharp, hard pencil (see book, p.64), and mark with a cross the areas which are to be cut away.

Work over all the design lines with a small running stitch, to 'pad' the embroidery. Then work the main lines of the design in buttonhole stitch, making sure that the knotted edges are against the cut away areas. Complete all the other embroidery stitches before cutting away the cutwork areas (see book, p.100).

MAKING UP

Join the front and back of the camisole with French seams. Hem the lower edge. Make a vertical slit about 1cm long in the centre front about 5cm below the waistline and work buttonhole stitch around it.

Press a small turning under the long edges of the casing and sew this to the inside of the camisole, about 5cm below the waistline. Leave the short ends open until you have inserted the drawstring.

Make the shoulder straps and draw-string from rouleaux. The simplest way to make rouleaux is to cut strips of bias fabric then fold them in half lengthwise, right sides together. Stitch, leaving the ends open. Attach a length of strong thread to one end of the tube at the seam. Pull the thread gently through the tubing, using a large needle or bodkin, inserting the eye first.

Fix the shoulder straps neatly inside the front and back of the camisole, at the top,

adjusting the length as necessary. Thread the drawstring through the casing, bringing the ends out through the centre front hole.

Designed by Angela Dewar

KEY

— bullion knots
— buttonhole stitch
— trailing
— twisted chain stitch

▨ areas to be cut away

CUTWORK DESIGN

one square = ½in/1.25cm

CUTTING PATTERNS

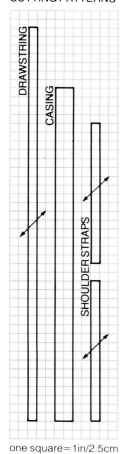

DRAWSTRING

CASING

SHOULDER STRAPS

one square = 1in/2.5cm

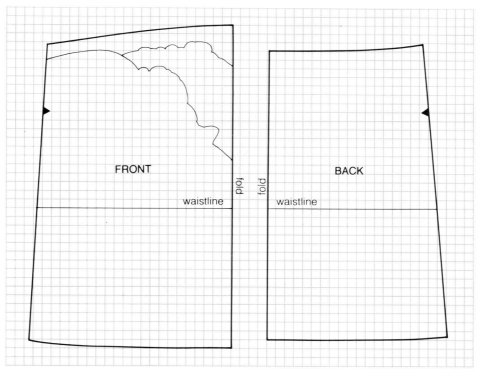

FRONT

BACK

fold

waistline   waistline

one square = ½in/1.25cm

CHOOSING THE DESIGN

Elevate a simple, shop-bought cardigan into the 'designer hand-knit' class with some clever embroidery. The design for the embroidered panels was inspired by, and adapted from, that found on a hand-knitted and embroidered cardigan discovered in a shop selling antique clothes. The original design has been simplified to make the front right and left sides mirror images of each other.

The embroidery is simple cross stitch in 3- and 4-ply yarns and is worked on a plain white woollen cardigan purchased from a chain store. It is important that the background fabric is predominantly woollen (at least 70 per cent wool to 30 per cent man-made fibres), so that any distortion caused by the embroidery can be corrected by lightly blocking and steaming the garment back into shape. Since knitted and other non-woven fabrics can stretch and 'give', the embroidery is worked through a canvas mesh to give a firmer backing. This is later dismantled.

MATERIALS

1 plain white knitted cardigan (this one is in pure wool to fit bust 95cm, size 14)
Tapestry wool
1 skein in each of the seven colours – pale blue, pale green, mid green, shell pink (pink I), salmon pink (pink II), yellow, lilac
2 skeins black stranded wool, used as either 1-strand or 2-strand

Tapestry needle, medium size
50cm rug canvas, 90cm wide (5 holes to the inch)

METHOD OF WORKING

Cut a piece of canvas to size for the first embroidered panel: calculate the required dimensions by counting the number of stitches in each direction and adding one or two extra rows to allow for tacking the canvas down. Loosely tack it into place on the cardigan over the area to be embroidered.

Work to the colour-coded charts below, embroidering one panel at a time. The whole area is worked in cross stitch except for the black outline, which is done in single-strand back stitch at the end.

To start work, make a back stitch on the back of the cardigan – a knot would pull through the knitted fabric. Finish off threads by running them through the back of some embroidered stitches.

When all the cross stitches in one panel are worked, dismantle the canvas by snipping and pulling it away *one thread at a time*. Then work the back stitches in single-strand black wool to form an outline.

Complete each embroidered panel in this way, then work buttonhole stitch around the neck and front edges of the cardigan, using 3-ply black wool.

FINISHING OFF

Place the embroidered front on a soft pad (such as a folded towel) to prevent the embroidered area becoming flattened as you press. Then, using a damp cloth or a steam iron, lightly press the embroidered areas from the back, to smooth away puckering.

OPTIONS

Any cross stitch or canvaswork design could be embroidered on to a garment in this way – look at samplers or old needlework books to get ideas.

To scale the embroidery down to a smaller size, for example on a child's cardigan, simply use a smaller gauge canvas, such as 10 holes to the inch.

The colours could be varied, but make sure you use compatible shades: all subdued, all brights or all pastels.

The technique could also be used on an evenweave fabric, using cotton or silk threads.

Designed by Janet Haigh

KEY

CROSS STITCH
- ✕ pink I
- ○ pale blue
- • pale green
- ● mid green
- ◣ yellow
- ◹ pink II
- ▲ lilac
- ■ black

BACK STITCH
- □ black

FRONT OF CARDIGAN
(reverse for right-hand side)

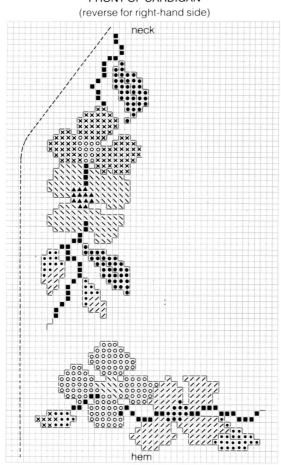

neck

hem

five squares = 1in/2.5cm

BACK OF CARDIGAN

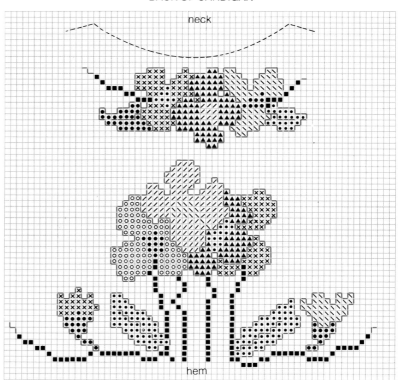

neck

hem

CHOOSING THE DESIGN

Blackwork is a traditional form of embroidery, but its graphic look gives it a modern appeal. The basket of fruit is a perfect motif for blackwork, since it has a well-defined outline and the varied textures of the fruit and the basket are depicted through different patterns and densities.

MATERIALS

1.6m evenweave linen, 140cm wide (20 threads to the inch) for the tablecloth; 50cm for each napkin
1 skein stranded embroidery cotton, black
1 reel sewing thread, white
Tapestry needle, size no. 22
Fine sharps needle
Tracing paper or graph paper

Finished size: the cloth measures 141cm by 150cm; the napkins are 48cm square

METHOD OF WORKING

The tablecloth

Find the centre of the fabric by folding it across the length and the width. Mark the centre point, then withdraw three threads 20cm from the point on all four sides to form a central square measuring 40cm. Weave about 2.5cm of the withdrawn threads back into the fabric to prevent fraying. Work any of the drawn thread patterns shown in the book on pages 106–9, using one strand of black thread.

Hem the edges of the cloth by working three-sided stitch or an edging stitch of your choice.

Trace the motif from the Pattern Design below, either by tracing through the fabric with a water-soluble fabric-marking pen as for canvaswork (see book, p. 123) or by drawing up the design on graph paper and counting out each stitch on to the fabric. The latter method is more accurate.

If you use 2.5cm square graph paper there will be two threads to each small square.

Work the outlines of the design in Holbein (double running) stitch (see book, p. 103), using one or two strands of thread depending on the effect desired. Complete the design with filling stitches, either those indicated in the design or any of those shown in the book on page 104.

The napkins

Cut out a square of fabric 50cm by 50cm for each napkin. Double-hem the edges invisibly using one strand of white thread and tiny hemming stitches. Mark out a triangular area in one corner as shown by withdrawing three threads for 13cm on each side; work over them using the same stitch as for the tablecloth. Position the design within the triangle as indicated and work it as for the tablecloth.

Designed by Caroline Davis

PATTERN DESIGN

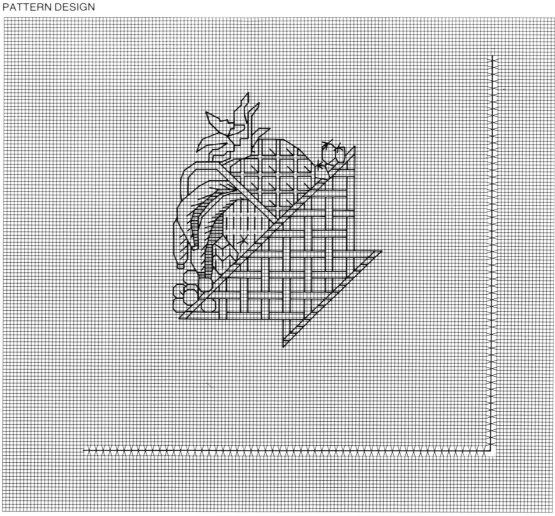

each square = one thread

CHOOSING THE DESIGN

This form of embroidery, known as needle-point lace, derives from cutwork and drawn thread work. The design is based on a grid formation, using the warp and weft threads of the fabric. The open areas are filled with detached buttonhole and picot bars.

MATERIALS

Fabric
25cm evenweave linen, 90cm wide, 30 threads to the inch in a natural colour
25cm satin, 90cm wide, contrasting colour
Small quantity terylene wadding
Small piece plastic cloth, 8cm square

1 spool linen lace thread (see book, p.144)
Sharps needle, size no.6; tapestry needle, size no.22
Thimble, sharp embroidery scissors, pins
Sewing cotton for tacking

Finished size: the pincushion measures 12cm square, the lavender bag 19cm high

WORKING THE PINCUSHION

Cut out two 13cm squares of linen along a thread of the fabric, checking that each is absolutely square by folding diagonally.

Work the front. For the hem, mark two threads 2cm from all edges with pins. Snip these threads at the centre of each side and withdraw them (see book, p.107) until they meet at the corners, but do not completely remove them or cut them off. Turn under 5mm at the outside edge, then fold hem back to meet the withdrawn threads, turning the opposite sides first. The corners are worked square, with any surplus bulk trimmed inside the hem. Pin, tack and then slip stitch the hem invisibly, using the sharps needle and linen thread, and secure the corners.

Following the diagram overleaf, which

is shown actual size, and working towar the middle of the square, leave fou threads and withdraw two on all side Neaten the work by tacking the withdraw threads to the corner of the hem ther using the tapestry needle, work doubl four-sided stitch (see book, p.108) ove four threads, making the stitch smaller a necessary as you reach the corner.

To mark the inner square, withdraw tw threads as shown, leaving ten, then leav four and withdraw two. Neaten the work a before, then work four-sided stitch aroun this square, using the tapestry needl Now leave four threads and remove one t meet at the corners. To make the cros count the threads, find the middle three i each direction and remove the outer tw threads of the three, both ways.

Padded roll
Mount the linen on the plastic square, fir pinning it and then back stitching aroun the inner four-sided stitch square, makin sure the centre three threads cross at rigl angles. To work the padded roll inside th four-sided stitch, first overcast the fou thread area outside the stitching with sma slanting stitches, as shown, then cut length of linen thread three times th length of the whole square to form th padding.

Knot the thread at one end, cut any loop at the other, lay it over the overcast stitche and work a close satin stitch over botl cutting away the surplus linen just befor stitching. Take care not to cut the centra three threads of the cross, which will for the foundation for the cutwork lace. Mak the stitches even and smooth and catch i any loose ends as you sew. Try to stitc into the threads of the fabric, not betwee them, and regulate the tension on th square by pulling gently on the paddin threads as you go. Work a tight stitch a each corner to hold the padding firm Finish at the last corner by trimming th padding threads flush and working a fina stitch to cover the ends. If you run out c thread during the work, run off the ol thread into the overcast stitching and ru in the new one in the same place.

Cutwork central square
Cut away any surplus linen from th centre, again taking care not to cut th centre cross. Begin to work the lace fillin

For the centre three bar, lay a reinfor ing thread across, going through the ro on both sides and oversewing the ba closely (see book, p.108). Repeat this vei tically, making sure the cross is exactly i the middle. For the spokes, lay thre threads diagonally and oversew then stitching through the cross to hold the ba secure each time you cross the centre.

At the centre, work a bullion knot star a follows. Lay a single-thread ring 7.5m from the centre by passing through th spokes three times. Work three buttor hole stitches, then one picot and anothe three buttonhole stitches between eac spoke, and one buttonhole stitch on th spoke. To work the picot, make a buttor

hole stitch on the bar, then another into the top of it. Make a tiny bullion knot (see book, p.78) into the top of the second stitch and come back through the top of the first one.

Lay another ring outside the first and 1.5cm from the centre by passing through the spokes three times. Work a petal between each spoke by working nine buttonhole stitches on the inside edge, then returning to the starting point with backward buttonhole stitches. Work a second row of eight stitches and a third of six, then work one buttonhole stitch on the spoke ready to start the next petal.

For the corner bars, lay three threads across the corner, going through the roll and the diagonal bar each time. Work three buttonhole stitches, one picot and three buttonholes in each space as before, with one buttonhole stitch on the bar. This completes the lace.

FINISHING OFF

Neaten the withdrawn fabric threads at the corners by folding them back over the hem and making a line of small running stitches to hold them flat. Trim the threads to 2.5mm, then make a backward buttonhole stitch back to the beginning as shown; work buttonhole stitch to cover the cut ends. Repeat for the corners of the four-sided stitch surrounding the cutwork square.

Make the hem for the back of the pincushion as for the front, then press both pieces under a damp cloth; allow to dry.

Stitch three sides together with bullion knots spaced about 5mm apart; work two at each corner. On the fourth side work the bullion knots on the front only. Make a small cushion pad of satin, 10cm square, fill it with wadding and place inside the linen. Slip stitch the fourth side to close.

WORKING THE LAVENDER BAG

Cut out a piece of linen 38cm by 13cm and remove the threads as shown in the diagram. Note that the hems on the short edge have a finished depth of 2.5cm. Count 10 threads in from the bottom and sides and mark the square from these points. Embroider as described for the pincushion.

Press, then make four woven bars in the 12-thread space to take the cord. Tack in the lining and sew up both sides to the deep hem, using bullion knots spaced about 5mm apart. Continue around the opening.

Make a twisted cord (see book, p.141) from the linen thread, slot it through the woven bars and knot. Make a small lavender bag from the remaining lining fabric.

**Designed by Gail Marsh and
Jacqueline Blackburn of *Bottom Drawer***

PINCUSHION

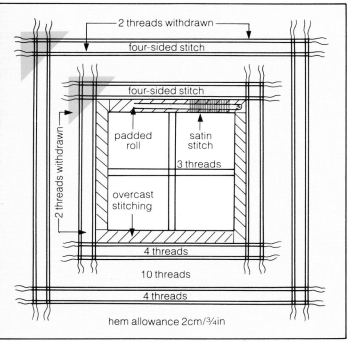

2 threads withdrawn
four-sided stitch
four-sided stitch
2 threads withdrawn
padded roll
satin stitch
3 threads
overcast stitching
4 threads
10 threads
4 threads
hem allowance 2cm/¾in

NEATENING THE CORNERS

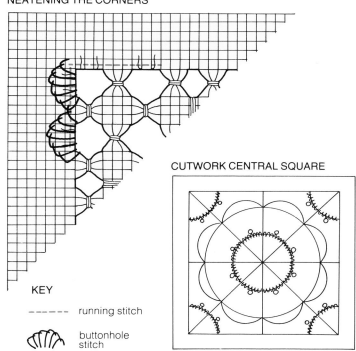

KEY

------ running stitch

buttonhole stitch

CUTWORK CENTRAL SQUARE

LAVENDER BAG

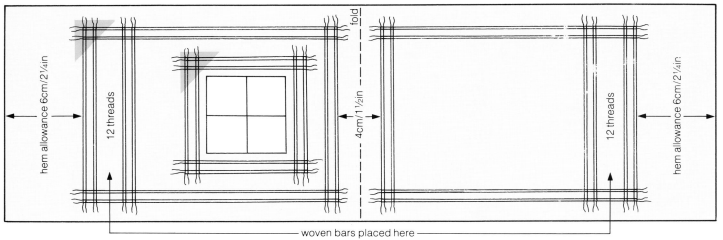

hem allowance 6cm/2¼in
12 threads
fold
4cm/1½in
12 threads
hem allowance 6cm/2¼in
woven bars placed here

CHOOSING THE DESIGN

Pulled work is a counted thread method of embroidery, which the designer finds both restful and therapeutic. The stitches were chosen not only for their inherent suitability, but because they can be neatened on the back satisfactorily, an important consideration in table linen.

MATERIALS

For four mats
50cm evenweave linen
5 skeins stranded embroidery thread (white, pink, green, lilac, blue)
1 reel silver lurex embroidery thread
Tapestry needle, size no. 22

Finished size: each mat measures 42cm by 26cm

METHOD OF WORKING

Cut a piece of fabric for each mat measuring 46cm by 30cm (the finished size plus 2cm for the hem). Lightly oversew the edges to prevent fraying while working. Tack the vertical and horizontal centre lines as a guide to positioning the central eyelet stitches.

Working from the chart below, mark the position of each eyelet stitch. Each one is worked over six threads, and is separated from its neighbour by two threads. Work the eyelet stitches (see book, p. 111) using three strands of the main colour, taking each stitch into the same central hole.

Next work the four sided stitch (see book, p. 111), using a single strand of the main colour. Note that this is separated from the eyelets by four threads, and the outside rows of border stitches are separated from each other by two threads.

Work the satin stitch over two threads, using three strands of the main colour. Then work four sided stitch over two threads, using one strand of white thread.

This completes the border rows. Now work cross stitches (see book, p. 103), between the eyelets, using two strands of white thread.

Picot edge and hem
Work the picot edge as follows.

Approximately 17 threads from the edge, and on the wrong side, work stem stitch (see book, p. 70) twice over three threads, using three strands of the main colour. Turn to right side and fold the fabric on the stitch line. Using the silver thread, work two satin stitches between each picot, pulling the satin stitches tight to accentuate the scalloped effect.

Mitre the corners (see book, p. 140), turn 5mm under, and secure hem by pin stitching (see book, p. 87) to edge of outer border row.

OPTIONS

The basic design can be varied in many ways. For instance, the eyelets could be worked in a different colour to provide contrast with the borders, the cross stitches could be omitted altogether, or a whole central area worked in cross stitch, with the borders made more dramatic by working the stitches over four threads instead of two.

Designed by Margaret Darby

KEY   each line = one thread

⌒ picot stem stitch
⊏⊔⊔ satin stitch
− − hem-pin stitch
⊏⊐⊏ four sided stitch (single strand)
||||| satin stitch
⊏⊐ four sided stitch (single strand)
⊏⊐ four sided stitch (double strand)
×× cross stitch
❋ eyelet

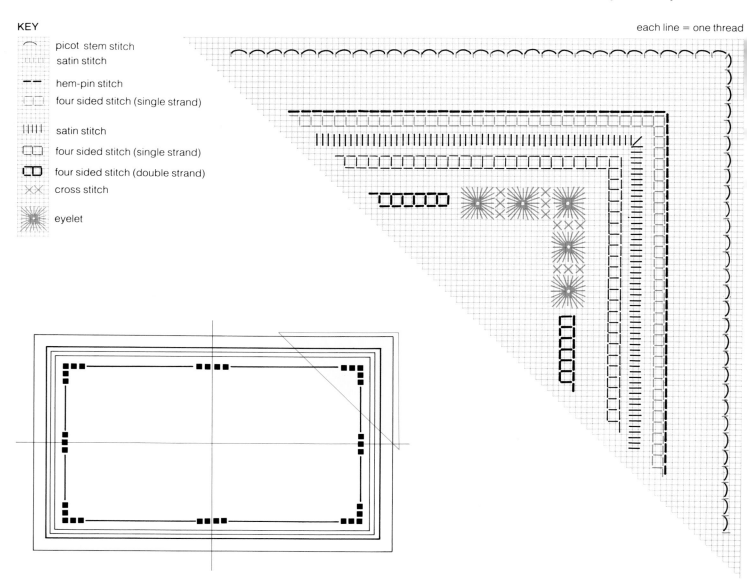

CHOOSING THE DESIGN

This sailor collar was designed to be soft, delicate and feminine, and the materials and technique were chosen accordingly. The fabric is a fine cotton lawn, the embroidery is drawn thread work. To enhance the impression of softness, the collar was made double, with a small, lighter collar lying on top of the larger one.

MATERIALS

50cm fine white cotton voile, 90cm wide
White stranded embroidery cotton or machine embroidery cotton
White pearl cotton no. 8
Very fine crewel needle

Finished size: the outer collar measures 36cm wide, 40.5cm from front to back and 14cm deep from the facing to the edge. The inner collar measures 27.5cm wide, 32 cm from front to back and 9.5cm deep.

METHOD OF WORKING

Outer collar

Cut an oblong of voile measuring 50cm by 45cm for the main collar piece. Withdraw one thread along all four sides 2cm from the cut edge. Withdraw a band of threads 5mm wide 6cm from all edges, as shown in the Pattern Design diagram overleaf. Leave a band of 10 threads, then withdraw another band 5mm wide, to join with the first one. Again leaving 10 threads in between, withdraw a third band the same width as the first and to join the first band.

Fold the fabric along the single, outer withdrawn thread, then fold again so that the fold aligns with the outside edge of the first withdrawn band. Tack with a soft, fine thread.

Using a single strand of embroidery thread, work herringbone stitch over the two bands of threads remaining, gathering the loose threads into bundles of four. Using pearl cotton, and working in coral stitch as shown in the Outer Collar diagram, tie bars in the centre strips into clusters of three.

Using one strand of embroidery thread, work hem stitch on both inner and outer edges of border, mitring all corners (see book, p. 107).

Inner collar

For the inner collar piece, which forms a layer on top of the one already worked, cut a piece of voile 40cm by 35cm and withdraw one thread for the hem as before. Withdraw a single band of threads, 5mm wide and 6cm from the edges. This forms the border. Work the hem as before, but hem stitch only on the outer edge of the withdrawn band. Using pearl cotton, work cross stitch over about four threads on the inner edge. This will divide the bars in half, creating a zigzag effect.

MAKING UP

Place the two oblongs together so that the edges of the small one lie just inside the inner edge of the border of the larger one.

Cut the neck and back openings in the collar as shown in the Pattern Design diagram. Cut out the facings from a left-over piece of the voile, using an enlarged version of the Cutting Pattern.

Cut an oblong of voile the length of the back opening and 3.5cm wide. With right sides together, seam to back opening 1cm from the edge as shown in the diagram for binding the back opening. Turn to right side, fold under 5mm on the raw edge and hand hem on the first stitching line.

Join back and front facings with a 1cm seam. With right sides together, join facings to collar, then snip carefully to seam on curves and turn to right side. Finish edges with hand hem stitch or machine stitch.

Designed by Gisela Banbury

CUTTING PATTERN

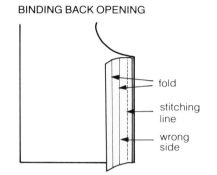

one square = 1cm/⅜in

BINDING BACK OPENING

fold
stitching line
wrong side

PATTERN DESIGN

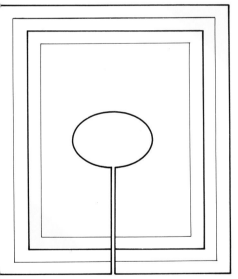

KEY

- coral stitch
- herringbone stitch
- hem stitch
- cross stitch
- voile

OUTER COLLAR

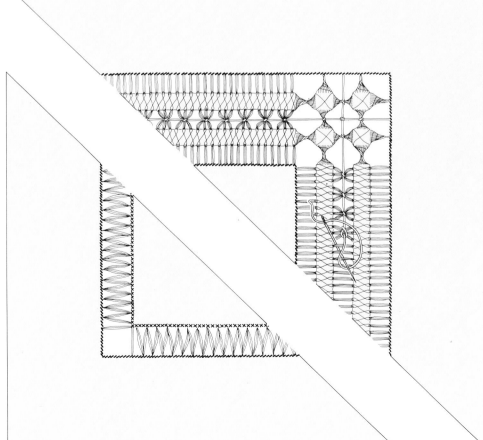

INNER COLLAR

CHOOSING THE DESIGN

Your choice of smocking motif is deter
mined by the limitations of the technique
itself, in that smocking is carried out in
straight lines, not curves. A completely
round motif, for example, will not be suc
cessful, and any animal or picture motif
has to be simplified and stylized to take
these limitations into consideration. Bear
in mind that such a motif also has to be
supported by lines of back smocking.

MATERIALS

1.75m cotton lawn or cotton/polyester mix
90cm wide
Threads
4 skeins stranded embroidery cotton, one
in each of the main colours used: yellow
dark blue, light blue, white
Small amount of brown and black stranded
embroidery cotton
1 reel light blue sewing thread

3 small yellow buttons
1m narrow yellow ribbon
2 pairs press fasteners

Finished size: to fit chest 55cm
approximate age $1\frac{1}{2}$–$2\frac{1}{2}$ years

METHOD OF WORKING

First make a paper pattern by enlarging
the outlines given overleaf; pin this on to
your fabric and cut out the pieces.
    Work all the smocking before starting to
assemble the dress.

The smocking

Refer to the section on Smocking in the book (pp. 112–15) before embarking on this. Gather the front skirt into eight rows of closely worked gathering stitches, 1cm apart, starting 1.5cm down from the top. Leave 1cm at each side for a seam allowance.

Work the smocking stitches as shown in the key below, using three strands of thread. Remove the gathering stitches.

MAKING UP

With right sides together, join front yoke to back yokes at shoulder seams. Join front facing to back facings at shoulder seams. Join front and back yoke to front and back facings at neck edge and centre back. Clip corners, turn to right side and press. With right sides together, attach front yoke to skirt front at top of smocking, taking a seam of 1cm. Turn under 1cm on front facing and slip stitch in place.

Attach the back skirt placket as follows. Turn under one long edge of strip by 5mm and press. Mark position of placket, in the centre of the skirt back and 11cm from the top edge; stitch, as shown, to reinforce seam, then slash to top of stitching. Pin right side of placket to wrong side of skirt and stitch all the way around on the previous stitching line, lifting the machine foot and pivoting the fabric to enable you to stitch down the other side. (The diagram

below gives a simplified view of this stage.) Press seam towards placket, turn placket to outside along fold line, and stitch pressed edge over seam. Bring folded edges of placket together, as shown, and stitch across diagonally, then turn front to inside and tack across upper edge.

Gather back skirt, but do not take gathering across placket, and attach to back yoke pieces as for the skirt front. Join front and back side seams from hem to bottom of armholes with a 1cm plain or French seam. Neaten seams if necessary.

Turn a 5mm hem on the bottom of each sleeve piece twice and hem, then attach ribbon 5mm from the edges. Join each sleeve with a 1cm plain or French seam, and neaten if necessary. Gather sleeve tops, adjust gathering to fit armhole. Tack in place and then sew. Neaten seam.

Sew ribbon in place around neck 5mm from edge, turning it over by about 1–2cm

at the back. Make three evenly spaced buttonholes 5mm from edge of right back yoke; sew on buttons in corresponding position on left back yoke. Sew on press fasteners above the top and below the bottom button. Turn up hem to desired length and slip stitch in place.

OPTIONS

To make a dress for a bigger child, either increase the dimensions of this pattern all over, or buy a simple child's dress pattern for the right age and size and enlarge the skirt front to accommodate the smocking. As a rough guide, allow three times the eventual width for the smocked part of the garment.

Designed by Penny Rawlings

TOP OF BACK SKIRT

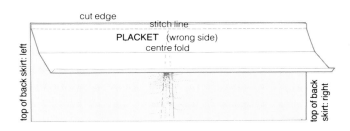

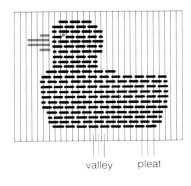

DUCK MOTIF KEY
- cable stitch (yellow)
- French knot (blue)
- oversewn beak (orange)

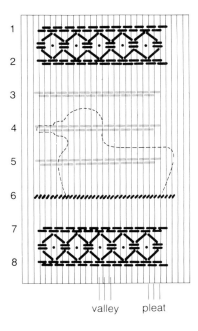

SMOCKING KEY
- cable stitch (yellow)
- back smocking (cable stitch)
- diamond stitch (blue)
- back stitch (white)
- stem stitch (blue)

CUTTING PATTERN

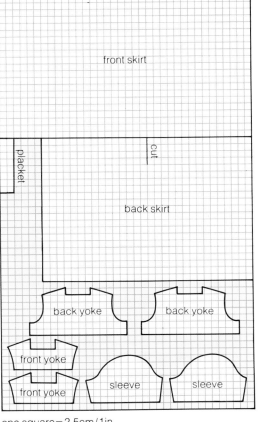

one square=2.5cm/1in

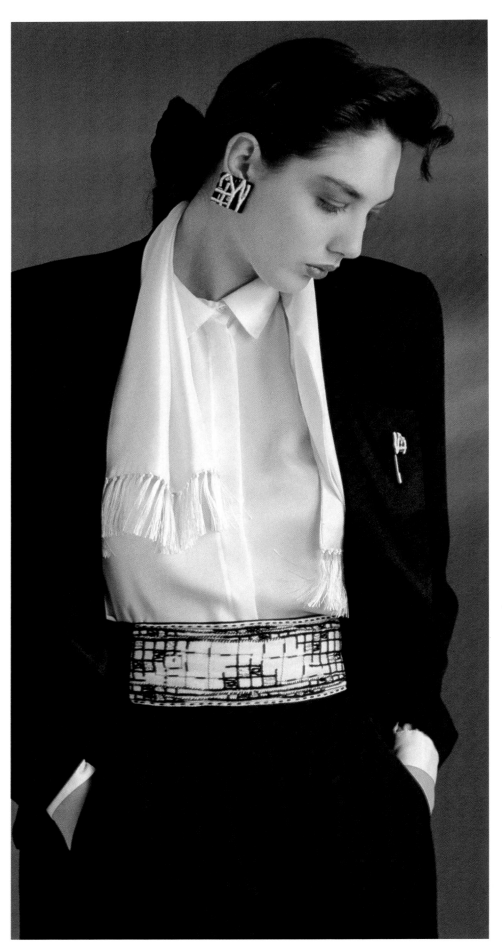

CHOOSING THE DESIGN

The original inspiration for this embroidery came from drawings of seaweeds, shells and fish, which were cut into squares and composed as a collage. Based on this collage, free machine embroidery samples were produced. These were then refined into the design used here.

The black and white colour scheme was chosen partly because the stark contrast emphasizes the design and partly because the black and white combination is a fashion classic that can be worn with many different colours and outfits.

MATERIALS FOR CUMMERBUND

Fabric
30cm white cotton muslin, 90cm wide
40cm black silk dupion, 115cm wide
15cm heavy sew-in interfacing, 90cm wide
Threads
1 large reel black 100% spun polyester thread
1 reel white cotton machine embroidery thread
1 skein black pearl cotton no.5

3 self-covered buttons, 11mm diameter
Sharps needle, size no.7; machine needle, size no.80
Beads: 25g each of black seed beads; clear cut-glass beads; black bugle beads (medium and small); silver bugle beads.

MATERIALS FOR EARRINGS AND PIN

Fabrics, threads and beads from allowance for cummerbund
10cm square foam sheet, 1cm thick
Small quantity cardboard, 1-2mm thick
Pair glue-on clip earring fittings
Glue-on stick-pin fitting with felt pad
Instant adhesive; fabric adhesive

Finished size: the cummerbund is 60cm long, but can be adjusted to fit desired waist size. The earrings are 3cm square, the pin 2cm square.

WORKING THE CUMMERBUND

Cut a rectangle of muslin measuring 90cm by 26cm. Transfer to it the pattern of fold lines at the top and bottom of the central panel shown in Diagram 1 overleaf, using the machine method. These lines act as a guide to the free embroidery as well as being used to fold the fabric when the embroidery is complete.

Select the area to be embroidered and mount the muslin on a ring frame about 25cm diameter. Set the machine up for free embroidery and, using the size no.80 needle and the black polyester thread, first work the partial grid pattern for the central embroidered panel shown in Diagram 2. This can be exactly as shown or varied slightly. When all the areas have been worked, fill in individual squares and emphasize the line with random free machine embroidery.

The beads are applied next, either following the pattern or varying as you prefer. Sew them on by hand, using the black polyester thread and the sharps needle. Make lines of oversewing stitches between beads as shown in the photograph.

Turn under the top and bottom edges of the muslin and machine stitch 2mm from the edges using black polyester thread. Fold the muslin as follows to make one fold above and below the central panel alternately. Take fold line A to points B; take fold line B to points C; take fold line C to points D, and fold line D to points E.

MAKING UP THE CUMMERBUND

Oversew the eight folded edges of muslin using the black pearl cotton. Cut out the dupion piece according to Diagram 3; cut out the interfacing 1.2cm smaller all around. Tack the interfacing to the wrong side of one of the dupion pieces inside the 1.2cm seam allowance. Place dupion pieces right sides together and seam 1.2cm from the edges, leaving the ends open for adjustment. Turn to right side.

Place the embroidered panel in the centre of the dupion. Turn the raw edges under and press. Stitch the edges of the panel to the dupion, using small hem stitches and black thread. Press the cummerbund under a cloth. Top stitch top and bottom edges of dupion to correspond with the hemmed edge of the muslin panel, then apply small black bugle beads along the top and bottom edges as shown. Cover the buttons as instructed by the manufacturer and stitch in place as shown on the Cutting Pattern diagram. Make loops to correspond with the buttons. Remove tacking.

WORKING THE JEWELLERY

Cut three pieces of cardboard, two 3cm square and one 2cm square. Mount an off-cut of dupion in the small ring frame and draw around the cardboard pieces, spacing them as far apart as the frame will allow. Using white embroidery thread, and with the machine set for free embroidery, follow the pattern given in Diagram 4 below. Apply beads using black thread.

Cut three squares of dupion about 1cm larger all around than the cardboard pieces. Spread one side of each thinly with fabric adhesive; glue to dupion squares and leave to dry. Fold edges of dupion over and tack the corners as shown below. Cut pieces of foam sheet to the same size and cut out embroidered squares, leaving a 5mm allowance all around to be turned under. Place foam on tacked side of square with the embroidered square on top, fold the edges under and sew around them. Glue earring clips and stick-pin fitting to backs.

Designed by Vanessa Richards

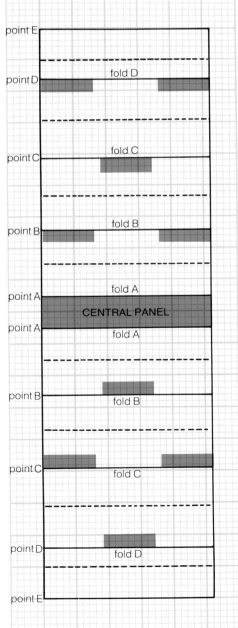

DIAGRAM 1: FOLD LINES

point E
fold D
point D
fold C
point C
fold B
point B
fold A
point A
CENTRAL PANEL
point A
fold A
point B
fold B
point C
fold C
point D
fold D
point E

five squares = 5cm/2in

KEY

○ clear bead   ▬ small black bugle   ━ free embroidery
▭ silver bugle   ▬ large black bugle   — free embroidery
▪ seed bead   ▨ free embroidered areas

DIAGRAM 2: CENTRAL EMBROIDERED PANEL

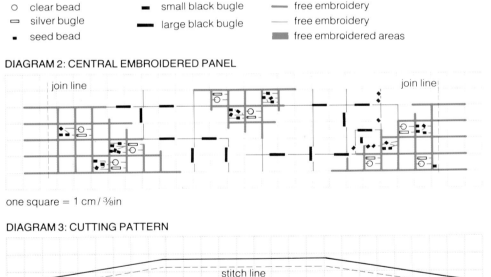

join line   join line

one square = 1 cm / ⅜in

DIAGRAM 3: CUTTING PATTERN

stitch line

one square = 2.5cm/1in

DIAGRAM 4

EARRINGS   PIN

  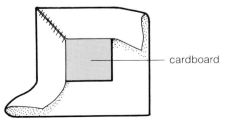

cardboard

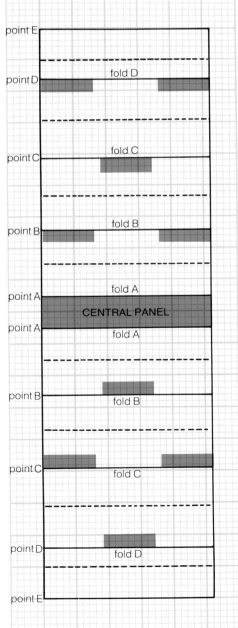

CHOOSING THE DESIGN

The original idea for this free machine embroidery came from a collection of photographs, postcards and sketches the designer had built up over several holidays. The final design was achieved by trying out various simple images, then placing these within borders to emphasize the picture-postcard theme.

MATERIALS

60cm unbleached calico, 60cm wide
Threads
Machine embroidery threads in 500cm reels: 2 mid-green; 1 each of pale blue, mid-blue, dark blue, dark green, yellow, white, pale pink, red, burgundy, dark brown, light brown

Tracing paper and transfer pencil
Piece of hardboard 25.5cm by 21.5cm

Finished size: the picture measures 25.5cm by 21.5cm, unframed.

METHOD OF WORKING

Transfer the design to the calico, so that it is placed centrally (see book, p. 64). Stretch the calico in a bound ring frame (see book, p. 116).

The technique used is free machine embroidery worked in close lines to form solid blocks of stitches. Set the machine up for free embroidery (see book, p. 116) and start working from the centre, filling in each area in the colour shown in the photograph. Let the outline of each area dictate the direction of the stitch, as though you were drawing with coloured crayons. The tree trunks, for example, are worked vertically, while the stitches for the leaves echo the shapes of the leaves themselves. (If you have not done this form of embroidery before, it is advisable to practise on some spare stretched calico before embarking on the design.)

Keep the work drum-taut or the thread will gather and break, and operate the machine at a steady, even speed, moving the frame fairly slowly and smoothly. Work the design outward to the borders. Work a border in green, measuring about 3.5cm wide at the sides and 2.5cm wide at top and bottom.

FINISHING OFF

Stretch the work by lacing it over the piece of hardboard (see book, p. 138). It can be mounted and framed if desired. The frame in the photograph has been bound with stranded cotton, using double-sided tape (see book, p. 52). The bright colours chosen match those used in the embroidery.

Designed by Kay Lynch

CENTRAL DESIGN

CHOOSING THE DESIGN

This bright, bold canvaswork frieze of clowns, each performing a separate act, was designed specifically for children. The idea originated from a Christmas decoration. To execute it, the designer first made detailed drawings on tracing paper and then plotted them out on graph paper. The idea of jack-in-the-box clowns is carried through by placing each one in a separate box.

MATERIALS

Double-thread canvas, 71cm by 28cm (10 holes to the inch)
Threads
Embroidery wool: 3 skeins deep yellow; 2 skeins royal blue; 1 skein each cornflower blue, grey-blue, dark green, mid-green, light blue-green, dark red, cherry red, pink-red, pink, bright yellow, light yellow, ginger-brown, black and white
Tapestry needle, size no.20

Finished size: the finished frieze measures 66cm by 21.5cm, unframed

METHOD OF WORKING

Mount the canvas on a stretcher frame (see book, p. 67). The embroidery is worked mainly in tent stitch, with the hats in cross stitch and the flowers for the right-hand clown in French knots. Borders, corners and some other pattern elements, such as the balls for the juggling clown, are worked in long straight stitches.

Work from the chart, following the stitch and colour keys, and working all the background stitches first. Note that the straight stitches are worked between the double threads as well as between each pair of threads, as shown in the Pattern Design. Start each new stitch at the end of the previous one, since this is more economical. Work the corners as shown. When all the background has been covered, work the flowers in French knots, and work small straight stitches over the background stitches for the jug handle, the straws and the third clown's mouth.

FINISHING OFF

Remove the work from the frame and press it (see book, p. 136). It is recommended that the embroidery be framed professionally. A little of the border may be lost in framing, but this can be minimized by working a few rows of tent stitch around the edges.

OPTIONS

The clowns can be worked individually, as a set of cushions, for example, or four separate pictures. Vary the colours to suit personal preferences.

Designed by Louise Lovell

DOUBLE THREAD STITCHING

CORNERING

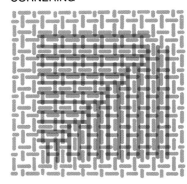

PATTERN DESIGN

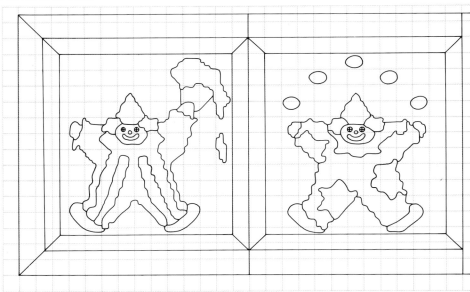

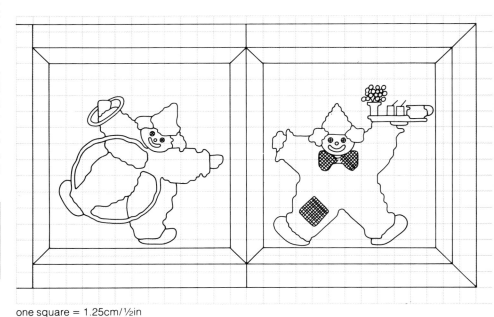

one square = 1.25cm/½in

CHOOSING THE DESIGN

The design for this canvaswork picture was based on a garden in rural England. The designer took several photographs and later made drawings from them, concentrating on the idea of a picture within a picture. The selected drawing was then transferred to graph paper to establish the scale and to make any necessary simplifications and modifications.

This designer is particularly interested in the contrasts between textures and areas of flat pattern. Both are combined in this embroidery.

MATERIALS

Single canvas, 24cm by 24cm (18 holes to the inch)
Crewel needle
Threads
Stranded embroidery cottons: 2 skeins black; 2 skeins dark grey; 2 skeins mid-grey; 2 skeins each in three shades of pale grey; 1 skein each of white, olive green, leaf green, bright green, mid-green, light yellow-green, pale green-white, light blue-green, off-white, pale blue, sky blue, deep blue; 4 shades of red from bright to dark.
1 skein white coton à broder

Finished size: the picture measures 18cm by 18cm, unframed

METHOD OF WORKING

Enlarge the design from the chart overleaf. Transfer the outlines to the canvas, then stretch the canvas over a stretcher frame.

Work the embroidery from the line chart, following the key that clarifies the stitches. The chart indicates which colours to use, but you might also refer to the photograph. Use three strands of cotton throughout, except for the inner border, which is worked in a single strand of coton

broder, and the sky, in which one strand
f each of the three pale greys are used in
he needle. Work the black, white and
rey areas first, followed by the white bor-
er, the coloured inner picture and finally
he outer border.

Block the finished work (see book,
. 136) and mount it by stretching it over a
iece of hardboard. (Or have it stretched
nd framed professionally.)

OPTIONS
The central picture could be worked in
black and white and the outer area in
colour. The design could also be enlarged considerably and worked on a
coarser canvas with wool threads.

esigned by Liz Mundle

MAKING UP

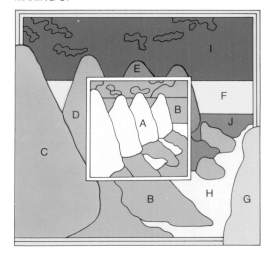

STITCH KEY
A = French knots
B = tent stitch
C = mosaic stitch
D = jacquard stitch
E = cross stitch
F = diagonal satin stitch
G = small chequer stitch
 (combination of mosaic and tent stitch)
H = tent stitch, reverse direction
I = long and short satin stitch
J = oblong cross stitch with
 back stitch at edges
INNER BORDER = diagonal satin stitch

STITCH CHART

CHOOSING THE DESIGN

The design consists of a trellis pattern enclosing diamond shapes. The trellis, in four toning shades of grey, is worked in diagonal satin stitch, giving a smooth background against which the orange diamonds, each filled by a double leviathan stitch, stand out as areas of texture.

The pattern repeat is quite small, so the design can be used for any size of chair seat. Tapestry wool has been chosen for the embroidery, since it is hardwearing, mothproof and fade-resistant.

MATERIALS

Single thread canvas, 75cm by 75cm (16 holes to the inch), or sufficient for the frame being used
Tapestry wool: 16 skeins orange; 11 skeins each of dark grey, mid-grey, and two shades of light grey
Tapestry needle, size no. 22
Sharps needle
1 reel sewing thread

Finished size: the embroidery for the chair shown measures 54cm along the front, 43cm along the back and 54cm along each side, to fit the chair seat measuring 42cm by 31cm by 42cm and approximately 5cm deep. The size will vary according to the chair seat being covered, but always allow for a 10cm surplus of unworked canvas around the design.

METHOD OF WORKING

Before starting the embroidery, remove the old chair seat covering and use it to work out exactly what area of the canvas needs to be stitched; to avoid excess bulk at the corners, leave unworked those parts that will be overlapped and work only the area that will show when the seat is in position. Any final adjustments may well have to be done after making up.

Mount the canvas in the frame or pin or staple it to the stretcher, taking care to keep the grain straight and the canvas square. Using sewing thread, tack the horizontal and vertical outside lines of the design on to the canvas. Then tack between these two lines to mark the slanting side edges. Mark the centre of the design in the same way.

Work the trellis pattern from the chart below, starting at the centre of the canvas and using one shade of grey over the whole area at a time. Work the satin stitch (see book, p. 125) over three vertical and one horizontal canvas intersections, all in the same direction. When the trellis background is complete, work a double leviathan stitch (see book, p. 131) in each diamond.

MAKING UP

Block the embroidery (see book, p. 136) to even out any distortions; let the work dry.

Trim the surplus canvas around the embroidery to 5cm, and lay the work right side down on a clean, flat surface. Position the seat centrally over the canvas and fold the edges of the canvas over the seat.

Insert one staple or tack at the centre of each side and check that the embroidery is in the correct position. Staple or tack the canvas to the chair seat around the edges, folding the corners in as neatly as possible. Trim away the canvas to within 1cm of the staples or tacks. Drop the covered seat into place on the chair.

> ### OPTIONS
> The trellis could be worked in dark colours, with the diamonds in bright primaries, or pastel shades used throughout for a more traditional look.
>
> Since this design has such a small repeat, it can be used for many other items such as cushion covers, bags, spectacle cases and pincushions, worked in either tapestry wool or stranded cotton.

Designed by Jan Eaton

STITCH CHART

CHOOSING THE DESIGN

The bowl of flowers is a traditional embroidery theme, but here an unusually subtle and interesting effect has been achieved by an ingenious choice of stitch and colour combinations. For the tent stitch background the designer has used a series of gently gradated colours echoed in the outer border, where the colours are arranged to give the effect of a Florentine pattern. The stylized Clarkia flowers are worked in straight stitches of varying lengths with four strands of wool so that they stand out in semi-relief.

MATERIALS

Single mesh canvas, 46cm by 46cm (13 threads to the inch)
Tapestry needle, size no. 20
Crewel wool: 11 skeins off-white; 5 skeins white; 4 skeins palest yellow; 3 skeins shell pink; 2 skeins each sky blue, bright rose pink, orange-red, pale lilac; 1 skein each mid-green, 2 shades leaf green, 2 shades royal blue, 3 shades rose pink, pale ochre, scarlet, flesh pink, palest grey.

Finished size: the picture measures 33cm by 33cm, unframed

METHOD OF WORKING

Mount the canvas on a stretcher frame (se book, p. 6) or bind the edges with maskin tape.

Draw the outlines of the main borde and mark the centre of each side with fine, indelible marking pen (see book p. 123). The central square is worked over 104 threads, and the border over 3 threads. Make a note of the lengths of th outer sides for reference when stretchin the finished work.

Work the straight stitch from the cha for the central square first, referring to th line chart for the lengths of stitches and the colours used, and using four strands of wool throughout. Then, using three strands of wool, work the tent stitch background from the same chart. Finally, work the outer border in eight sections, referring to the border line chart for the colours and stitch lengths.

The colours used in the charts have been exaggerated to clarify the 'Florentine' pattern of the border and the colour changes in the background. Refer to the colour photograph to note the subtle shades used in the actual picture, or work out your own combinations from the yarns you have.

FINISHING OFF

Remove the work from the frame, if used, and block it (see book, p. 136). Lace the embroidery over a piece of hardboard or have it professionally framed.

Designed by S. Martin and S. Windrum

BORDER

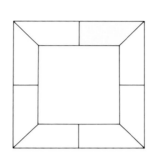
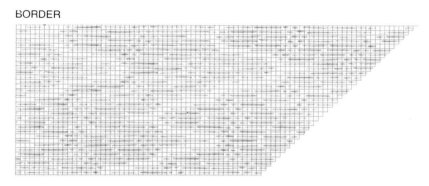

CENTRAL SQUARE

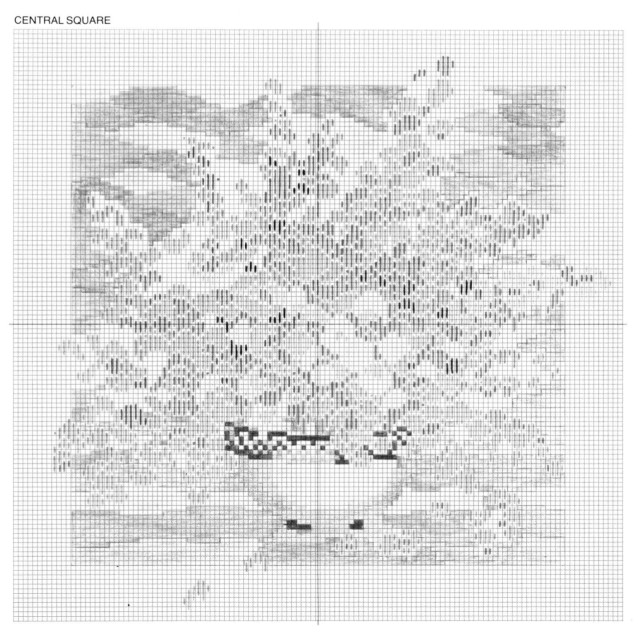

CHOOSING THE DESIGN

The inspiration for this 'lily cushion' came from a series of drawings entitled 'A beautiful bunch of lilies,' which the designer completed for a series of greetings cards and wrapping paper. The design was drawn straight on to the canvas with coloured pencils, the aim being to achieve a fresh, spontaneous approach. The illustrative style of the design, and the bright colours used, bring a fresh, modern quality to the traditional technique of canvaswork.

MATERIALS

Fabric
50cm single canvas, 60cm wide (10 holes to the inch)
50cm pink furnishing fabric (cotton/linen), 90cm wide
1m fabric for piping, 90cm wide
Tapestry wool
15 skeins pink I (background pink)
5 skeins white
2 skeins green I
2 skeins green II
2 skeins lilac
2 skeins turquoise
1 skein yellow
1 skein pink II
1 skein pink III

Tapestry needle, size no.20
2m piping cord, 6mm wide
1 reel pink sewing thread
1 feather-filled cushion pad, 38cm by 38cm

Finished size: the cushion measures 38cm by 38cm

METHOD OF WORKING

Mount the canvas into a frame (see book, pp. 66–7) if desired, and work in tent stitch (see book, p.125), following the colour-coded design chart.

FINISHING

Block the canvas (see book, p.136) before making it into a pillow. Cut the piping fabric into bias strips and join them together, then encase the piping cord as shown in the book on page 139.

Attach the piping to the canvas front, then join the back of the cushion to the front, following the instructions for Making Up given on page 140 in the book.

Designed by Julie Arkell

KEY

- ▨ white
- ▢ pink I
- ▨ pink II
- ▢ pink III
- ▨ turquoise
- ▨ yellow
- ▨ lilac
- ▨ green I
- ▨ green II

ten squares = 2.5cm/1in

CHOOSING THE DESIGN

Childhood memories of happy days at the seaside were the original idea behind this design. The designer then referred to pictures and photographs, and the basic outline came from a photograph of a beach that she knew well. From a list of personal seaside associations the most suitable elements were chosen to be included in the border. A number of rough sketches were made before arriving at the final design and layout. The design was then plotted out in pencil on graph paper, and the smaller details worked out at this stage.

The colours were chosen to give the impression of a hot sunny day in midsummer. They are stronger than they would be in reality, since the intention was to convey a mood rather than a strict representation of a scene.

MATERIALS

1m double-thread canvas, 60cm wide (10 holes to the inch)
1 skein tapestry wool in each of the colours shown on the key below, plus 1 extra skein of crimson
Tapestry needle, size no.18

Finished size: the picture measures 26.5cm by 35.5cm, unframed

METHOD OF WORKING

Cut the canvas to size; it should be at least 36cm by 46cm, but may need to be cut larger to fit on a frame. Mount the canvas on the frame (see book, pp.66–7). Work the design in tent stitch (see book, p.125), following the colours shown on the chart.

Accentuate the outlines around the fishes' mouths, the sunglasses, the crosses on the flags, the bucket handles and the poles of the windbreaks by working back stitch over the tent stitch. Refer to the colour photograph as necessary.

Work the people on the beach in only two strands of wool, using vertical stitches, positioning them as indicated on the chart.

FINISHING OFF

Press the work on the wrong side, using a cool iron. Hold it up to the light to make sure there are no missing stitches: if there are, fill them in.

If you wish to mount the picture yourself, stretch it over a piece of hardboard, lacing it at the back as described in the book on page 138. Some of the plain outer edge of the border will be lost in framing. If you are having the picture framed professionally, this will usually include stretching the canvas.

OPTIONS
The various elements of the design could be used in a number of other ways. The central scene could make an effective picture on its own, and would be much simpler to execute. Alternatively, you could use one of the borders as a repeating frieze for a child's room.

Designed by Louise Lovell

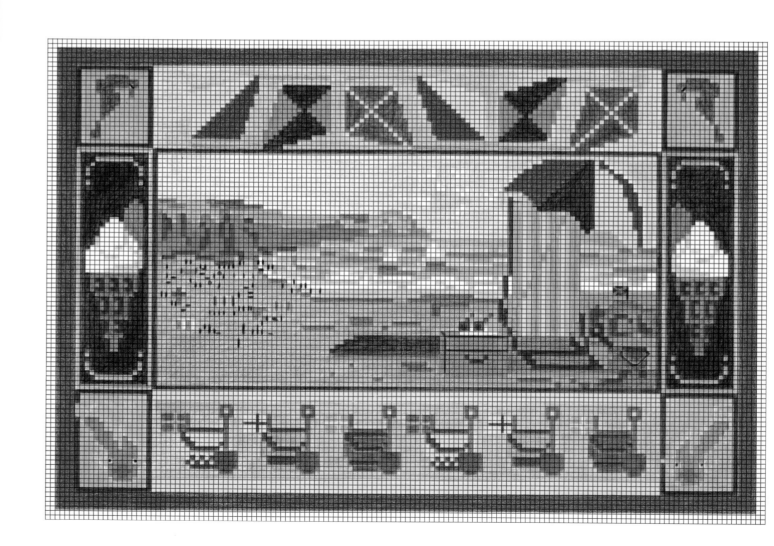

CHOOSING THE DESIGN

The design of this unusual canvaswork resulted from a long series of experiments with colour. The effects are created by the technique of optical colour mixing, in which pure colours are laid side by side so that they appear to blend. In this piece, six colours of thread—two reds, two yellows and two blues—are laid on canvas over different sizes of squares. The order of working the colours produces a wide variety of both colour 'mixes' and shapes— squares, diamonds and triangles.

MATERIALS

Single-mesh canvas, 23cm by 23cm (12 holes to the inch)
Pearl cotton size no.5: 1 skein each bright red, dark red, bright blue, dark blue, bright yellow and yellow-orange
Tacking thread
Tapestry needle, size no.22

Finished size: the finished embroidery measures 14.5cm by 14.5cm, unframed

METHOD OF WORKING

Mount the canvas on a small slate or stretcher frame. The design is based on nine squares of 21 by 21 holes each, the three squares on the left then being sub-divided into smaller squares. Mark the nine squares with tacking thread: first count 10 threads to left and right of the central hole to give the vertical lines, then repeat the process for the horizontal ones.

Working the large squares

Lay a grid of 10 dark blue threads verti-cally on the central square, leaving two threads between each stitch, as shown. Fasten off, then work 10 diagonal stitches in bright red, leaving two threads be-tween each one as before. Work another 10 diagonal stitches in bright yellow. Work 10 bright blue stitches horizontally, then work diagonally halfway across from the top left-hand corner with the yellow-orange. This completes the central square.

Work five other squares above, below and to the right of the central square in the same way, butting them by starting each one in the hole in which the previous square finished. Use a different colour each time for the foundation stitches, as shown in the Pattern Design, and vary the succeeding layers of colours so that there are never two adjacent blocks of the same colour.

Working the small squares

Each of the squares on the left is divided into four. The total is worked as 12 small squares over 10 threads each. Work the foundation stitches of each group of four squares in dark red, dark blue, bright blue and yellow-orange, as shown, then complete as for the large squares, taking care to arrange the colours to contrast with those adjacent to them.

Working the edging

Using two strands of the dark and bright red and the dark and bright blue, lay long threads from corner to corner as shown in the edging diagram, leaving two threads between the outer and inner laid threads. Using single strands of each of the colours in turn, work across the laid threads with vertical stitches.

FINISHING OFF

Remove the work from the frame. It should not need blocking if it has been framed correctly. Lace it over a piece of hard-board and mount and frame as desired (see book, p. 138), or have this done professionally.

Designed by Jennie Parry

WORKING THE LARGE SQUARES

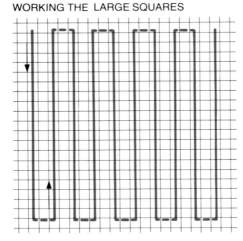
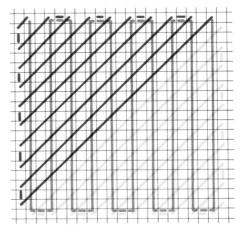

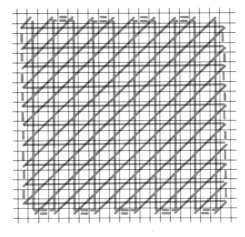
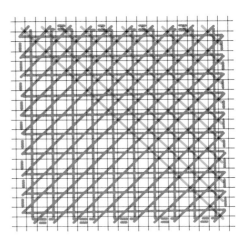

WORKING THE FOUNDATIONS

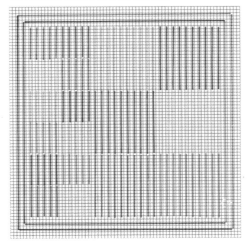

WORKING THE EDGING

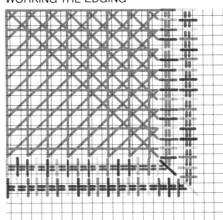

CHOOSING THE DESIGN

The idea for the central part of this design came originally from a patterned piece of ribbon seen twisted on the floor. The embroiderer sketched this out as a symmetrical motif on graph paper and then charted the whole design, working outward to echo the shape in the centre. The stitch used is Florentine, worked over four and six threads, and is quite simple and quick to work (see book, pp. 128-9).

MATERIALS

Single thread canvas, 56cm by 42cm (14 holes to the inch)
Tapestry wool: 4 skeins dark brown, 4 skeins mid-brown, 2 skeins light brown, 9 skeins dark cream, 5 skeins light cream
Tapestry needle, size no. 22
Piece of carpet felt or similar for backing
Spray glue (optional)

Finished size: the mat measures 48cm by 34cm

METHOD OF WORKING

Find the centre of the canvas by folding it across the length and the width and mark the point. Mount the canvas on a stretcher frame or bind the edges with tape.

Work from the Pattern Design chart, starting in the centre with the lighter cream thread. Note that this area is worked over four threads throughout. Continue working outward from the centre, following the colours indicated, over four or six threads as shown.

The background area also alternates the length of the stitches, with the row outside the light brown zigzag line being worked over six threads, the next row over four, the next six again, and so on.

The border is worked in interlocking long and short stitches worked over six, four and two threads as shown.

FINISHING OFF

Block the work if necessary (see book, p. 136). Trim the canvas to about 1.2cm outside the stitching and turn under the edges. Cut the carpet felt to the same size and either fix it to the back of the embroidery with spray glue, or stitch all around the edges with button thread or a double thickness of sewing thread.

OPTIONS

The design could be adapted to a full-scale rug, using rug wool and a heavy gauge rug canvas. It could equally well be reduced, for a much smaller item worked in embroidery threads. The colours could be varied as you please, and a wider range could be used: for instance eight or ten toning shades would give a more traditional Florentine look as well as making the pattern appear more intricate.

Designed by Gisela Banbury

MAKING UP

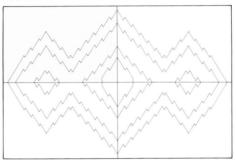

BORDER

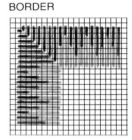

PATTERN DESIGN

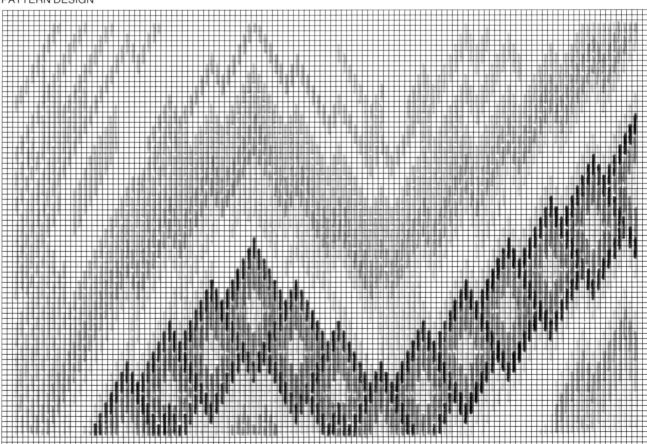

INDEX

ACKNOWLEDGMENTS/USEFUL ADDRESSES

SUPPLIERS' CREDITS
The publishers are particularly indebted to Dunlicraft Ltd of Leicester, the sole distributors in the UK for DMC threads, who provided the threads for many of the patterns in the Embroidery Design Collection as well as for the embroidered samples illustrated in the book.

10/11 **C.J. Graphic Supplies Ltd.**
13 Threads: DMC/Dunlicraft Ltd, Leicester; Royal School of Needlework, London Beads: Ells & Farrier
14/15 Sewing equipment and canvas samples: Royal School of Needlework, London
63 Embroidery frame: Royal School of Needlework, London

PATTERNS
2 Fountain pen: Philip Poole, Pen & inkwell: Mansfield
5 Table: Country Pine
7 Shirt: Simpson Scarf: Aquascutum
9 Jumper: Benetton 012
17 Cutlery: David Mellor
18 Box: Antiquarius/Gerald Mathias R3 Hat pin: Antiquarius/Persiflage Y8 Threads: Royal School of Needlework
20 Dress made by Avril Farley
22 Tuxedo: Dickins & Jones Shirt: Jaeger Scarf: Aquascutum
23 Handbound frame by Zilda Tandy
25 Frame: The Court Gallery
26 Chair kindly loaned by Suzanne Tandy
27 Frame: The Court Gallery
28 Lampshade: The Reject Shop
29 Frame: The Court Gallery
30 Frame: The Court Gallery

PHOTOGRAPHIC CREDITS
1 Roger Phillips; 3 Roger Phillips; 4 Peter Rauter; 8–9 embroidery: Peter Rauter; surrounding objects: John Barlow; 10–11 Roger Phillips; 12 John Barlow; 13–14 Roger Phillips; 15 John Barlow; 23 Roland Lewis; 25–29 John Barlow; 31–33 Roger Phillips; 34–35 Peter Rauter; 36–37 John Barlow; 38–39 Roger Phillips; 39 John Barlow; 40–41 John Barlow; 42–43 Roger Phillips; 44–45 John Barlow; 46 Roger Phillips; 47–49 John Barlow; 50–52 Roger Phillips; 53 John Barlow; 54–55 Roger Phillips; 56–57 John Barlow; 60–63 John Barlow; 69–135 Grade One Photographic

PATTERNS
Peter Rauter 3, 4, 10, 23, 24, 25–27, 29–31
Christine Hanscomb 1, 2, 5, 7, 9–13, 17–19, 21, 28
John Barlow 6, 14
Heinz Lautenbacher 15, 16, 20, 22

ARTWORK CREDITS
Key: t top; b bottom; l left; r right; c centre
16–17, 18–19 Richard Phipps; 19 (colour butterfly) Alan Male/Linden Artists; 21, 22 Richard Phipps; 23 tr Hayward & Martin; bl Terry Evans; 24 Richard Phipps; 25, 27 (collage) John Bigg; 29 tr, cr John Bigg; b Hayward & Martin; 30, 31 (line drawings) Richard Phipps; 40 (colour swatches) John

Hutchinson; 44 (rubbing) Jenny Chippendale; 52 Richard Phipps; 58–59 Favorite Charted Designs by Anne Orr/Dover Publications Inc.

64–141 Special thanks to Coral Mula for all the step-by-step illustrations.

All pattern diagrams and charts drawn by John Hutchinson

EMBROIDERERS' CREDITS
Key: t top; b bottom; l left; r right
1 Margaret Horton; 3 Irene Ord; 4 Jennie Parry; 8–9 Louise Lovell; 31–33 Irene Ord; 34 Jennie Parry; 35 Chris Crilly; 36 Sheila Miller; 37 Patricia Few; 39 Jenny Chippendale; 42–43 Irene Ord; 44 Jenny Chippendale; 45 t Isabel Dibden; 45 b Robin Giddings; 46–47 Jenny Chippendale; 48 t Irene Ord; 48 b Avril Farley; 49 t Diana Thornton; 49 b Judith Groves; 50–51 Margaret Horton; 52 Irene Ord; 53 Liz Cooksey; 54–55 Jenny Chippendale; 55 Barbara Siedlecka; 56 Jenny Chippendale; 57 Liz Mundell; 60 tl Jan Eaton; 60 tr Jenny Chippendale; 60 bl Margaret Horton; 60 br Jenny Chippendale; 61 tl Irene Ord; 61 tr Gisela Banbury; 61 bl Angela Dewar; 61 br Diana Thornton; 63 Helen Conrad; 69–87 Irene Ord; 88–95 Angela Dewar; 97–99 Caroline Davis; 100–101 Angela Dewar; 103–105 Caroline Davis; 107–108 Helen Conrad; 109–111 Margaret Darby; 113 Gisela Banbury; 115 l Pauline Brown; 115 r Gisela Banbury; 116–121 Diana Thornton; 124 Eleanor Van Zandt; 125–135 Gisela Banbury

DESIGN EQUIPMENT, FABRIC DYES AND PAINTS
Atlantis Art,
Gullivers Wharf, 105 Wapping Lane, London E19 RW
(art supplies by mail order)
L. Cornellissen & Son,
22 Great Queen Street, London WC2
(dyes and paints by mail order or from the shop)
Candlemakers' Supplies,
28 Blythe Road, London W14 0HA
(tie-dye and batik materials; fabric paints)
Dylon International Ltd,
Lower Sydenham, London SE26 5HD
W.H. Smith & Sons for art materials, drawing equipment and paper
George Weil & Sons Ltd,
63–65 Ridinghouse Street, London W1P 7PP
(dyes and paints by mail order)

FABRICS AND THREADS
Mary Allen,
Wirksworth, Derbyshire DE4 4BN
(evenweave linens by mail order)
John Lewis,
Oxford Street, London W1 and branches
Liberty of London,
Regent Street, London W1
MacCulloch & Wallis,
25–26 Dering Street, London W1
(threads and general haberdashery by mail order or from the shop)
Silken Strands,
33 Linksway, Gatley, Cheadle, Cheshire SK8 4LA

(threads: send S.A.E. for shade cards and price list)
Seba Lace,
76 Main Street, Addingham, Ilkley, W. Yorkshire LS29 0PL
(linen lace thread and other specialist threads by mail order)
Shades,
57 Candlemas Lane, Beaconsfield, Bucks. HP9
(mail order for metallized and other specialist threads)
Whaleys (Bradford) Ltd,
Harris Court, Great Horton, Bradford, W. Yorkshire BD7 4EQ
(fabric for dyeing and painting by mail order)

GENERAL AND SPECIALIST EMBROIDERY SUPPLIES
The Camden Needlecraft Centre,
High Street, Chipping Camden Gloucestershire
de Denne Ltd,
159–161 Kenton Road, Kenton, Harrow, Middlesex
Ells & Farrier,
5 Princes Street, London W1
(beads and trimmings)
Mace & Nairn,
89 Crane Street, Salisbury, Wiltshire
(materials for metal thread embroidery)
Royal School of Needlework,
25 Princes Gate, London SW7

CANADA
Belding Corticelle 1982 Inc.,
617 Denison Street, Markham, Ontario L3R EB8
J & P Coats (Canada) Inc.,
Station 'A', P.O. Box 519, Montreal, Quebec H3C 2T6

AUSTRALIA
Coats Semco,
Semco Park, 8A George Street, Sandringham 3191, S. Australia
Olivier (Australia) Pty. Ltd.,
47–57 Collins Street, Alexandria, NSW 2015 Sydney

NEW ZEALAND
Coats Patons (New Zealand) Ltd.,
P.O. Box 6149, Wellesley Street, Auckland 1
Warnaar Trading Co.,
376 Serry Road, P.O. Box 10567, Christchurch 2

SOUTH AFRICA
J & P Coats S.A. (Pty) Ltd.,
4 Wol Street, Homelake Extension, Randfontein, Transvaal
South African Threads and Cottons Ltd.,
56 Barrack Street, Capetown 8001